LAND ROVER EXPEDITIONS

WHERE TO GO OFF-ROADING IN THE UK

LAND ROVER EXPEDITIONS

WHERE TO GO OFF-ROADING IN THE UK

LAND ROVER
Owner International
M A G A Z I N E

Materials © Emap Automotive Limited 2004
Compilation and cover design © Haynes Publishing 2004

First published in 2004

A catalogue record for this book is available from the British Library

ISBN 1 84425 141 1

Published jointly by

Haynes Publishing, Sparkford,
Yeovil, Somerset BA22 7JJ, England
Phone 01963 440635, www.haynes.co.uk

and

Emap Automotive Limited,
Wentworth House, Wentworth Street, Peterborough PE1 1DS, England
Phone 01733 213700, www.emap.com

Designed and typeset by Bookcraft Ltd, Stroud, Gloucestershire

Printed and bound in England by J.H. Haynes & Co. Ltd, Sparkford

Contents

Foreword by John Pearson

**Editor-in-Chief
Land Rover Owner Magazine**

FROM GENTLE DRIVES by the Suffolk coast, to the hidden beauty of Shropshire's byways, from off-road drives just a mile or two from London's busy traffic, to the wide open spaces of the Lincolnshire Wolds, they're all great places to see beautiful Britain by Land Rover.

Photograph: Bob Atkins

And if you can't be out there driving, delighting in new views and enjoying nature in all its beauty, the next best thing is to be admiring photographs of off-road driving locations and reading about them as a prelude to planning your next trip. Which is where this book comes in.

Written and photographed by Land Rover Owner International magazine's experts, we've explored, discovered, mapped and assessed many of the finest drives through this country's most beautiful landscapes. We'll bring to

life areas you have never visited, and cast new light on your favourite destinations.

We've sourced and checked all the practical information, from the maps you'll need to where to stay for the night, plus useful addresses, and recommended routes, to make your next trip as easy and smooth as it could be.

All you have to do is find a space in your diary, book the time off, lace up your boots and head out for the finest greenlaning Britain has to offer.

Follow the Off-Road Code

Only drive greenlanes that have known vehicle rights – after studying your Ordnance Survey map. Check the definitive map at the local county council or contact the local Land Rover club's rights of way officer or GLASS (Green Lane Association) representative.

1 Avoid badly rutted or sodden tracks. You'll only make them worse and provide ammunition for those who would like to see us banned.

2 Drive slowly (max 12 mph). Pull over and stop if you encounter walkers or horses (and switch off your engine for the latter).

3 Travel in groups of four vehicles or less.

4 Don't damage trees or hedgerows, except for cutting back overhanging branches.

5 Take recovery gear/spade in case you get stuck.

6 Don't travel alone – you might get stranded.

7 Open gates should be left open – and closed ones should be closed again after you've gone through.

8 Take your litter home.

9 Supervise dogs and children at all times, especially when you're near livestock.

10 Avoid all waterways unless you're certain there's a public right of way.

11 Avoid aggro with other greenlane users. Don't argue but explain politely that you're there legally.

Location Map

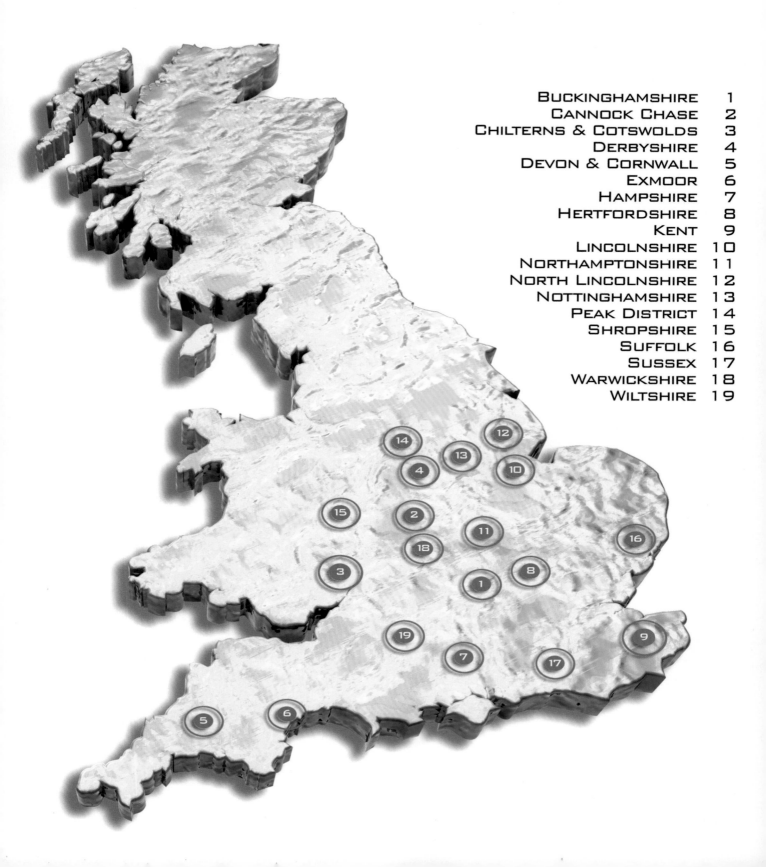

Surf and Turf

We explore Devon and Cornwall in three 90s, and find flooded roads, steep hills, breathtaking views and lots of red mud ...

Words: Dan Stevens
Photographs: Fiona Richardson

THE SIGN READS 'Tidal road – impassable at times'. It has just gone 3pm and, according to my tidal book, at this time of day the sea has filled up all the rivers, estuaries and beaches in South Devon. Which means that the road, snaking along the banks of the River Avon, should now be completely flooded – there won't be any normal traffic taking this route for the next few hours. But we'd be stupid not to try ...

Even if the water is too deep, there's no chance of getting stuck because, although it looks like a river, this is a proper metalled road. Short, isolated stretches of tar

stick out of the water in huge lumps – drivers trapped by the advancing water have been known to take to these islands to sit out the rising tide.

So I drop the Land Rover into second low, which should provide just enough momentum to keep a respectable bow wave moving off the front of the vehicle, and plunge in. The water's just up to the sills, and I can hear the tide lapping at the bottom of the doors.

Passenger Ben – it's his first time in a Land Rover – is looking nervously at the floor. 'Any water coming in yet?' I ask. 'No,' he says, relieved that his boots are still dry.

As it happens, the water doesn't get any deeper than headlamp height, and the door seals hold. Just. Vehicles wading on this road can't be an uncommon sight (it does actually go somewhere), but we've still provided some entertainment for an elderly couple peeking out of the windows of their bungalow on the water's edge. And technically, we haven't even gone off-road, so nobody can come and shout at us.

So if that's what the surfaced roads are like in the South West, what the hell are the unsurfaced ones like?

Although Devon and Cornwall don't have many byways and RUPPs (roads used as public paths), the two counties make up for this with miles of UCRs (unclassified roads) that snake across the rolling countryside. These are the white roads you see on OS Land Ranger maps, and at that scale they're indistinguishable from tarred roads.

Get an OS Explorer though, and suddenly what looked like surfaced lanes become off-road tracks, shown by green dots along the route. Devon has more miles of road than any other county in the UK, and most of these are tiny, single tracks bordered by hedges that dwarf even a Land Rover. In early summer, every plant and tree is bursting with foliage as they shrug off the torpor of winter and bask in the warm weather that flows from the Gulf Stream. The South West is one of the wettest and warmest places in the UK, and don't those plants know it.

Which means that by the time we arrive at our first lane, it's a battle between Land Rover and hedgerow. The 2001 Foot-and-Mouth crisis hit the South West hard, and many of the routes we'll be driving haven't seen much use since the end of 2000. Great for the plants, but not so good for off-roaders and horse riders, and soon we're pushing through rampant greenery as we track a series of UCRs that wiggle across the hills west of Dawlish. It's not threatening the Defender's bodywork, but the (already shabby) paintwork's taking a battering as branches screech down the sides of the hard top. The trees are closing in.

Just as I'm beginning to think we'll never get out of this alive, the track opens out and we're on top of a hill overlooking the Exe estuary. And yes, we can see the sea for the first time. There's something about that initial sighting of the wide blue ocean (or in this case, the murky English Channel) that brings back childhood memories, the feeling of sand between your toes, and the sound of the tide splashing against a sandy foreshore in the late afternoon sun.

Hills and views are two of the defining characteristics of this part of the UK, and wherever you go you'll be able to see something green in the distance. The other is the colour of the mud, a subject close to all of our hearts. It's red. Not brown, or grey, or any of the other assorted

Most of Devon and Cornwall's tracks are UCRs, so they're public highways. This sign has no place here.

archetypal mud colours, but a deep, russet red that stains everything it touches. And when it rains, puddles look like something's died a death in them. Its uniqueness adds to the colour and vibrancy of the landscape. And it's all over my boots.

The lane we're on soon returns to tarmac when we reach Dawlish, and we skirt the edge of the slightly run-down Victorian seaside resort, heading back inland.

Finding the entrance points to these tracks is not easy. They're not signed, because they don't have any special status; often the start of the track is massively over-grown, and you have to look hard to distinguish it from the hedge. LRO photographer Fiona Richardson, nor-mally a demon navigator, is having problems finding the exact location of the paths, and we take a couple of wrong turns, nearly ending up in a field full of cows.

We're trying to locate a bunch of roads near the village of Ideford, and if we can just stop driving through the cow's lunch, then we might be able to get some more driving done before the weather breaks. Not that we're averse to a little rain, but it tends to make photography difficult.

The rain holds off until we get onto Dartmoor. There's no off-road driving on Dartmoor – the fragile ecosystem of this unique wilderness makes it too harmful – but the views and atmosphere are worth the journey. Even in the English equivalent of a tropical downpour the moor still looks incredible – bleak, but beautiful.

It puts a stop to our fun, though. Dark skies mean problems with photography, and we're not inclined to get soaked for the sake of it. At times like this, there's only one thing to do – sit out the rain in a pub. My choice would be The Rugglestone, a tiny two-room hostelry with no pumps (beer's served from kegs behind the bar), in the beyond-picturesque village of Widecombe-in-the-Moor. But at 4pm it's closed. Time to return to the low-

The warm, wet climate means plant life goes crazy in the summer.

A journalist, a teacher and a map. Confusion reigns …

lands and catch the latest weather forecast.

The rain doesn't clear until late evening, so it's not until the next morning that we get out again. We've met up with Neal Daniel, rights of way representative for the Cornwall and Devon Land Rover Club. He's going to join us to drive a network of UCRs that radiate out from Totnes, in the South Hams. Neal pilots a V8 90 County Station Wagon, a rare machine even when new. It's in near standard condition, but Neal says it's going to need a gearbox very soon.

Now I've got a confession at this point. I grew up around these parts, and at some point in the past fifteen years I've walked most of the tracks we're planning to drive. But I've never driven them, so this is going to be a learning experience for me. It will also be a first for Neal, who hasn't explored them either. We don't know quite what to expect – after all, a washed-out gully that you can simply sidestep on foot can bring a Land Rover to a wheel-spinning, traction-defying halt.

The first problem, though, is much more devious than something as simple as a gully. We turn onto the UCR (past a helpful 'road closed' sign that's obviously been swiped from some nearby roadworks and propped up against the hedge), and meander down the track. It's solid under the tyres, and the recent heavy rain hasn't turned it into a mudbath.

Then the track starts to close in a little, and Neal, who is leading, stops. 'It's really narrow here,' he says, 'and the bank rises up to one side.' Not normally enough to stop a Land Rover, but the catch is the stream on the left. If the 90's rear wheels slip even just a couple of inches to the left – which the banking on the right will force them to do – then the back end will slide into the ditch the stream runs through.

The drop is about four feet – easily enough to incapaci-

tate a Land Rover. And if it did go over, I can't see the farmer – who we presume put up the 'road closed' sign – being too keen on the idea of coming to pull us out.

Neal reckons he can get through, with me guiding him. The 90's running on relatively narrow rubber, and if he's careful there should be just enough room. Gingerly, he feeds it over the troublesome ground, as I try simultaneously to watch the front and rear wheels and to give hand signals. He glides the Land Rover through, with little bother, in one go.

Now it's my turn. I hate doing this sort of thing. Ever since I nearly capsized our Discovery in Kent on an equally innocuous lane (marathon two-hour recovery involving two rescue vehicles and fence removal), I've been ultra-cautious and maybe a little afraid when it comes to obstacles like this. To make matters worse, the Defender is shod with 285 section tyres, which are about two inches too wide for the track.

It's very, very close. Inching the Defender forward, and following every move of Neal's hands, I put the rear wheels onto the bank. 'Stop!' shouts Neal. 'The back nearside tyre is about to go over. Give it full opposite lock, and it might bring the rear up a bit.'

With the kind of delicacy normally reserved for repairing Rolex watches, I ease the wheel round and trickle a little power to the axles. It works, and I can pull forward, the rear wheels thankfully following the front onto the track. Without making too much of a drama out of it (this is South Devon, not South East Asia) we feel pleased, and relieved that we've got through. But I wouldn't attempt this one again, and I don't recommend driving this lane at all.

Which is a shame, because the rest is straightforward and very beautiful. Bluebells, campion and cowslip are bursting from the banks, and the smell of wild garlic is

A spot of impromptu road building is needed to fill this gully.

intoxicating. At the end is a house, with another misappropriated 'road closed' sign next to it, and the track continues across a tarred road.

And that's where the washed-out gully appears. There's absolutely no way we're going to get up there, with just six inches of flat ground for the tyres to contact with on one side. To climb it you'd need a winch, and if you need a winch you're greenlaning in the wrong place.

Defeated, we drive back through Totnes and head down the other side of the River Dart through the riverside villages of Tuckenhay and Cornworthy. Nestling in the steep valleys are more UCRs, and we're going to find them.

On the way we find a decaying Series III dumped in a field, that I know was complete and on-the-road two years ago, and also an 80-inch Series I that's been parked in the same yard for at least fifteen years. It used to have a companion 80-inch, but all that remains of it are a few forlorn components peeking out of the junk strewn across the yard.

Strangely, the next track also has a 'road closed' sign, informing us that the water board is carrying out work for the next 42 days. Well, we can always turn round if we have to.

This is the narrowest lane so far, and I lose my door mirror head to the clutches of the hedgerow. It gets tighter, but week-old tyre tracks going in the opposite direction, left by another Land Rover-sized machine, indicate that we should get through. It's worth the climb for the view, visible through a gateway, of the Dart meandering through the valley it has cut for itself over thousands of years.

As we descend, we're coming down the side of that valley, and the lane opens out, with a thick canopy of trees above us. It's wide – almost wide enough for two cars to pass – but that doesn't impress the dog walker we meet there, who point-blank refuses to engage us in any eye contact.

He doesn't say anything, but he obviously disapproves of off-roaders. I've got an urge to tell him I grew up and went to school here, and have as much right to be there as him, but I know that these conversations go nowhere. He carries on walking, and we carry on driving.

A brand-new driverless Toyota Land Cruiser blocks the next lane, and the one after that runs into a locked gate. It also meanders through the middle of a farmyard, so we decide to move on. The lane after that is a no-hoper, but only because ahead of us is a Ford Escort, which trundles confidently down the lane. Not really much point in driving down there if an Escort with its six-inch ground clearance can make it.

We've got to get a move on as well, because we're going to meet CDLRC's other greenlane rep, Roger James, in Cornwall. Neal's got to get back to the real world and work, so we strike out for the Tamar Bridge, which crosses the river that divides Devon and Cornwall.

You can avoid the A38 dual carriageway by taking the back route to Plymouth, which just happens to run through Aveton Gifford (pronounced, as is so often the way, nothing like its spelling – try Awton Jifford), which just happens to have that tidal road. Show a Land Rover an impassable road, and it will show you a way through.

By the time we reach Roger's cottage, right in the middle of Cornwall, the rain is falling hard enough to break glass and the wind is so strong the force can be felt from within the Defender. Greenlaning is out for this afternoon, so we pass the time drinking tea and talking greenlanes.

'Cornwall County Council tends to neglect our lanes,' says Roger. 'It waits for a UCR to get totally overgrown, then declares it too dangerous to remain a highway and closes it. We've lost several like that.'

He also says some tracks have been closed thanks to the efforts of an idiot off-roader minority, who did their utmost to destroy delicate surfaces and generally charge around like they owned the place. Needless to say, they weren't from Cornwall.

One advantage of being so far south is that bad weather blows through quickly on its way north, so the morning dawns are clear, if not so bright. We hook up with Roger and his battered but authentic 90 in the village of Lerryn, to explore the dozens of UCRs scattered across the countryside. And yet again, we find the first track blocked by a parked car. Roger's out of the Land Rover and knocking on the door of the nearby house before I can even get the handbrake on. The owners move it without hesitation, saying that they always leave the track open at weekends. Well, it is 8.30am.

These lanes are very similar to the Devon tracks, but they're much more overgrown. At one point the view from the Defender's driving seat is completely obscured by foliage. We'll be picking bugs out of the bodywork for days after this. Although there is definitely a track in

Driver Profile

NAME	Neal Daniel
VEHICLE	V8 90 County Station Wagon

V8 90s are rare, so Neal Daniel's holding onto his – even if it does need a new gearbox. Neal, a teacher from Ivybridge in Devon, bought the 90 18 months ago. It had been stolen and then recovered when it was 18 months old, and had lost its engine and chassis numbers along the way. It took a lot of work to return it to a legal state, but Neal's really happy with it. Apart from the leaky roof, rotten bulkhead and worn gearbox, that is.

The roof leaks from where it joins the hardtop sides, and the LT85 gearbox, which only went into V8s, is on its way out, and predictably, they're the most expensive type to replace. The rest of the Land Rover's in great shape though, and it's all original.

there somewhere, if the foliage is left any longer it will become a wood – a Land Rover is the only way of getting down here.

The good news is the surfaces, which are in good condition and solid. Like Devon, Cornwall is a land of rock and hills, so the water drains off quickly, and there's not much soil to turn to mud anyway. Axle twisters and washouts are the biggest hazards, along with fords.

Which is what we encounter when we drive the track to Muchlarnik – one of the most beautiful lanes I've ever driven. You start on a narrow, overgrown lane that runs between two fields, and then descend through a pine plantation. Okay, so it's hardly a traditional English setting, but the tall trees, the clear light and the feeling of space make it a very special place. If we had a picnic with us, this would be the place to eat it.

The track's hardly demanding at this point, but to get to it you do need four-wheel drive and ground clearance. And to keep going you'll need it as well, because there's a deep ford to navigate and a steep climb. Crossing the ford is easy, but on the other side Roger decides to walk up the hill.

I see why when we get halfway up. Rainfall and erosion have conspired to remove large chunks of ground, leaving a steep gully to one side and plenty of bare, exposed rock. Further up it gets steeper, and the rock becomes stepped. To climb it would involve airing down tyres (and then inflating them at the other end), and not a little frus-

tration and damage. Vehicles have been up, and down, recently but we're not going to try it.

We do get up the next lane though. It's another steep climb, this time with the added attraction of a hairpin turn. Roger's some way ahead, and disappears round the bend at the top before I'm halfway up. Ben's in the passenger seat holding on as the 90 bucks over the rock. Then it stops.

The front tyres have pushed up against a sheer piece of rock, and they're just spinning. Failed hill climb drill kicks in, except the engine's not dead, so it's handbrake on, grab reverse and let the clutch out fast. We lurch back, tilting as I reverse the 90 round the tight downhill right-hander. 'Err – how far will these things go before they, err, go over?' asks Ben. 'Oh, a lot more than this,' I breezily reply. I don't think this reassures him.

Next try, and we've got more momentum and a little bit more power. The 90's tyres scrabble purposely on the rock and pull the Defender over the top, suspension banging and creaking as the rear axle follows the front. Now Ben's got a smile on his face, and when we catch up with Roger he tells me he'd actually quite enjoyed himself.

And as is always the way, just when it's time to go home, the weather gets better. It takes a long time to get from Cornwall to, well, most places really, and we've got a long way to go. Now the rain's gone, and I think the sun is attempting to put in an appearance.

It's at times like this, when the sun is shining and the air's warm, that the South West comes into its own as one of the most beautiful parts of the UK. The clarity of the light, even on an overcast, dull day always makes the place feel special. The greenlaning in this area is superb, with masses of variety and plenty of easy tracks to try out. The South West – it's not just for holidays.

Cornish lanes are very similar to Devon routes – overgrown, but with unbeatable views.

Land of Contrast

From desolate Exmoor to the watery wastes of the Levels, a wealth of greenlaning fun awaits you in Somerset

Words: Dave Phillips
Photographs: Mark Dixon and Dave Phillips
Additional reporting: Mike English

This beech-lined lane starts near Minehead and leads to the uplands of remote Exmoor.

THE GREAT STAG lifts its magnificent, antlered head and sniffs the breeze. Our approaching convoy of Land Rovers isn't yet in sight; but he knows we're coming while we're still nearly a mile away, bouncing gently along the rocky track.

Around him, the dozen or so does and lesser young bucks graze on, picking out the sparse tufts of grass among the heather. But, sensing their leader's agitation, they edge down the hillside, their grey winter coats blending easily into the drab winter colours of the moor.

By the time we arrive, a few minutes later, the herd of red deer is at least 300 yards away but, with binoculars, we're able to marvel at the sight of Britain's biggest wild animals in their natural habitat.

Today, we're on safari. But this isn't the sun-baked plains of the Serengeti or the lush swamps of the Okavango Delta. It's an English winter and we're on the desolate uplands of Exmoor, where the wind, armed with icy daggers, races right at us.

Wherever you are in the world, there's always something exhilarating about

being high above the tree line, meeting the elements head-on. And there's nowhere quite like Exmoor.

Yet this great, craggy plateau is just one small corner of Somerset, the county we're exploring this month. We're in an area steeped in history and marinated in scrumpy cider. This is the land of Arthurian legend and the Glastonbury Festival, where vast sweeps of flat wetlands are suddenly punctuated by improbable-looking steep hills, which are inevitably topped by an ancient monument.

And if all that isn't enough, Britain's answer to the Grand Canyon – the Cheddar Gorge – is here to impress us all.

There's clearly much too much to squeeze into the two days available to us. But, hey, we'll try our best.

Our adventure begins in the gorgeous little town of Dunster. Here, on the northeast corner of Exmoor, sparkles an unspoilt medieval jewel.

In former times, Dunster was the centre of a thriving wool industry and its 550-year-old yarn market still stands in the middle of the market place, flanked by

The castle dominates the skyline above the attractive old town of Dunster.

buildings equally old. At one end of the main street, atop a huge mound, towers Dunster Castle. At the other end, on a steep hill, is a complementary folly.

It would be easy to lose a day exploring this charming town; but we're up early, heading for the high moor. Our convoy is led by Duncan Waller, a Land Rover fan who turned his hobby into a business six years ago when he and his wife, Alison, set up Barle Valley Safaris.

In their fleet of Defender 110s they take visitors to parts of the wild moor that lesser vehicles just wouldn't be able to reach. And once there, they're treated to glimpses of the famed herds of red deer, wild ponies and birds of prey.

There's a buzzard with us now, as we skirt south of Minehead on a track over Gravis Hill. It soars above us, its kitten-like cry carried off the wind that's buffeting the tops of the gnarled, ancient beech trees.

Photographer Mark Dixon has brought along his venerable 1971 Range Rover, while LRO Adventure Club leader Vince Cobley is giving his new Td5 90 its first off-road outing. Peter Graves is also at the wheel of a Td5 90, while the second-generation Range Rover DSE of Richard Greenway and the Td5 Discovery of Richard Towell make up our happy band.

Driver Profiles

NAME	Duncan Waller
VEHICLE	1997 Defender 110 300Tdi

DUNCAN WALLER carries up to eight passengers in his Defender 110 on his Barle Valley Safari tours of Exmoor, using seldom-used tracks and byways.

NAME	Richard and Jim Ballance
VEHICLE	1999 Discovery Td5

RICHARD'S DISCO has been fitted with full steel bumpers to accommodate a dismountable winch. Guards fitted to the front axle, rear differential and fuel tank allow him to make the very most of Somerset's many off-roading opportunities.

NAME	Richard Greenway
VEHICLE	Range Rover 2.5 DSE

RICHARD GREENWAY and his friends Susan Hall and George Gosney joined us to test the off-road capabilities of Richard's Range Rover, which he has only owned for six weeks – but he still wasn't bothered about getting it muddy.

That's one more vehicle than we would normally take on a greenlane adventure, so we split into two groups, just meeting for the photos. The people we meet along the way, including horse riders, walkers and even a naturalist out conducting a census of the local dormouse population, invariably greet us with a cheery wave and stop for a chat.

Unlike neighbouring Devon, where the RUPPs (roads used as public paths) have been relegated to bridleway status, Somerset has maintained the status quo. And rightly so, since these historic rights of way date back to the days when horse-drawn carriages traversed them, their passengers no doubt wary of the lawless robbers who roamed the wild moors. One such family of outlaws, the notorious Doones, terrorised Exmoor back at the time of the English Civil War. And it was their exploits that inspired R.D. Blackmore's romantic novel, *Lorna Doone*.

Our convoy is descending into a lush, alluvial plain called the Vale of Porlock, where we head for the grand-sounding village of Wootton Courtenay, its cottages built of the pink-blushed local stone.

From here, we head for the bleak moorland of the Holnicote Estate, where Duncan tells us we're sure to see red deer. *En route* we stop at a high outcrop known as Webber's Post, where there's an impressive panoramic view across Exmoor. In the near distance is Dunkery

Exmoor ponies are a tough breed – they have to be in this bleak landscape.

Beacon which, at 1700 feet above sea level, is the highest point in Somerset.

It's cold and exposed up here, and most of the farmers' beasts are tucked up in their quarters, leaving only the very hardy (and woolly) Swaledale sheep out in the elements.

Despite the harsh environment, even a few trees manage to survive up here. Most of them are the spindly sessile oak, introduced here hundreds of years ago for its bark – used in the leather tanning industry – and local charcoal burners. Both were thriving industries in bygone times, when these wild, lonely hillsides were more heavily populated than they are today.

Despite being such a bleak, inhospitable place, human settlers have favoured Exmoor – right

Above and left   Panoramic – the lanes give us great views across the moors.

back to 4000 BC, when Bronze Age tribes farmed the moors and buried their kings in hilltop graves known as barrows, many of which still survive to this day.

Today, life here is little easier. Many of the hamlets here only got mains electricity very recently. Rural life in Somerset revolves around agriculture and was devastated by the Foot-and-Mouth outbreak of 2001. It still hasn't recovered.

Farmers, still reeling from that trauma, are reluctant to rely upon the meagre profits of dairy production and sheep rearing: diversity is the farmers' buzzword up on the moors and leisure activities are seen as the way forward.

Off-roading is just one of the new uses they are finding for their fields. Meadows are being bulldozed to create exciting hills, water holes and mud pits. Milking parlours are being converted into heated clubhouses, where 4×4 drivers can exchange tales after a day's exciting sport.

Richard Greenway has promised to take us to his own course tomorrow, but for now we're enjoying our moorland drive. The wild waters of the Bristol Channel are in view now.

This is Porlock Bay, where an Atlantic storm breached the sea defences a few years back and flooded the low-lying fields beyond. Nobody has ever bothered to reclaim them and today they have reverted to wildlife-rich salt-marsh.

Porlock is famous for its 1 in 4 hill out of the village. Coaches and caravans have to take an alternative route but, of course, it's no problem in a Land Rover.

Now we head inland over Winsford Hill, liberally dotted with Bronze Age barrows and grazing ponies. These hardy beasts are a unique breed, as close to the original wild pony as it's possible to find. They are regularly culled to remove cross-breeds and keep the genetic integrity of the herds. Nearly 400 still roam the 265 square miles of Exmoor.

Our ears pop as we descend steeply to Liscombe and

Assorted Land Rovers make easy work of the ford at Tarr Steps.

The harbour at Porlock Weir.

another verdant valley, this time with the delightful River Barle at the very bottom. We ford the river beside the famous Tarr Steps – a stone-built clapper bridge that some historians believe dates back to prehistoric times. But others claim it's Roman – and yet more reckon it was built in the Middle Ages. Either way, it's pretty impressive, with some of the individual limestone slabs weighing over two tons each.

On the other side of the river we're faced with the daunting climb up a RUPP to Penny Bridge, which involves a climb of nearly a mile up a 1 in 3 gradient over mainly loose shale. At the top, we're out of Somerset and in neighbouring Devon – but only briefly, mind – as we head for the coast again.

Our final destination is Porlock Weir, a small harbour which is reached via Withypool village, once home of those dreaded Doones. Despite the biting cold, we linger here into darkness, savouring the atmosphere as the rollers crash on to the shifting shingle.

We spend the night in Dunster, at the lovely but very reasonably priced Yarn Market Hotel. It seems a shame to miss the delights of the local scrumpy, but strong cider and a long day's driving the next day don't mix. Instead we sink a couple of pints of local real ale and swap Land Rover stories before retiring.

The day before, while buying Ordance Survey maps at the local post office, I got chatting to the postmistress – who told me her teenage son, George Mills, was LRO's

biggest fan. Today she's let him take a day off school to join his hero (honest – I'm not kidding ...) Vince Cobley. Young George is grinning from ear to ear as he climbs up into the 90.

We head out of Exmoor, taking in some greenlaning as we head south-east to Wiveliscombe, where Richard Greenway takes us round his new off-road site at Sharp's Farm. It's so impressive that Vince pledges to run some LRO Adventure Club events there in the future. With more than three miles of exciting tracks through 247 acres of open farmland, and with great views all around, it's sure to prove a highly popular venue.

From here, we head across country to Glastonbury via the rolling countryside of the Quantock and Mendip Hills. We'd dearly love to visit Cheddar Gorge, the sheer walls of which cut a great canyon, more than 400 feet high, through the limestone – but time is short and it will have to wait for another visit.

The lanes here are narrow and flanked on either side by sturdy earth banks, topped by hedges – so typical of so many of the roads throughout the West Country. But we make leisurely progress to the great plain of Somerset, where Glastonbury Tor rises enigmatically out of the flat levels. The place is redolent of myths and legends of King Arthur of Camelot; and the myths and legends of the Isle of Avalon and the Celtic Otherworld.

Joseph of Arithmathea is reputed to have brought the Holy Grail to Glastonbury – and from his staff is said to

A typical track between the man-made waterways of the Levels.

Raising the suspension on the Range Rover improves ground clearance for rutty driving.

have sprung the Glastonbury Thorn. A great abbey was founded here in 700, but in 1191 it was largely destroyed by a fire. Later, while clearing up the ruins, the monks claimed to have found the bones of King Arthur and his queen, Guinevere, in the abbey grounds.

This is another place where it would be all too easy to spend a day exploring, but we're on the move again,

Legendary landmark – Glastonbury Tor can be seen for miles across the flat countryside.

Young Blood

GEORGE MILLS has restored a scrapyard Series III and taught himself to drive off-road. It's his fourteenth birthday this month.

Restoring a £50 scrapyard Series III to MoT pass standard is a tough task, but managing to do it yourself before your fourteenth birthday is amazing.

George Mills won't be able to drive on the road for another three years but he hasn't let this dampen his enthusiasm for all things Land Rover. He has eaten, slept and loved Land Rovers ever since he picked up a copy of LRO four years ago. Since then he's bought every issue – and two Series IIIs!

The first, a 109-inch, cost him just £50 from a local scrapyard. The chassis of the former recovery vehicle was riddled with rust, but he replaced the rear crossmember and welded in plates to get it roadworthy before turning his attention to the 2.25-litre petrol engine.

That's academic, of course, as George has at least three years to wait before he ventures on to the public highway. In the meantime, he's taught himself to drive in his second Land Rover – an 88-inch SIII diesel that he keeps at a local farm, where he has persuaded the owner to let him take it off-road in a disused quarry.

LRO's Vince Cobley was so impressed that he allowed young George to take the wheel of his brand-new 90 for an off-road spin. 'He's an excellent young driver,' was Vince's verdict.

determined to try out some UCRs (unclassified roads) across the marshy levels. Once a flooded morass, they were drained by man hundreds of years ago to create what is now some of the finest pastureland in the entire British Isles.

But you can never truly defeat nature: the recent heavy rains had flooded these flat fields. Although the waters had largely drained away by the time we ventured on to the levels, vast flocks of wildfowl filled the air as we disturbed them from their feeding on the sodden grass. But the lanes, with underlying stone beneath the rich, black peat, were easy going and we caused no damage.

We eventually stopped atop a bridge over a ruler-straight drainage channel, watching the watery, winter-afternoon sun sink low over the equally watery landscape. It was the end of an all-too-brief trip to this fascinating corner of the world, but I suspect it won't be too long before we return to explore some more.

Vince allowed fourteen-year-old George to take the wheel of his new 90 around the off-road site.

THREE HOURS AGO I was standing on top of Wiltshire, looking out over the dramatic sweep of the chalky downland, skylarks wheeling overhead, unexpected winter sunshine on my face. Now I'm at a standstill on the M25, inching the mud-spattered Discovery forward through the stacked-and-racked traffic as darkness falls over the London Orbital. The ancient drove roads of Wiltshire seem like another country now, and I know where I'd rather be.

Wind back two days and that's where I am, climbing the side of White Sheet Hill north of Mere on a perfect morning, the rough gravel of the lane crunching under the LRO Discovery's tyres. Ahead of me is the Series III of our guide for the trip, local Land Rover enthusiast and green-laner Jim Talbot, and behind is the 110 V8 of Charles May, who's come along for the ride. We're going to spend the next two days exploring the greenlanes of South Wiltshire.

Chalk and Trees

Off-roading in unspoilt Wiltshire is a secret world of chalk downs, ancient routes — and lanes so overgrown they're like Hobbit burrows; join us in a Discovery, a Series III and a 110 V8

Words: Dan Stevens
Photographs: Peter Gathercole

It looks like marshland, but it's actually a legal byway.

Wiltshire is still a truly rural county, where agriculture plays a large part in daily life, and where most of the countryside remains unspoilt. It's also peppered with byways, and the county council has a refreshing attitude towards four-wheel drive users. In neighbouring Dorset, many byways have been reclassified as footpaths, but in Wiltshire the council appears determined to keep them open for all types of traffic. And all of this makes it an ideal place to enjoy a bit of greenlaning in some of Britain's most idyllic countryside.

As England continues to disappear beneath retail parks, multi-storey car parks and motorway service stations, counties like Wiltshire provide a haven from the commercialism of modern life. And you can get even further away from it all if you've got a Land Rover and an OS map.

Reaching the top of the hill we climb out, buffeted by the strong wind blowing across from the south. Despite the sun it's cold. Views are all very well, but I'm back in the Disco quickly and we're off down the lane. The surface is compacted flint and gravel, but it's washed out in places, leaving big dips full of water. They're not especially deep, but they do provide a nice chance to get the wheels dirty. The amount of chalk in the ground means this water is going to play havoc with wheel bearings, and I remind myself to pencil in a regrease before too long. There's nothing like a bit of preventative maintenance, especially when it comes to elderly Land Rovers.

Jim's Series III is already suffering, from a worn universal joint in the front driveshaft. It's not desperate, but Jim's aware of the fact that it might get worse over the next two days, so we may have to retire the 88-inch and double up in the Disco and the 110. Jim's son William has had to leave his SIII at home, thanks to a failed water pump. He's just finished rebuilding it, and he's a bit disappointed at not being able to bring his own vehicle. Still, Jim's SIII has L-plates so Will's going to be able to drive some of the lanes.

We're crossing farmland on tracks that run alongside the edge of the fields, defined by no more than a pair of thin, shallow ruts that mark the bright green of the grass with a deep, rich brown. Underneath, the earth is a much firmer surface, and there's never any danger of sinking into a bottomless pit. It's possible that when this route was in regular use there would have been a graded, hard surface, regularly maintained to keep the coaches running.

We pass a milestone sticking up out of the grass, dated 1750, declaring Old Sarum to be XXII miles away (22 miles in new money). The distance to London has been obscured by some old graffiti, the initials WC scratched into the granite surface.

This track is now a gated road, separating fields. As passenger in the lead vehicle, Jim's wife Francis has to do the honours. With many of the hedges removed to make way for agribusiness the fields are big here, but the curves of the hills break up the wide-open spaces of green. Yet we're not far from the busy A303, traffic hurtling past below us. Another milestone, this time intact, says we've travelled a mile – Old Sarum is now XXI miles, and London is XCIX (119) miles.

Then we're rejoining the A303, slipping into the busy traffic, mud flying up from the tyres, pattering against the Discovery's wheelarches. It's a short hop along tarmac to the next lane, which climbs the side of Chilmark Down, the main road peeling off to the left as we follow the line of the hedge.

I can feel the Discovery's tyres squirming on the wet grass and slippy mud, the back end twitching out a little as I apply the power. They're new Goodyear Wrangler ATRs, a 50/50 road/off-road tyre, fitted in place of the previous Toyo Tranpath road tyres. They look much better, with pronounced side cleats, and they're working really well. The wet mud, although not deep, is doing an admirable job clogging up the treads, but the Goodyears are still gripping on whatever they can find, keeping the Discovery in a straight line.

Then the defined track gives way to a field, and it's not clear where to drive next. Jim, however, knows these lanes, and has driven them before. He confidently points the Series III across the middle of the field, heading for a gate in the hedge. He's spent precious time in council offices researching the routes to find out if they're legally driveable, and it makes a difference. Instead of having to stop, pore over maps, then attempt to find the right path without knowing for sure if we're definitely allowed to use it, we can keep going. It's good to know that what you're doing is lawful, and it takes away that irritating uncertainty about what's going to happen next.

Suddenly the lane becomes heavily overgrown. The roof rack on Charles' 110 is catching foliage and branches, and I can hear the tangled growth laying into the Disco's

It's a V8, and that's a lot of water. Pass the WD40, Miguel.

paintwork. But we resigned ourselves a long time ago to the fact that it was going to pick up some damage, because we regularly use it off-road. And what's a Land Rover, any Land Rover, without the odd scratch?

Jim halts the convoy, and Francis gets out to remove a branch that's fallen across the path. This is responsible greenlaning at its finest – there's no point in driving over something, or round it, when you can move it easily. We push on through the undergrowth, emerging into another field where the track runs alongside the stubble remains from the year's harvest.

Over tea and sandwiches, we discuss the greenlanes of the area, and Jim's fascination with their history. He's been studying the area's byways since he bought his Land Rover, and he keeps producing little gems of information about the route we're on. 'This was a drove road and

coaching route – at one point there would have been 60 or 70 coaches a day passing through here,' he says. He points up the track. 'Further on we'll drive past the site of a couple of coaching houses – one still stands, but the other is long gone.'

In fact, we're on the M4 of the 18th century. These days it probably handles less traffic – and at a more sedate pace, their drivers and passengers travelling for the sake of it, not because they have to.

Then it's down into the woods, descending the side of the hill. The trees form one long, continuous arch above us, and leaves litter the track, making it greasy. 'It gets progressively tougher now,' warns Jim, pointing down the track into the wood. 'Last time I was down there it was really sticky, with deep ruts and water.' We bump over an axle twister, tyres slipping a little on the mud-and-leaf surface, lights on in the gloom of the wood. I'm ready for a bit of mud now.

Dan gets the back out at a life-or-death 2 mph.

The disco encounters its progress-stopping mystery object.

A woman's work is never done, especially when she's out greenlaning.

Except that it's not mud. It's tarmac. Someone has come in here and laid a load of the stuff, which is not what you expect to find in the middle of a Wiltshire greenlane. It's not compacted or rolled, but it is definitely tarmac. 'Well, it was mud the last time I came down here,' mutters Jim. Somewhat disappointed, we press on.

A properly-surfaced road bisects the lane, and we suddenly emerge from the woods onto a blind bend. Gingerly crossing over, we take up our route again, at first broken tarmac, later giving way to earth. We cross another lane and head uphill; the Series III leads the way over a couple of hillocks with deep ruts on either side. The 88-inch bounces over the top with ease, despite its limited ground clearance (Jim runs it on 6.50×16 tyres). The Discovery, however, doesn't. It stops as I point the bonnet up the hill. I grab first. Nothing doing; the vehicle's not going to go forward. Something is catching on the underside.

I reverse, and in second low give it a bit more gas to clear the hillock. The Discovery sails over the top, but photographer Peter wants me to do it again, slower this time, for the camera. Predictably, the Discovery stops again, the mystery object fouling the underside. It doesn't seem to be the towbar, which is the most likely candidate on any Discovery, and the diffs aren't touching the ground either. So I take it again in second low, and it clears it with no problems. I never did find out what was causing the holdup.

Then we emerge from the woods into the back end of a housing estate in the town of Wilton. That's the intriguing thing about greenlaning – you never quite know where you're going to end up next. Sure, OS maps give you an idea about what's coming around the next bend, but the way it's possible to be driving through the middle of a seemingly isolated wood one minute and then into a housing estate the next always fascinates me. The difference between old and new really highlights how these roads were once major thoroughfares.

This is in direct contrast to the next lane we drive, after our short detour through Wilton. Leaving Salisbury and a magnificent view of the cathedral (which has England's tallest spire at 404 feet) behind us, we take another track that was once … a racecourse. In the 17th century the local lord used it to race horses on, and planted a lime tree every mile as distance markers. They've all gone now, as have the coaching houses that used to line the route in the 18th and 19th centuries.

The sun's starting to set now, and we're driving right into it. All I can see is the outline of Jim's SIII 20 feet in front of me, and the steam rising off the underside as he splashes through the puddles. It's very pretty, with the deep glow of a setting sun filtering through the trees and casting long shadows – even if it is difficult to see exactly where I'm going.

We've come to another White Sheet Hill and, as the sun begins to sink below the downs, we stop for the perfect photo opportunity – Jim's SIII disappearing off into the sunset. Then I notice that the Discovery's front offside tyre is bulging. We all stand and stare at it for a minute, and come to the conclusion that yes, it's definitely getting flatter. A flurry of action produces a mini electric compressor, which Charles and I hook up to the tyre.

We wait. While it's not getting any flatter, it's not getting any more inflated either. I can see a dusk tyre-changing moment coming on here, in rapidly dropping temperatures, and I'm not entirely sure where the thing that unlocks the wheel-locking device on the spare is.

'You can't use a hi-lift jack on this, can you?' asks Charles, reminding me of the fact that Discoverys come with an only-slightly-better-than-useless bottle jack, which are slow and difficult to use.

So, in the light of that lot, and in the absence of light, we tighten the valve core (with our handy valve core tightening device) and turn round to find our rooms for the night. I'm driving slowly and carefully, listening for the characteristic thumping of a flat tyre running off the rim, but when I stop a mile later the tyre's looking just fine. It's still plump and fully inflated two hours later. Valve core tightening tools' … indispensable.

We're forecast rain next day, as winter approaches from the north. But it dawns bright and clear, and as we drive up between Trow Down and Pincombe Down, I can't help but feel lucky to be here, looking out over the Wiltshire countryside, with warm sun filling the Discovery's cabin. We stop so that William can take the wheel of Jim's 88-

The prospect of a wheel change brought much avoidance of eye contact and staring at the floor. Eventually the tyre stayed up anyway.

inch, then head off down a grassy track, with wide and fairly deep ruts that look like they've been cut by tractors. Our Land Rovers traverse them with ease, because again the mud is lying on a solid surface of flint, which means there's plenty of grip. Turning downhill, having fought our way through some thick hawthorn trees which hung over the track, we pass a converted barn, the only access to which is via a greenlane. Fittingly, there are three well-used Land Rovers parked outside.

Land Rovers are commonplace in this part of Wiltshire, and almost every farm has an example of the marque in the yard. Negotiating the tight, downhill track, we pass two Defenders in an adjacent field, two men carrying shotguns standing next to them. Further on, a man standing next to the track is holding a gate open. How very thoughtful, I think, until I look back. Lined up in the field, waiting to cross the track, are five brand new, black Range Rovers, with blacked-out windows. One of them has the window down, with a faintly familiar face looking out at our convoy of muddy Land Rovers (by contrast, these five are spotless). I wave – he looks tentative, and then raises a hand, a little uncertainly. The pheasant shooting season has started.

Charles, in the lead, cuts across from one set of ruts to another, and the 110 fights for grip on the grass, the back end crabbing across the track. I try to make a better job in the Discovery, concentrating on getting the rear wheels to follow the front as I guide the vehicle into the ruts. They don't, and the Disco slides along the grass until the Goodyears find something they can get a grip on. They don't have quite enough side cleat to bite into the soft grass; but then Charles' 110 is shod with Trac-Edges, and they didn't do it either.

Now we're skirting the edge of the Rushmore Estate and Chase Wood, which in the mid-morning sunlight looks as perfect as any woodland could. The ground is uncultivated and rough, but we're following a well-worn path, with clearly defined ruts that have already seen traffic today. The byway peters out at the bottom of the hill, and we're back on tarmac again. We wend our way

Truly an idyllic moment – Land Rover pootles gently into the sunset.

through a couple of small, sleepy Wiltshire villages, and then take another greenlane at Tollard Royal, climbing again. There are plenty of walkers out today, and I'm expecting the odd sour look, maybe even a challenge to our presence. But without fail, everyone we pass gives a wave or a smile – one elderly couple stop to talk, interested in where we're going and maybe a little puzzled as to why we've chosen to drive instead of walk.

This byway was once a drove road, used to take livestock from Weymouth to London: sheep, cattle and even geese were herded along here, and fish packed in ice hauled inland from the coast.

Our minds are on something more contemporary – the Queen of Pop. Jim points into the valley below where Madonna is rumoured to have bought a house, once owned by artist Cecil Beaton. I can just make out the tip of a roof, the rest masked by the thick trees that cover the valley. It's beautifully concealed, an ideal place to escape prying camera lenses and nosy journalists. Suddenly, Charles clicks with something earlier on. 'Those Range Rovers back there – I could have sworn one of the men in them was Guy Ritchie' (Madonna's film director husband). Could it have been him who waved to us?

We're not getting starstruck though – we've got a lane to finish. We cross the top of the drover's track with most of Wiltshire laid out in front of us, steeply-terraced fields sloping away into the pastureland below. This is Win Green, the second highest point in the county, and on a clear day you can see The Needles on the Isle of Wight to the south. A Series I chugs around the corner, a working vehicle driven by a ruddy-faced man in a cloth cap who gives us a cheery wave. Here, even the oldest of Land Rovers is still used for its intended purpose.

Real life returns – I realise that we're going to have to leave for home now, to beat the inevitable commuter slog on the M25. We leave Jim, Francis, William and Charles on the side of Win Green in the late autumn sunshine, and head north.

Meet Your Greens ...

Words and Photographs:
Chris Rudge

Chris Rudge tackles Hampshire's glorious woodlands with his Series II

SPRING HAD ARRIVED at long last, releasing the singing birds and giving new life to wintered trees. The long-awaited warm weather provided the perfect opportunity for an afternoon's greenlaning with my wife, Michelle, and our two boys. Our Series II is in desperate need of a new set of springs – to the extent that it is leaning over on the driver's side. Still, I thought I'd squeeze the last bit of money's worth out of the old springs before it goes up on the jacks.

Luckily for us, we live in the middle of Hampshire, which has a good network of byways and unclassified roads – unlike many parts of the country – and if you fancy getting out and having a stroll, the whole place is bristling with footpaths and bridleways.

We decide the old market town of Alton is a good starting point as it's only down the road from our home. Its name comes from the Saxon for 'village of the great spring', referring to the source of the River Wey on the outskirts of town. There is a rich history attached to the place, having been the scene of battles during the Civil War in the 1600s. The damage caused can still be seen on the doors and walls of St Lawrence church. Oliver Cromwell lived just over the road for a while and Quakers had set up at the other end of town some years before. Much has happened in this area over the years with not only Saxon, but Roman presence as well.

One of the attractions today is the Watercress Line steam railway, which starts where the normal commuter line terminates. Running a number of steam and diesel engines on a stretch of line between Alton and Alresford, it uses an old route of the Alton to Winchester line, and can be found operating over most of the summer and weekends in winter. If you're lucky you might catch a sight of Thomas the Tank Engine when he comes to visit!

Council Clearance

We head north past St Lawrence Church heading towards Odiham, and pick up our first and favourite lane. It's only a short way out of town and we always keep an eye on its condition and use. Last year the council had it cleared as it was getting very overgrown, and the improvements for access either by vehicle or foot were quite dramatic. The main gain from that work will hopefully mean the usual huge mud holes will dry up during the summer – in previous years water has remained at the top end of this lane, even during the driest summers.

We drive about 100 yards away from the road and have to put the SII into low ratio due to recent rain – ruts are deep and full of water. This is a popular route with four-wheel drive folk looking for a bit of off-road use. My son, Adrian, had previously come back with a tale of woe during January, when he and one of his mates tried unsuccessfully to help extract a Suzuki driver out of this same mud. So I take it cautiously, as large holes can be dug out by a wheel spinning continuously, and I don't want to get stuck – even if we're not far from home!

As it turns out, the track's okay; deep ruts, but the 750 Firestone SATs pull us through with ease. This particular lane is almost on top of a hill to the north of Alton, and when the weather is clear, which is the case today, a good view can be had over to the South Downs. At a number of points along this trail, places can be found to pull over and take a stroll or make a brew.

The whole length of this lane is around one mile, and at just over the half-way point, we decide to turn round and go back. One reason is that the upper end, although having been cleared, is extremely water logged with deep mud holes and, being a 'lone Landy', I don't fancy getting bogged down. The second reason is that if I do go through, my passage would only help trash the surface even more, and not give it a chance to recover. At this point there is ample room to turn round, so we return the way we came.

Arriving back on the road, we soon find another lane. This one is steep and prone to being somewhat rocky due to heavy rains washing out the surface soil. In the past I've found great difficulty stopping on this gradient, as loose stones keep propelling the vehicle downhill, although the wheels are stationary. Better check it out first! Another bit of fun is getting out at the far end, which is risky, unless someone else can see you on to the road. It exits from a very steep rocky slope, which requires first low, onto a fast main road. You have to choose just the right time to go!

We decide to go for it, and are rewarded by only a small slide down the slope, followed at the bottom by a hard right through a gap just big enough for the 88-inch and up a 45 degree muddy incline. No problem! A bit worrying at the other end though; I had forgotten about the side slope to the right as well as the 30 degree decline. Just in case, the others get out and follow. This stretch is only a couple of hundred yards long, but it has to be taken carefully.

We make it across the main road, and straight on to the next stretch which is semi-metalled due to access required for private houses further along. Just past the last house is an immediate closing in of undergrowth, and we push through. Half a mile later it opens out again, as this bit is used as a farmyard track, and we end up on a small lane.

Gliders and Elephants

As it was Sunday, we went for a sedate drive around the spring (tarmac) lanes – let's face it, you can't race a 1960 Series II – and we pull into Lasham Airfield. Originally

Woodland gives way to asphalt, and a trip to Lasham Airfield's WWII Aircraft Preservation Society ... sporting few, if any, WWII aircraft.

built during the Second World War as a fighter and Mosquito base, it is now used as an aircraft repair facility and is one of England's premier gliding schools. I read a while back that a touring circus troupe wintered here in the 1940s or 1950s. During their stay, one of the elephants died and is buried somewhere in the airfield.

We hang around for an hour or so to watch the launch of gliders by both air tow or ground launch. It's great fun, and they do trial flights for a reasonable fee if you want to whet your appetite for glider flying. I recommend it; there's a whole new perspective on the world from 2,000 feet up.

Up at the far end of Lasham Airfield is the Second World War Aircraft Preservation Society. The most extraordinary thing about this display is that there are no aircraft from the Second World War, although the small display of restored and partially-restored aircraft are quite fascinating. The nearest to Second World War vintage appears to be a part-restored Army Auster, looking like the engine and front end has gone away for a refurbishment.

When leaving Lasham Airfield, tucked away in the hedgerows we can see remaining air raid shelters. In a month or so, they will vanish from sight under thick undergrowth when summer arrives ... I can't help wondering where that elephant is buried!

Consulting the OS map, we find we are adjacent to another greenlane, but as I had done some research during the winter months, I knew this RUPP was an effective dead end, as the original lane it led to had been reclassified to a footpath some years back. There are a number of potential routes in this area which are marked on the very useful and easy to use Explorer series OS maps as a byway, but have been reclassified – so beware. Most are marked with Hants County Council wooden right of way signs, especially the recently reclassified routes, but even some of these are misleading.

As we were not going to get anywhere with that one, we head back through Shalden village and across the A339 to a lane I haven't got around to driving yet. Finding the entrance near the main road junction, we strike out up the hill. This one is quite overgrown already; it will be a bundle of laughs to get through here at the tail end of the summer – not recommended for nice shiny paintwork. Pushing through overhanging holly and thorn bushes will leave some lovely patterns for you to admire for months to come!

No problem, until we get to the top of that incline and find agricultural use has churned it up a bit, leaving it looking very boggy. I check it out and decide to risk it. The SATs pull us through, but road-type tyres would have a few problems here.

Back out on the A339, we drive north towards Basingstoke, and cut across on a small road heading west. Taking a byway on the right, approximately half a mile away from the A road we just left, we again head north through a wonderful bluebell carpeted woodland. Stopping some way in and getting out to stretch our legs, we were hit by the full force of that almost-hyacinth smell of bluebells. That's one of the reasons we head for this route – bluebells are guaranteed at this time of the year, and it's a sight not to be missed.

Nothing too testing presented itself ...

and bluebells lined the woodland rides.

32

Agricultural use has churned the track up a bit, leaving it boggy.

Further down the track we find the ground has been deeply rutted. I pop the Landy back into low ratio again to pull us through, even though the general slope of the lane is in a downhill direction. Most of the byways in this area are extensively used by the landowners and their employees for access to fields and woodland – this is worth remembering when encountering a tractor or similar, and I try to give way when possible.

At the bottom of this section, there's a junction of bridleway, footpath and private drive, which is where part of the now-dismantled Basingstoke to Alton railway ran past. A small brick-built tunnel and some of the track bed are still in place, together with an old railway building. If you travel the A339 from Basingstoke to Alton, there are still a great number of clues to the original route of this railway which finally closed in 1936. Some may remember the Will Haye picture, *Oh Mr Porter*, which was filmed on the line in 1937 before it was finally pulled up forever. The only parts found intact are used by the Watercress Line steam railway in Alton.

After driving through the tunnel, we are back on the A339 … afternoon over! It's amazing how much green-laning can be packed into one afternoon. We are lucky enough to have it on our doorstep, though, and long may it remain there.

Journey's end, and a trip worth waving for.

Testing Tracks

Leafy Hampshire has a neat network of well-maintained highways and byways – LRO joins the Shire Land Rover Club on a tour of the area's Test Valley

Words: Craig Cheetham
Photographs: Nick Dimbleby

34

IF YOU ABUSE them, then you're going to lose them. That's the rule when it comes to greenlaning and, unless we all act responsibly, it could become a hobby of the past, with frightening consequences for Land Rover enthusiasts all over the world.

Luckily, some greenlaners are hugely responsible and take a real pride in repairing and maintaining the lanes in their area, none more so than the Shire Land Rover Club (SLRC) in Hampshire. And they want to show us what they do. So, without hesitation, I headed along the M4 in LRO's Discovery to join them for a morning's greenlaning.

It's early ... very early. It's also a cold Saturday morning in the middle of December when I swing into the Land Rover-infested driveway of Julian and Alistair Read, who, along with Julian's girlfriend Vicky, are the brains behind today's event. These guys are serious Land Rover nuts. As well as the LRO Disco, the front of the house is home to a Camel Freelander, a Range Rover Vogue, a V8 Hybrid, a multi-coloured Lightweight and Vicky's rather queezy purple bobtailed Range Rover. There's also a 90 in the back garden, while Ali's workday Peugeot is banished to the parking in the street – one round the corner to be precise. It obviously doesn't have the pedigree to park on the Reads' driveway.

Vicky greets me with a welcome cup of strong coffee. Julian and Ali, apparently, are already on their fourth cup. They've been up since the early hours putting the final touches to the day's route.

With coffees finished and adrenaline kicking in, we drive in convoy to the event's starting point, the Old Forge Inn at Otterbourne. I take up the rear in the Disco, behind Julian and Vicky in the Freelander and Ali in his well-used Range Rover.

We swing into the car park and already there's at least ten vehicles waiting for us, ranging from Jeremy Dale's pristine Range Rover 2.5DSE to a posse of bent and battered Range Rovers. Their owners are looking forward to the afternoon; a free run on a private off-road site where the odd roll or tree shunt is classified as fun.

'That's the good thing about these events,' says Julian, as he caresses the frumpy front of his Freelander. 'Our club is full of people from different walks of life, with various levels of off-road experience. People can choose how tough they want to get, whether it's just a gentle drive in the country or a blast round the private section at the end.'

And that diversity is no more apparent than in the vehicles assembled. The oldest is Dave White and Mick Harris's grey Series II; the newest a six-month-old Freelander belonging to Dave Rawlings and family. There's even a choice of

The Shire Land Rover Club gather for a briefing before jumping into their vehicles.

routes, with some of the tighter and muddier sections bypassed by more gentle lanes for those enthusiasts with shinier vehicles or those lacking the confidence to try the tougher stuff.

Before we set off, marshal Ashley Parsons takes his orange Range Rover for a trial run along the first lane, behind the villages of Silkstead and Compton. Apparently, the lane can get very slippery and, after a night of torrential rain, there's one area that's very dangerous, not to mention potentially damaging to both the vehicles and the lane.

Ali clambers onto the crooked tailgate of the Range Rover. Six months ago it was pristine, but over the past couple of months it's been used in anger. The nearside front wing picked up a ding on a previous off-road excursion and the offside took a knock the previous evening while the lads were out doing a last minute recce of the course. But Ali isn't bothered – he bought it to be used as Solihull intended. And the rear tailgate is also the perfect platform for delivering drivers' briefings, which Ali does with immense pride. He's the main man behind the Shire Land Rover Club and, with such good turnouts to these events and such a brilliant atmosphere, he has every right to be proud.

Mad, Raving Mad!

BROTHERS JULIAN and Ali Read have been involved with Land Rovers since they were wee nippers, and both have owned a plethora of Land Rover products.

They're hugely enthusiastic club people and, between them, have nurtured the SLRC into the 250-strong organisation it is today.

Much of the unseen work is carried out by Julian's girlfriend, Vicky Cumming (centre), who looks after membership details and enquiries, runs the administrative side of the club and is an enthusiastic off-roader herself, using a lurid purple Range Rover as her own off-road toy. The trio is also behind the successful launch of the newly-formed Freelander Club and will be organising similar events for Freelander owners in the near future.

The SLRC has an excellent relationship with local Land Rover dealer, Hunters of Southampton, which includes parts discounts and assistance with club events. They also arrange a number of social events for members, as well as off-road trips.

Sadly, we discover the first lane has to be cancelled – the ground is too soft and using it would only result in damage or injury. Instead we opt to start a mile or so down the road at the village of Compton End.

The first lane takes us through a pair of muddy fields – the track here is slippery, but the deep ruts keep the vehicle straight and controllable. Furthermore, the track is kept in excellent condition, thanks to continuous lane repairs carried out by the SLRC.

'We believe very strongly in keeping the routes in good condition,' says Julian. 'If we use them for off-roading, then it's only reasonable that we ensure that any damage is repaired. After today's event is over, we'll be back to

Ashley Parsons' Range Rover has gone from being pristine to picking up dings and knocks all over the place – the result of testing lanes before other vehicles drive them.

check all the lanes and repair any damage incurred. There's many complaints about off-roaders at present and, by treating the countryside with respect, we're doing our part to keep a good image in the area.'

And he's right. Despite our route crossing by several farms, not one farmer complains about our presence. Indeed, a couple even greet us with a cheerful wave as we pass by their doors. They obviously recognise the efforts the SLRC is going to, by keeping the area passable for four-wheel drives. No doubt the continuous repair scheme is helping them with access to their own land, saving them plenty of effort in maintaining the lanes themselves.

Sadly, the same attitude isn't shared by the irate chap we meet at the end of the lane. He wants to take a short cut home via the same route in his Toyota Land Cruiser, but going the other way. The presence of our vehicles, travelling in no more than groups of three, is causing him some annoyance.

'How many of you idiots are there?' he barks, as I roll down the Disco's window. I shrug my shoulders and tell him there's quite a few. I'm not here to be called an idiot, and certainly not by a hypocrite who is only there to use the lane himself.

Undeterred, he calls us all a 'bloody disgrace' and heads off to call the police. The club members aren't in the slightest bit bothered – the local constabulary already know we're using the lanes today and that we have every right to be there. Not surprisingly, they don't turn up.

Our route brings us out onto the A3090 at the hamlet of Oliver's Battery. The tiny village sits upon a hill from where Cromwell's Roundheads attacked the Royalists of Otterbourne and Winchester during the English Civil War of the 17th century. Today it's idyllic, with only a rural petrol station and the odd car as an obvious reminder of modern life.

There's a short road section before we join the Clarendon Way at Teg Down. We're making good time, with only a minor dispute between me and photographer Nick Dimbleby threatening to halt progress.

Joining the road section we follow Julian's Freelander and I'm so intent on following the leader that I'm oblivious to Nick's instructions. Julian disappears down a short cut to get ahead of the pack and I almost swerve down after him, despite Nick's protestations.

Luckily, it doesn't come to fisticuffs and I begrudgingly agree to listen to my navigator, who takes us out on to the Clarendon Way.

This route runs from Winchester to Salisbury and is a 24-mile network of lanes and footpaths, crossing the Test Valley. Most of it is an old Roman road and parts of it are still open to all traffic. Others are byways with supposed free access, but you need a Land Rover to cross them; there are deep ruts, tricky descents and plenty of loose rock. Recent rain means there's quite a few bonnet-high water splashes to contend with, but none of us are deterred. Even the Freelanders are happy as they speed through the water splashes, flinging mud like American presidential candidates.

The lane brings us out at the edge of Farley Mount Country Park, which boasts, among its attractions, some of the most diverse wooded areas in the country, with yew and beech, coppice woods and a modern plantation covering the area.

The 'tread lightly' rule is taken very seriously by the SLRC. After each off-road event they revisit the lanes and repair any damage.

Rising above the park is a distinctive triangular folly, which marks an ancient burial mound. The folly itself was built as a memorial to a horse which, 200 years ago, survived a dramatic fall into a chalk pit with its owner. Apparently, the horse subsequently won a local race under its snappy new name, 'Beware Chalk Pit'.

Silly names for racehorses might still be in vogue, but the landscape around Farley Mount has changed considerably over the years. It's a no-go area for most vehicles, but there's a byway on the southernmost end of the park

which is still open. This cuts through a short wooded path and across the open lanes of Pitt Down, where plenty of chalk pits are waiting to catch out unwary Land Rover drivers and dozing racehorses.

From Pitt Down we head along a short road section to the longest part of our route, where, once again, we're confronted by a hostile local.

Nick and I are leading the pack in the Disco. We stop in a lay-by just before the start of a RUPP (road used as public path) leading through Parnholt Wood to allow some vehicles past, with a view to photographing some of the other vehicles in the convoy.

We're parked legally in a recognised public parking space, yet our actions raise the hackles of a local lady in a Peugeot, who is furious that I've taken the space she usually uses when she comes to walk her dogs. 'Excuse me young man,' she says, finger wagging merrily in the breeze, 'but I must park my car there.'

I say she can, and I'll be moving on in just two minutes if she's prepared to hang on. She isn't, and instead she parks her Peugeot bang in the middle of the lane and wanders off for a walk, yapping dogs in tow.

To her annoyance, she's left enough room for us to squeeze past, but not without splashing mud against the side of her illegally-parked vehicle. To make matters worse, one of her corgis makes a suicide dash under the wheels of the LRO Disco. I slam the brakes on and miss the daft mutt by inches. The woman thinks her dog's death-wish is my fault and scribbles down our registration number. The police have yet to get in touch.

Our new lane offers a variety of driving styles and conditions. It starts off gently, with loose rocks and thin mud covering nearly level ground – certainly nothing too taxing. Deeper into the lane, however, it turns into huge fun. The mud gets thicker and deeper, while some evil twists in the lane require forethought and proper vehicle positioning. I'm having so much fun that I've abandoned our photographer half a mile away and have forgotten about him. It's only when he arrives at the bottom end

The route runs along Farley Mount Country Park which boasts some of the most diverse wooded areas in the country.

There is a great variety of different tracks to tackle, from non-taxing level ground routes to thick mud lanes which require forethought.

of the lane in the passenger seat of Jeremy Dale's Range Rover that I remember he's with me.

I offer him a packet of crisps as penance, which seems to do the trick. Our snack-scoffing antics mean we miss one of the highlights of the day, as Dave White comes bumbling down the track waving his Series II's steering wheel out of the window.

Dave brings the SII to a safe, if wayward, halt and sets about some typical Land Rover repair work. This involves a large rubber mallet and a lock nut the size of a boxer's fist. 'It's always bloody doing it,' he says, with a shrug of his shoulders, as he lovingly wallops the wheel back into place.

We follow Dave for the next couple of miles, up through the villages of Up Somborne and Crawley. He obviously isn't too bothered about the steering wheel. His SII makes light work of the twisty country lanes, with the Disco struggling to keep up thanks to its vast proportions.

Emerging from Crawley, which has buildings dating back to the first century, we swing on to our final and most taxing lane of the day. The thick, wooded area across Brockley Warren is marked as optional on the map, but two-thirds of the competitors, Freelanders included, are prepared to give it a go.

I reluctantly resign the LRO Discovery to an attack from branches and brambles, knowing I'll have to spend a long Sunday afternoon with a bottle of polish before handing it back. But this lane is too much fun to worry about small things like scratches and paint blemishes. My mind is made up when the Disco in front – a rather tasty Camel Trophy vehicle owned by Andy Marshall – opts to follow the tricky route.

Andy's chuffed to bits with his Camel. He had intended to buy a standard Discovery but the sight of the beast on a dealer's forecourt took his fancy. Apparently, he got it for a knock-down price.

The dealer said it would fetch more if some idiot hadn't stuck all the funny stickers and off-roady gear on it. It was just the vehicle Andy wanted, so he snapped it up.

The lane across Brockley Warren is far too much fun to worry about scratches from branches and brambles – even for newer Range Rovers!

The ground underfoot is very greasy and the Discovery's Toyo road tyres, while excellent for motorway use, are really struggling, with the back end sliding all over the place. The worst moment comes when we slide out of some ruts and the front end lifts on to a bank, missing a barbed wire fence and gatepost by a matter of inches. Luckily, a bit of power snaps it back into shape at the right moment, and the only damage is to my embarrassed pride.

The track leads us deep into the undergrowth, dipping through natural troughs in the ground and tilting the vehicle over by 25 degrees in places. We round a corner and are confronted by Andy's Disco, stationary in the lane. Ahead of him, a queue of Land Rovers has formed, indicating problems ahead.

Word comes back that the lead vehicle, Jackie Clarke's Defender 90, has suffered a puncture. But, with a gaggle of committed Land Rover enthusiasts on hand and a dozen or so high-lift jacks at the ready, it's a matter of

minutes before Jackie and her husband, Dave, are fully inflated and mobile again.

We wait for the convoy to break up – making sure we obey the tread lightly rules – before heading deeper into the lane. Our next obstacle is a low branch, which hangs too low for the Discovery to pass under. There's a small path around the edge of the tree, just wide enough for a vehicle but, as Andy proves, it's difficult to negotiate. He has to shunt the Discovery back and forth a few times before he can beat the obstacle, and the front of the vehicle comes within an inch of clipping the tree.

Then it's my turn. The tyres on the LRO Disco don't afford the same grip as the Camel's, but in this case it's a blessing, as the back end slips round and positions itself perfectly for a simple reverse turn. We're through in seconds, leaving the guys with mud tyres to shunt and shove their way through in our wake.

From here, the lane gets easier, although the dense undergrowth presents a problem for those with shiny paintwork. It's not a real issue, however, as Jeremy Dale proves by barrelling £30,000-worth of Range Rover DSE through the trickiest parts of the track without so much as a shrug.

You Can Do It Too!

ALL THE ROUTES covered in this section can be found on Ordnance Survey Landranger Map 185 (Winchester and Basingstoke, Andover and Romsey).

LRO stayed at the Gateway Hotel in Eastleigh. Alternatively, there are several pubs and guest houses in the area, as well as campsites for when the weather gets more friendly.

Although it's possible to do the route yourself, it would be quicker and much easier to join the SLRC on a trip. Guests are welcome and the routes are already planned for you. For more information call 07980 589944 or 023 8090 0261.

A Camel vehicle reminisces as it splashes through rain-filled ruts.

Even our four-legged friend enjoys an off-road adventure atop a Series vehicle.

Reluctantly, we pull off the track back on to tarmac and bring our morning's greenlaning to an end, opting instead for lunchtime refreshment at a traditional pub in the village of Goodworth Clatford, near Andover.

But the off-roading action isn't over. This afternoon, the SLRC has booked a private off-road site just up the road, and here we'll have plenty more thrills and spills.

The venue is a Second World War bomb site on the outskirts of Andover and, rumour has it, was the result of a German bomber choosing not to drop his bombs on Southampton, as instructed. Instead, he apparently dropped them in a deserted rural area, where he would cause minimal death or destruction. No doubt the Germans would have had him shot if they'd found out, but the man is probably responsible for saving hundreds of lives and preventing extensive damage.

The forgotten hero has also left a superb off-road site in his wake, with three large pits in which SLRC members have often been known to roll their Rovers over.

Sadly, our entry is restricted when we discover that some joyriders have abandoned a car bang in the middle of the access road to the site. But with a fleet of Land Rovers on hand, a burnt-out Rover doesn't present much of an obstacle. Cue SLRC member Steve Marsh

and his trusty Series III, fresh from the workshop with a new set of parabolic springs. Steve's enjoying his day's off-roading, claiming the parabolics do wonders for his SIII's ride comfort and axle articulation, but shifting the stricken Rover is by far the highlight of his day. As if the poor car hadn't suffered enough by being stolen, trashed and burnt-out, it suffers the final indignity of being shovelled off the track by a snorting Series III tena years its senior. Result: Rover, nil; Land Rover, one.

I'm unaware of the surprise the SLRC has in store for me. Mad Phil Hicks has a spare seat on the passenger side of his slime-green hybrid and he's determined to crack a side slope he's failed to conquer for the past two visits to the site.

I try all manner of pathetic excuses: I've just developed a bad back, I won't fit inside the tight racing harness and, er, I've got a bit of a cold. But none of these wash as the SLRC members mercilessly gang up on me and strap me into the bright-green fright machine. And, to make matters worse, the hybrid has already lost a battle with a tree today, something which Phil shrugs off as a minor inconvenience.

An entertaining quiz designed by the SLRC keeps everyone busy throughout the day.

41

A WWII bomb site provides the perfect venue for some serious off-roading.

Steve Marsh and his Series III creep slowly into a rain-filled hollow.

The next ten minutes are quite possibly the most frightening of my life, as 3.5 litres of Rover V8, a madly grinning Phil and my stomach do battle with physics.

On the first run, the off-side rear wheel drops of the edge and into a ditch, with Phil stopping the hybrid just in time to avoid a roll. Second time, it's a similar story, but Phil is unperturbed. Ali suggests we take a run at the course from a slightly steeper angle, to allow the rear end to slide further down the bank.

Phil slams the beast into reverse, takes a much longer run up and we're off, exhausts growling, gearbox screaming and passenger wishing he'd packed another pair of boxer shorts.

Amazingly, the hybrid scrabbles its way to the top, missing the drop by a couple of centimetres and almost flattening Nick Dimbleby and Julian Read in the process. I escape, vowing to never get in a car with Phil again, yet with the ultimate respect for his driving abilities. He and Julian are regular competition safari drivers, and boy does Phil show it.

There are plenty more off-road days with the Shire Land Rover Club being planned. If you're in the area and fancy joining one, it'll be the best fiver you ever spend.

Defenders of the Realm

Nobody knows the Sussex shoreline and greenlanes better than the coastguards, who drive Defenders at work and play

THE CHALK CLIFFS of England's southern coastline are a symbol of national defiance. To the foreign visitor arriving by sea, the first glimpse of our green and pleasant land is actually white.

They're a natural deterrent to would-be invaders. It's nearly a thousand years since William the Conqueror landed near Hastings and lived up to his name. None has managed it since, including Napoleon and Hitler.

Today the cliffs are largely a peaceful place, but they're also dangerous – they overlook the busiest shipping lane in the world. The English Channel is the maritime equivalent of the M25, where the juggernaut tankers weigh tens of thousands of tons and the lanes see a heavy flow of traffic.

In the midst of this mayhem, people go to play in the fast lane. Weekend yachtsmen and fishermen weave between the heavy shipping, jagged rocks and dangerous shallow sand bars, while swimmers all too often get swept away by treacherous currents.

All in all, a very busy place for the men of Her Majesty's Coastguard. Volunteers all of them, they risk their own lives to save others on a daily basis. And they do all of this in Land Rovers.

Not any old Land Rovers, either. Uncompromising Defenders are, appropriately, the first choice for these no-nonsense defenders of the realm. The machines and the men who drive them are rugged and get to the places others wouldn't reach.

Only coastguards and the insane would ever consider taking their 90s to the edge of those crumbling cliffs, in inky darkness, during a huge gale. And who would care to winch themselves over the edge into the cauldron of crashing waves and spray, hundreds of feet below, to pluck a stranger to safety?

Yet in kinder times, when the sea's calm and there are no souls to save, these brave men leave their working

The Land Rover-loving coastguards watch over one of the busiest beats in Europe.

Words: Dave Phillips
Photographs: Peter Gathercole and Dave Phillips

vehicles at coastguard HQ and climb into their own motley collection of Land Rovers, for greenlaning jaunts and off-roading adventures in the picturesque South Downs.

The Newhaven-based coastguards are kept busy. Their watch includes the estuary of the Sussex Ouse which, despite being incredibly narrow, happens to be the entrance to the Newhaven harbour, where huge cross-Channel ferries and ocean-going ships disgorge their cargoes.

They pick their way there through hidden channels, dredged out of the shallow mud and sandbanks. Get it wrong and it's only a matter of minutes before you'll be swept on to those treacherous rocks and cliffs, which include the famous Seven Sisters – towering chalk out-crops that get progressively higher before peaking at Beachy Head, at 530 feet the most famous and formi-dable cliff in Britain. Fifty-seven people decided to end their lives there last year. The grisly job of recovering their bodies fell to the coastguards.

No wonder they can't wait to get into their Land Rovers and fill their lungs with the bracing air of the chalk downs. This is brilliant greenlaning country, where many lanes are driveable through most of the year, thanks to the hard, well-drained surface of chalk and flint.

Trevor Cutler and Nick Stanyard are the keenest Land Rover drivers of them all. They also happen to be employed by Newhaven Port as pilots. Life is normally quiet for coxswain Trevor and mate Nick, with just the occasional inexperienced ship captain to guide in and out of the harbour. But in a full-blooded storm, they are on constant call. Today, one such storm is steadily brewing …

We have to wait until the second day before the wind drops enough for them to take us on the promised green-lane tour.

It starts at the workshop of the Allen family – dad Chris and sons Rob and Chris jnr, all Land Rover fanat-ics. They drive them, repair them and restore them from their barn at Peacehaven, which is also the base for their agricultural engineering business. Chris proudly shows off his Defender 110, which he's converted into a mobile workshop, complete with arc welder powered by a PTO-driven generator. With it, he can drive into the middle of a muddy field to repair tractors, combine harvesters – in fact, anything that's mechanical and broken.

But today it's son Rob – another coastguard – who is joining our posse. From his workshop at Hoddern Farm, he takes us up a surfaced UCR to Piddinghoe, where we head north for two miles along a minor road to Southease, before turning right and across a rickety wooden bridge over the River Ouse. Here we wait for permission to cross an unmanned level crossing (there's a phone by the barriers).

A quarter of a mile up the road we join the A26 north for just over a mile before turning on to another surfaced UCR that ends at a T-junction with a byway. The surface is good and it gets even better after a quarter of a mile, when the byway status ends and it becomes a minor road, which eventually ends at the main A27, just south-east of the town of Lewes.

We head east for about half a mile before turning right down a minor road to the village of Firle. We eventually meet a great byway (clearly signposted), which runs along the bottom of the South Downs for five miles. This terminates at the village of Alfriston, on the Cuckmere River. All the time, the open grassy fields of the high downs are in sight, while the marshy lowland fields are full of wading birds.

Despite brimming ditches, the going is good. There are no ruts to speak of and the chalk and small-flint surface isn't damaged by our passing. Sections that have suffered wear in the past show signs of being repaired by the conscientious county council.

This really is very driveable by any 4×4 and would easily be negotiated by a Freelander without chance of mishap. The byway is very much a working lane; busy, with farm traffic accessing the adjacent fields although, on one particular half-mile stretch, it's bordered by a brick wall marking the boundary of Firle Park.

So often on greenlaning adventures a new lane starts off very promisingly but deteriorates steadily until the point is reached where you have to admit defeat and turn back. Not so here – the opposite, in fact.

We note that the lane is getting better all the time and, by the halfway stage, we find ourselves driving on a perfectly levelled surface of rolled stone. It's better than many B-status roads I can think of. We find out why when we round a corner near the village of Alciston and find the lane is blocked by contractors working for the county council, carrying out lane repairs.

After a brief chat, in which they turn out to be genuinely interested in our little adventure, they kindly move their machinery to let us pass. But they also warn us to avoid the very end of the lane, which they tell us is rutted and muddy. Rather than risk getting stuck, we heed their advice and, instead of continuing, turn to the left down an unclassified road to the village of Berwick.

They're off, heading towards their first greenlane.

The Coastguards and their Land Rovers

| NAME | Trevor Cutler |
| VEHICLE | 1996 Defender 90 County Station Wagon |

TREVOR'S DEFENDER 90 is the latest in a long line of Land Rovers he has owned, including a Series III and three Discoverys. It's a standard 300Tdi, which doubles up as a family car as well as Trevor's toy for greenlaning.

| NAME | Chris Allen |
| VEHICLE | 1983 Defender 110 |

CHRIS ALLEN'S Land Rover is also his mobile workshop. It is one of the first One Tens ever built, and agricultural engineer Chris has owned it for the past 15 years. He has replaced the original diesel engine with the more powerful 200Tdi unit.

| NAME | Peter Leonard |
| VEHICLE | 1968 Series IIA |

PETER'S SERIES IIA is a pristine example of the restorer's art. It was a shabby wreck when he was given it as an 18th birthday present by his dad, but three years of painstaking work saw him finish it in time for his 21st.

| NAME | Richard Mercer |
| VEHICLE | Defender 90 Station Wagon |

RICHARD'S 90 STARTED life as a pick-up, but the rear body was added by a previous owner. Richard bought the turbodiesel a year ago, with 63,000 miles on the clock. An added bonus was the Husky winch, which he uses to launch his boat.

| NAME | Graham Easton |
| VEHICLE | 1998 Defender 90 300Tdi |

GRAHAM GOT HOOKED on Land Rovers two years ago when his wife bought him a day's off-roading as a birthday present. Once he'd driven a Defender off-road, he knew he'd have to have one.

47

The next port of call for us is another byway, which leaves the main A22 dual carriageway at Lower Dicker, two miles north of Hailsham, and leads to Chalvington, almost three miles away. But shortly after entering the lane we're greeted by a helpful Land Access and Recreation Association (LARA) sign, requesting users to avoid driving during wet winter weather.

Fellow LRO writer Mark Saville and I investigate on foot and confirm LARA's view: although much of the lane is hard and well-drained, there are soft clay sections with deep ruts. We don't want to cause further damage so we turn round and head for our next destination.

Just four miles south, on the outskirts of Hailsham, is a right-hand turn to Wilmington Wood. Take the first left into Robin's Post Lane and soon you're enjoying greenlaning at its best – a hard surface through picturesque woodland. Ignore the 'Unsuitable for motors' sign at the lane entrance. A Freelander will breeze through on this well-maintained byway, although there are one or two sections where you may wish to employ a pair of secateurs to prevent overhanging brambles scratching the paintwork.

The woodland here is mainly ancient coppice, where trees such as hazel were cropped regularly for their branches, which were used either for fencing or charcoal. Today, there are also modern conifer plantations. In the early morning or late evening you're likely to see roe or fallow deer, which roam these woods. We don't see any today, but there are plenty of songbirds, including yellowhammers.

Greenlaning isn't something to be rushed. Find time to stop your Land Rover, switch off the engine and let the sound of birdsong fill your ears.

Unfortunately there are also signs of that modern scourge, joyriding – and we find the burned-out wreck of a saloon car that has been there for a long time. I know that for a fact, because it was there when I travelled this route with Ray Mears a few months back.

The LARA sign helpfully warns drivers.

The byway ends after two miles, where you can proceed along a minor road for half a mile and take the first right to another byway complex south-west of Arlington Reservoir.

But we continue for another two miles, crossing the main A27 to the pretty village of Wilmington – a popular tourist destination for its views of the famous Long Man of Wilmington, a figure carved out of the chalk hillside in prehistoric times. An impressive sight it is, too.

We're here for very different views, though – because we're about to drive one of the most spectacular greenlanes up on to the South Downs. Just after the village church on the right, we turn left onto a RUPP (road used as a public path). The going is reassuringly firm, we're pleased to discover. Shortly afterwards, we stop briefly to clamber up the steep bank for a view of the Long Man. We then proceed along a chalky track, with the chalk uplands getting ever closer.

There are no ruts here to speak of, although the centre of the lane is badly eroded on the steeper sections by washouts from the recent storms. They're no handicap – in fact, they enhance ground clearance so there is absolutely no chance of fouling diffs (or rear exhaust hangers, in the case of Freelanders).

Happily, there are no areas of sticky clay, so it is easy going over the chalk surface, dotted here and there with small flints. We wouldn't hesitate to drive a Freelander here, but we'd have second thoughts about the new Range Rover. The lane is narrow in places and those branches and briars could damage the paintwork on a wide vehicle. Bring along a pruning saw, just in case.

After less than half a mile, the lane begins to climb up the hillside. About halfway up there's a wood on the right and a giddy drop to the left. There's a little mud in the shade of the trees, but nothing to worry about.

After a mile, the RUPP ends at Folkington Church. Happily, this is also where a byway begins. Again, the surface is chalky and very firm.

After a short drive through trees, the landscape opens up into typical open downland, grazed by cattle and sheep. Ruts are few and far between, but there are more deep washouts in steep sections. Yet there's nothing you couldn't drive in a Freelander.

After another mile or so, the lane eventually ends at the village of Jevington, where we celebrate with a glass of pop at the Eight Bells pub (open all day). Mark and I are in for a long, buffeting motorway journey back to the East Midlands through high winds, but it's very tame stuff compared to what the Newhaven lads face tonight. While Trevor and Nick are battling through mountainous waves to guide the 17,000-ton ferry from Dieppe into the harbour, the rest will be on standby, ready for every eventuality, and entrusting their lives to their Land Rovers.

A Clifftop Drama Unfolds (but it's only an exercise ...)

THERE ARE MORE than 3,000 brave volunteer coastguards around the UK, prepared to risk their lives to save others. They are respected as one of the best search and rescue services in the world.

The speciality of HM Coastguard at Newhaven is cliff rescue. And with the towering cliffs of Beachy Head and the Seven Sisters on their doorstep, that's just as well.

When LRO paid a visit, the Newhaven team were joined by colleagues from neighbouring Shoreham and Birling Gap stations for a clifftop exercise, which involved their Land Rovers and winching – winching a team member over the sheer cliff edge, that is.

The Coastguard Land Rovers are all Defender 90s, fitted with capstan winches driven by the PTO (power take-off). The current vehicles are all 300Tdi models, which are due to be replaced by Td5 90s. It is expected that these will be equipped with hydraulically driven capstan winches. 'Capstan winches are essential because we use ropes, not cables, for our work,' explains Trevor Cutler. 'Also, they have more control. We couldn't use electric winches in case of battery or motor failure in the middle of a delicate operation. Lives are at risk here.'

The capacious hard-top Defenders also house all the equipment the coastguards carry, which includes thousands of metres of rope, plus associated rigging, harnesses, pulleys, waterproofs and safety clothing.

The Coastguard Service has passed through many phases. There have always been people whose job it has been to guard and watch the coast, although the modern service has only been in existence for 150 years.

In Roman times, men patrolled the coast to watch out for Saxon longboats, while in Queen Elizabeth I's reign, men were posted on the clifftops to sound the alarm at the approach of the Spanish Armada.

When Napoleon threatened to invade in 1805 the coast was watched over, and the modern Coastguard Service performed the same duty during the Second World War.

The Coastguard Service came about when the various anti-smuggling services of the time were reorganised. Since then, it has undergone many further reorganisations, and it is now responsible for ship and coastline safety.

The Coastguard Service came into operation on 15 January 1822. Those early incumbents were posted away from their home towns for fear of collusion with smugglers. By 1829, the first 'Coastguard Instructions' were issued. They included a section on lifesaving and lifesaving equipment. In 1856, after the end of the Crimean War, control of the Coastguard Service came under the Admiralty. By this time, smuggling was dropping and the lifesaving role became more important.

The Coastguard had always performed some kind of duty involving wrecks, salvage and lifesaving apparatus. In 1866, they were finally authorised, by means of another Instruction, to 'take an active part in the workings of a lifeboat'. Another duty involved the reporting on movements of buoys, beacons and light vessels.

Over the years the service acquired a variety of different responsibilities, including assisting vessels in distress, taking charge of wrecks, operating lifesaving apparatus, participating in the lifeboat service, searching for mines and torpedoes lost at sea, and performing duties with signals, telegraphs, buoys, lighthouses, wild birds and rare fish washed ashore.

Since the First World War the Coastguard Service has changed hands five times. From 1923 it was controlled by the Board of Trade then, from 1939, by the Ministry of Shipping. For the rest of the Second World War, the Admiralty took charge, until 1945, when the Service was placed under the Ministry of (War) Transport. The most recent change was the Department of Trade taking charge, from 1964 to 1983, when it became part of the Department of Transport (now the Department for the Environment, Transport and the Regions).

A Winter's Tale

Dan Stevens gets stuck in with a spot of digging in the Garden of England

WHEN THE BACK end goes, I'm not surprised. The track is really greasy, and although we've only got 75 yards down it, the Discovery has been squirming about plenty already. I give the wheel a little flick and add a bit more power to counteract the rear breaking out, which should bring the front round and even up the Land Rover.

It doesn't. Instead, the Discovery's front follows the rear into the ditch, sliding slowly and smoothly sideways until it comes to rest against the undergrowth. I turn to look at Fiona in the passenger seat, which involves bracing my foot against the driver's door because the Disco is now leaning at an angle of about 40 degrees. 'It's okay,' I say confidently. 'I'll just drive it out.' First gear, low box, diff lock in, ease up the clutch, and the Discovery creeps forward. It stops after a foot. I try reverse, and it does the same thing. Back about two feet, and stops. Looks like we're stuck, then. We've been driving for about 35 seconds.

Getting out involves climbing up and out of the passenger door, and then I can see exactly what the problem is. There's a tree at the front, and there's a tree at the back. There's more of the Discovery over the edge than on the flat, so driving it out is not an option, luckily.

Towing is, and luckily we're not by ourselves. Up front is the Series II of Karl McCartney, whose idea it was to get us down to Kent to try some greenlaning in the Garden of England. His 1959 SII is very much a back-to-basics Land Rover, with multicoloured bodywork, cross-ply tyres and a slightly ragged tilt. And this is very much a back-to-basics trip — we've only got a couple of tow ropes and some spades, to show you don't always need air lockers, brush cables and winches to tackle Britain's greenlanes.

Although right now I'd quite like at least the winch, but Karl's SII should be up to the job of pulling the stricken Discovery from its precarious position. A short length of rope, plus low box, and the SII should be able to rectify my mistake in a couple of minutes. From the Disco's

Words: Dan Stevens
Photographs: Fiona Spencer

That's definitely stuck, then. Farmer turns up in a hybrid (not waving a 12-bore) to help out. Recovery attempt from rear fails. Driven mad by useless LRO staffers, Michael snaps and tries to remove the Disco's front wing in an attempt to get revenge for his fence.

driving seat I feel the rope go taut, and add a bit of throttle to help out. I don't move an inch. Karl tries again from a different angle, but the Discovery is too far over the edge for the SII. We try pulling from the back, but the Discovery is stuck fast in its ditch. The SII isn't heavy enough and doesn't have enough traction to pull the significantly lardier Disco over the ridge.

Then the farmer turns up. So far I've managed to total a row of fresh-out-of-the-box saplings, still with their protective plastic tubes wrapped around the trunk and block the track, and I'm dangerously close to crushing the fence. I prepare myself to be very, very humble.

But hold on – that's not the engine note of a Massey Ferguson. That's a Rover V8. The farmer has pitched up in a competition safari-prepared hybrid, and he's not waving a shotgun in my direction. In fact the farmer, whose name is Michael Goodworth, is a true Land Rover man. 'I saw you from across the fields,' he says. 'If it had been a Jap motor, I wouldn't have come out.' Without even so much as a 'get off my land', he breaks out a rope and connects the hybrid to the Disco's rear end. This does at least move the vehicle, but instead of pulling it clean out, it results in the back end further up on the track, and the front dipping further down into the ditch. From the outside it looks like a sinking ship, and from the inside it feels like a scene out of *The Poseidon Adventure*. In the driver's seat I'm very, very close to the ground, and I reckon the Disco is about to exceed the manufacturer's

stated limit of side slope stability. 'It's quite close to going over,' says Michael, with that practised air of one who has seen it all before, as he rocks the body from side to side. I hope he's just testing because I really don't want to have to end today picking pieces of broken Discovery out of the field, and then try to explain it all back at the office: 'Well, it just kind of slipped over and there was nothing I could do about it and I tried really hard to rescue it and ... I'll get my coat.'

The only way out now is through the field. It's Michael who suggests cutting the fence, and I mumble something apologetically about sending us the bill as he wrenches the posts out of the field. With the wires severed, I try to drive the Disco forward, but now it won't start. The angle is too severe for the fuel pick-up pump, so we resort to using the starter as motive power. With the hybrid pulling the back round from the front, the Discovery lurches down the ditch and out into the field. It turns out that Michael does team recovery events, so he's a very handy man to have in a situation like this. Even if it has taken two hours to extricate the Discovery.

We give up on that lane – it gets much narrower further down, and Karl reckons we'd struggle to get the Discovery through. Having already taken it much too close to the edge, I reckon it's a good idea to go and find something less challenging.

Kent is a county blessed with plenty of open countryside. Despite the presence of some of Britain's busiest motorways (M25, M20), there's a lot of it that hasn't yet been ruined by the relentless march of industrial estates, shopping malls and dual carriageway. Tucked away beneath the roar of the commuter traffic are tiny villages, orchards and hop fields, ancient timber-framed houses, Saxon churches and quite a lot of byways. Not a huge amount, but definitely enough to make for a couple of days' enjoyable greenlaning.

A blissful winter greenlaning trip (*previous page*) turns into a two-hour recovery nightmare (*left*)!

Two ropes, one pulling the back round and one keeping the Disco in place, mean that we get the Disco's back end round far enough to push the front end down into the field and drive it out under its own power – two hours later.

Karl's done the necessary and been down to see the nice people at the local council offices, to check out the status of the routes. Quite a lot of the byways in this area have traffic restriction orders on them, and several are inaccessible thanks to utility companies, which are busy digging everything up.

We meet up with Karl's log man, Shaun. He owns a 110 that has been modified for work, which involved stitching a Ford Transit tipper rear body onto the Land Rover's chassis. The Transit subframe went straight onto the chassis via a couple of brackets, and the tipper looks as though it was designed to be there. Shaun uses the 110 in preference to his larger Transit when he needs to negotiate driveways and tight spaces. He has also got a 90, but today it's the workhorse 110 that's coming with us.

We head for a short byway that shouldn't present any significant problems. It climbs the side of a hill, the sides of the lane thickly wooded and a thick carpet of leaves covering the surface. As we descend, the banks grow higher and the trees grow taller until the Land Rovers are dwarfed. It is quite beautiful. It's quite easy as well – actually, it's very easy – which is a welcome change from the morning's efforts. We exit the lane at the intriguingly named Rats Castle.

Next is a short section of byway that neither Karl nor Shaun has tried. After a few wrong turnings we find the entrance to the lane, which is heavily overgrown. Not seen much use, this one, although there is the telltale single rut left by trail bikes, and some horseshoe imprints. It looks narrow and overgrown, so Shaun and I walk down to find out what we're likely to encounter. Lots of overhanging trees, big trunks at about the right height to remove a Land Rover roof, some mud and a small stream at the end. But underneath the mud the ground is solid, and I reckon lack of use has caused the silt to wash downhill, creating a thick quagmire at just one point on the lane.

We're never going to get the Discovery or the 110 through – they're just too big. But the SII, which is narrower and lower, should make it. We all pile in, and Karl eases the venerable Land Rover through the thick brush, branches screeching down the side of the canvas. Karl's new to Land Rovers, having only owned the SII for six months, and he freely admits he doesn't know a vast amount about off-road driving. Maybe, but he's up for exploring some unknown territory.

When we get to the really narrow bit, where the ground rises on one side and drops away on the other, with a tree poking out over the track, he's obviously more nervous. Shaun and I guide him, and he gently brings the Land Rover through. The tree catches on the tilt frame at one point, bending the bar, but Karl shrugs it off with the stoicism of an old hand. I tell him it just adds to the vehicle's character, although if you gave this SII much more character it would end up hosting its own television chat show. It's great to see such an old vehicle out on the lanes, and if it was possible to detect such things I reckon it would be thoroughly enjoying itself. Its total absence of luxury, the way every component is slightly worn, the utter simplicity of the way it's built, all make it a strangely desirable machine. Back-to-basics suddenly seems like a good idea again.

Until Karl bogs the SII. He takes the mud at speed, or at as much speed as is possible in low range with a six foot run-up, and ploughs in. The Land Rover battles through until the diff grounds on the centre of the rut, and it comes to a stop. It will go back, though, so Karl coaxes the non-synchro' box into reverse and tries again. He gets further this time, but the wall of mud building up under the front tyres stops the Land Rover dead. 'Try it again,' says Shaun, 'but this time put it into low range.' Ah, that would explain why the SII won't go any further – it's in high box. This time Shaun and I have to push the Land Rover back to get it moving, and predictably I get covered in mud.

It goes up – and it goes down; one man and his home-made tipper.

Third time round and Karl gets further again, but he has stopped short of the firm ground. With more aggressive tyres he'd probably have made it, but right now the SII isn't going forward, or backward. Shaun, a man of few words but in possession of a quiet confidence, heads back up the track to get his 110. He drives it round on the road to the end of the track and reverses it back down to the point where we're stuck. I follow on foot with the rope, passing a family at the top of the track doing some gardening. They don't seem at all fazed by the presence of a large green Land Rover going backwards down the path outside their house, followed by a scruffy individual (me) covered in mud, brandishing a long length of rope. They even say hello.

We've got just enough rope between us to connect the two Land Rovers together, and after a couple of attempts Shaun gets the 110 close enough to join them up. I ask him what engine he has got under the bonnet: '200 Tdi,' he says, 'the old lifesaver.' Well, he's obviously done this before.

The SII pops out of the sticky morass on the second pull, and Karl looks faintly relieved we haven't pulled the front off his Land Rover. One rope, two Land Rovers and a bit of pushing. Who needs winches?

The entrance to this lane shows what happens when no-one uses byways.

Sometimes the only option is to push. All together now …

By now the light is fading, and it's getting cold, which means it's time to go home. That night we're joined by Michael, Shaun, Karl and fellow off-roader Martin, who farms and will only buy Land Rovers as working vehicles. I feel I owe them all several drinks after everyone's efforts to get us out of various sticky situations. We all consume beer until last orders.

Once More into the Breach …

I'm stuck again. This morning we'd taken this shortcut to bypass a badly rutted muddy section that would have had the Discovery flailing for grip, and now I've come to a halt on a seemingly innocuous straight stretch of byway, within sight of the main road. Karl hasn't noticed yet, and he's almost made it to the end when he stops. Obviously he has seen me, and he's coming back to find out what's happened. I run up the track – 'I'm stuck,' I shout. 'So am I,' he shouts back. Now there's a dilemma. Both vehicles immobile, 300 yards apart. Our recovery gear consists of two spades, and one of those is a mere shovel. Looks like this is going to be hard work.

Both Land Rovers are hung up on the diff, and they've both lost traction on more than one wheel. We elect to get the SII out first, because then at least we can use it to give the Discovery a pull. And there's only one way we're going to get it out, and that's to pack stuff under the tyres. If there's one thing I would like to add to our pared-down inventory, it's a set of traction mats.

We haven't got any, though, so we start digging around for rocks to jam under the tyres. There aren't too many big pieces of rock in this part of Kent, but then I find a pile of broken tarmac and some lumps of concrete dumped in the hedge. We can make our own road.

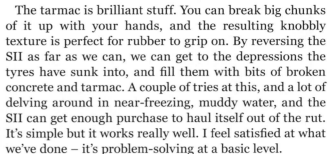

The SII risks its hood sticks to pass a vicious tree problem.

The tarmac is brilliant stuff. You can break big chunks of it up with your hands, and the resulting knobbly texture is perfect for rubber to grip on. By reversing the SII as far as we can, we can get to the depressions the tyres have sunk into, and fill them with bits of broken concrete and tarmac. A couple of tries at this, and a lot of delving around in near-freezing, muddy water, and the SII can get enough purchase to haul itself out of the rut. It's simple but it works really well. I feel satisfied at what we've done – it's problem-solving at a basic level.

We try the same thing on the Disco, but it's less successful – the tyres just spin on the concrete and pulverise the tarmac, so Karl reverses the SII back up the track (keeping out of the ruts) and hauls the Discovery out. We didn't mean to get stuck here, but we just couldn't help it.

Time to try something less demanding, and a byway near the village of Shadoxhurst, disappearing off into a rather pretty wood, is just what we're looking for. And it would be, except for all the junk that's strewn along either

Disco tyres won't grip on slippy surfaces.

side of the track, including a burnt-out Toyota Avensis, several electric heaters and the remains of numerous fitted kitchens. There's even a motorbike sunk up to its forks in one of the ruts, and I don't really want to risk driving over the top of so much buried rubbish. The ruts are quite deep as well, and there's nowhere to effect a recovery from, should we need to. We bail out, and turn round.

Only to get almost immediately stuck on the next byway. This looks good, a challenging long section that meanders through a large wood – the first bit is quaintly

Who needs fancy winches when you've got Dan-power?

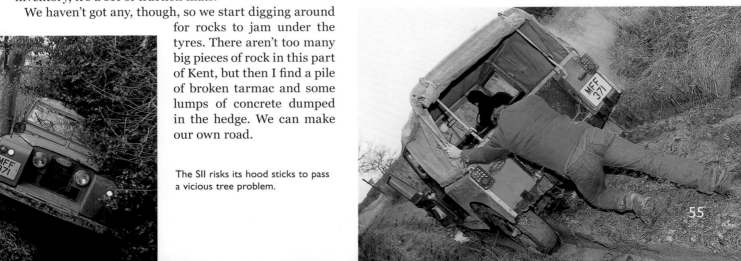

Driver Profile

NAME	Karl McCartney
VEHICLE	1959 Series II 88-inch

KARL'S SERIES II is a living embodiment of what's good about old Land Rovers. The patchwork panels and honest-to-goodness look of the thing give it real presence, and it's a capable off-roader.

He bought it because it was the ideal vehicle. He needed a hobby, something to use as a workhorse when renovating his house, and his wife Cordelia wanted something capable of transporting pieces of furniture for her antiques business. Oh, and he really wanted one as well.

MFF 371 came from Hastings, complete but without MoT or tax. 'Cordelia insisted on a short-wheel base if we had to have one, but she didn't say anything about it having to have a hard top,' says Karl. It still retains its slightly motheaten tilt. Under the bonnet the original two-litre diesel has been replaced with a 2.25-litre petrol.

Karl tinkered with MFF to get it through an MoT (leaking exhaust, seized brakes, worn shock absorber brushes), and now he uses it for fun, and for work. Greenlaning is a sport that he has just taken up, and he is keen to do more with MFF.

marked on the map as Duck Lane. Karl gets past the muddy entrance to the lane in one go, the SII bouncing over the top, and the rear cross-plys providing just enough grip to keep it moving, but the Discovery is less lucky. I'd laid a load of concrete slabs, found by the side of the track, over the top of the mud to make for some sort of solid surface. And it worked, until the front tyres contacted the clay and lost all grip. Trouble was, in order to avoid the tractor-size ruts directly in front, I had to turn left, and that caused the Disco to slip off the concrete.

It's back to digging and stuffing concrete and tarmac under the wheels (strangely, again there was plenty of tarmac dumped in the hedge – why?). And again, the best technique is to try to get to the dips the tyres have dropped into, and fill them with broken rock. It's smooth stuff that just makes the tyres slip even more. A piece of ragged fencing wire makes for a good traction mat under the back wheels, and after half an hour of bouncing and pushing and packing and digging, the Disco breaks free.

Oasthouses – built for the Kentish practice of storing oasts. What did you think they were for?

Just yards from the main road and we've entered the strange world of DIY roadbuilding.

Unfortunately, it has broken free in a backwards direction, and I'm not about to spend the rest of the day trying to cross six feet of mud to get to the other side. This is a shame, because the rest of the byway looks great, as it snakes off into the woods. But knowing when to stop is as much a virtue as carrying on regardless, and anyway, it's lunchtime.

It's also time to head for the Dartford Tunnel before the rush hour, and make our way home. Kent's thrown up some interesting surprises for me, and for the LRO Discovery, but next time I think I might compromise on the back-to-basics idea and take at least some traction mats. Then again, it was fun making our own road, and knowing that we had to make do with what we had. We were never in any real danger, and there's nothing quite like getting your brain around the problem of a stuck Land Rover.

RUPPs and Downs

Join the LRO team as we explore the hidden greenlanes of the Chilterns and Cotswolds in three Land Rovers

Words: Dave Phillips
Photographs: Fiona Spencer

58

A STARTLED BUZZARD flaps lazily from the branches of a gnarled oak tree as our trio of Land Rovers edges towards it, pushing through the long grass of an overgrown byway. We were up at the crack of dawn this morning to make the most of this weather and, after two hours of driving it's now 9am. I can't help sparing a thought for the poor souls dragging themselves into their offices and workplaces for another day of air-conditioned toil.

Out here the air is heavy with the dust of a hundred harvesters as the farmers make hay while the sun shines – or, rather, take advantage of the dry spell to gather in the corn. Like us, they can smell the freshening air from the south-west, and the pink-tinged sky on the horizon of rolling hills surely suggests rain is imminent. Time to press on …

This trip, on this occasion, was LRO photographer Fiona's idea. She was due to make a visit to Northampton

to snap all the Land Rovers at the town's annual hot air balloon festival and suggested we should join her and then head south to Silverstone to try out the off-road course at the famous Grand Prix circuit, before heading on south and west through Oxfordshire and Gloucestershire, exploring the Chilterns and Cotswold hills as we went. It sounded like a great two-day break, so we didn't take much persuading.

LRO art director, Peter Comely, had planned to bring his newly-restored Series IIA along for its greenlaning debut ('It'll be ever so gentle, Pete, honest. The ruts are very small and there are hardly any brambles to scratch the new paintwork …'). But the SIIA had developed a clutch problem, so he declined to bring his baby out to play – opting for the LRO Project Discovery instead.

I couldn't decide whether to drive my own Td5 90 or the

LRO Lightweight, so I did the obvious thing and brought along both. My neighbour, Jon Walker, whose own Series IIA is currently in bits on his workshop floor, awaiting a new chassis to accommodate it all, gladly volunteers to drive the extra vehicle. He even brings his girlfriend, Melinda, along for the ride.

Fiona is still enthusing about the colourful balloons of the previous day when we meet her outside Silverstone, but her attention soon switches to motor sport as we follow the perimeter track, shadowing the hallowed circuit, which is home to the British Grand Prix. Soon we arrive at the off-road course, situated alongside Hangar Straight, and within spitting distance of Stow, where Michael Schumacher came a cropper in the British Grand Prix two years ago, which ultimately robbed him of the 1999 World Championship.

But although I'm a great admirer of the German driver, I wouldn't rate his piffling little Ferrari for the task ahead of us. The Silverstone off-road course, developed in conjunction with Land Rover two years ago, is pretty impressive. There are some great man-made hills, white-knuckle descents, deep water for wading and even a jungle section. Just right to test the might of three very different Land Rovers.

Soon we're tackling the course with glee. The roof is off the Lightweight and Jon's enjoying his first taste of LPG-powered off-roading – despite the fact that the SIII gearbox is getting increasingly troublesome. Sometimes all the gears slip in sweetly, but more often the gearbox is notchier than Eddie Irvine's bedpost. Occasionally you find all gears bar first, then second and third disappear for a while. But first, of course, you have to catch the vibrating gearstick, which is like stirring a bucket of gravel with a poker.

But you know what? We love it all the same. The problem is probably something as simple as a knackered selector, which we'll get sorted when we get it home,

Silverstone – a brilliant, feature-packed off-road course situated within spitting distance of the legendary racing circuit. We reckon wet tyres would be best on this particular track!

but it all adds to the experience of driving a 17-year-old ex-military warhorse. And the great thing about a SIII Landy, of course, is that it keeps on going anyway.

And it doesn't get stuck, which is more than you can say for Pete. He takes one muddy climb just a little too slowly on the Disco's Toyo road rubber and soon he's bogged in. Luckily, a sharp reverse, followed by another attempt, with a lot more oomph, saves him the embarrassment of being towed out. It's great fun, so we spend a couple of hours at Silverstone before reluctantly tearing ourselves away. We've got a lot of ground to cover.

The obvious route to Oxford and beyond is the A43, but we don't fancy getting stuck in the trunk road holiday traffic and opt instead for a cross-country ride along tiny lanes, RUPPs (roads used as public paths) and byways. By now, I've prised Jon and Melinda out of the Lightweight, so that I can enjoy some wind-in-the-hair driving, accompanied by the roar of the gas-powered 2.25-litre engine.

It's great fun and the ride on the new parabolic springs would be comfortable – if it wasn't for those vinyl-covered utilitarian seats. It's a very hot day and soon my lower back is soaked from sweat, thanks to that unbreathable plastic. To hell with authenticity, it's time to get rid of those old military seats and get something more driver-friendly.

Lack of use on this RUPP, near Stow-on-the-Wold, means the undergrowth has encroached to the extent that it will soon be impossible to drive. Get out there and do it!

Stow-on-ye-Wolde has lots of antique and tea shoppes for ye tourists

We settle for a pretty sedate 50 mph as we follow our route, which passes Stow School, skirts the lovely county town of Buckingham, then bypasses Brackley and Chipping Norton. We make our first stop, in the archetypal Cotswold town of Stow-on-the-Wold, with its characteristic mellow stone buildings (and even more characteristic antique and tourist shops. Ah well ...). It's blazing hot now and we're in dire need of liquid refreshment, so we find the local supermarket, park up, and buy a case of bottled water. Saved from death by dehydration, I've got a smile on my face now. But not for long – the Lightweight won't start. I try it on gas, attempt to fire it up on petrol, all to no avail. Dan Stevens had warned me of its reluctance to start when hot, so I've no option

Three of a kind: Disco, Lightweight and Defender are very different vehicles, but all from the same Solihull factory.

but to sit it out for half an hour to allow it to cool down. Meanwhile, the others go sightseeing.

Even when they return, it still won't fire up. Jon and Pete get busy under the bonnet with screwdrivers (and Pete's treasured Kershaw multitool), but you'd need an ice bucket to cure this particular fuel starvation problem. Eventually I get it running on petrol, but the black smoke and sooty deposits on the exhaust tailpipe suggest over-rich running. It's difficult to get to the mixture screw below its tamper-proof cover on the Zenith carb, but the engine's running a bit rough, so we also adjust the idle.

The rich running is academic, anyway, as I flick the rocker switch to LPG. Now it's purring, sweet as a nut, as we continue our journey, following an old Roman road south-west to Bourton-on-the-Water, and making a couple of detours to explore some greenlanes. What an idyllic way to spend a summer's afternoon.

The sun is starting to sink on the horizon now and the light is at the red end of the spectrum, which sets the stone buildings aglow – nowhere better than in the choc-olate-box village of Windrush, which we visit *en route* to Burford and our eventual destination for the night, Lechlade. Tonight we sleep the sleep of the just, with the sound of water lapping against the boats moored on the adjacent River Thames.

After an early start, we're looking forward to another enjoyable day – and we're not disappointed. Fiona has researched some great RUPPs and byways, which provide brilliant yet non-damaging driving. Most of the terrain around here is very stony, with underlying limestone a few inches beneath the topsoil. As a result, there are no ruts to speak of and very little mud. A Freelander would

Top Stone roses – it's early evening and there's a warm blush to the mellow Cotswold stone in the picture postcard village of Windrush.

Middle If Hovis ever decides to remake its old TV advert, the steep High Street in Burford would make an ideal location.

Bottom The upper River Thames at Lechlade is very different to the muddy London reaches.

Dave and Pete are working out how to pick their way across the illegally-placed boulders. But watch out – the man in pink trousers is about to make an appearance.

The long grass suggests no vehicles have used this greenlane since Foot-and-Mouth restrictions were eased. In fact we didn't meet another 4×4 in two days of driving.

breeze through here – no problem.

The only obstacle we encounter is a pile of stone blocks placed across a RUPP at Ablington, near Bibury.

Pete and I get out of our vehicles and reckon we can easily pick our way over the rocks and continue along what is, after all, a public right of way. We're just planning our tactics when a shrill, elderly man comes into view, spluttering with indignation. He explains that the blocks have been placed there to prevent 'travellers' from gaining access. In truth, he's a NIMBY (Not in My Back Yard) of the highest order and he's hard to take seriously – after all, you don't meet many elderly, apoplectic men wearing pink cord trousers in the middle of nowhere.

While accepting that we had every right to use the route, he pleads with us not to, in case gypsies or new age travellers spot our tyre tracks and set up home down 'his' lane. And once that tactic fails, he tries to accuse us 'townies'

(we all live in the countryside, incidentally) of threatening his livelihood with Foot-and-Mouth disease.

By now we're getting bored with the confrontation – we want to get on with some driving – so we take a vote. The let's-turn-around-and-drive-somewhere-else contingent win narrowly, so the Man in Pink gets his way ... this time.

If, however, any adventurous readers would like to drive this lane, buy yourself a copy of Ordnance Survey Landranger map 163 (Cheltenham and Gloucester) and head for grid reference 100076.

Nearby Bibury was described as the most beautiful village in England by William Morris (1834–96), designer, socialist, poet and the father of the English Arts and Craft movement (says Pete, who knows these sort of things). The people who live here today, however, must rue his words, because it is now a nightmare of tourist-packed coaches.

We pause for a few minutes, feed the semi-tame trout in the crystal-clear waters of the stream that runs through the middle of the village, and depart without regret. Is all of Ye Olde England destined to become a glorified theme park to be captured on the camcorders of tens of thousands of Japanese visitors ... or am I too suffering from a touch of the NIMBYs? Must be contagious.

It's afternoon now and we're heading back for home. We'd decided beforehand that this would be a two-day break – the sort of trip Land Rover fans could do in a weekend – so we resist the temptation to explore further. The Forest of Dean is

The sleepy village of Shilton gets a rude awakening as the Lightweight negotiates the shallow ford.

enticingly close – just a few miles further west – but it will have to wait until another time.

We head north-east instead, again taking the tiny lanes through the open countryside, past Carterton, Witney, Woodstock, Blenheim Palace and Bicester before cutting across country to return to Buckingham and our starting point. As we drive into Silverstone, we can't help smiling at the village sign: 'Silverstone welcomes careful drivers'. Try telling Schumacher that.

Luckily, you don't need to be a racing driver to have a lot of fun in this part of the world. This is true Land Rover country – and it gets the LRO recommendation for a great weekend break.

Country folk have strong views on politicians and are not afraid to air them.

Up and Away

Words and Photographs: Fiona Spencer

DRIVING THROUGH THE morning mist, the serenity and quality of light made me once again curse the Foot-and-Mouth precautions which prevented the annual Northampton Balloon Festival from following its normal practice of allowing the balloons to fly wherever the wind takes them.

My hosts for the day, Tony Pinner and his crew from the Ballooning Business, were also cursing. It was a beautiful morning, but the forecast promised stronger winds as the day progressed. Eight knots or more would put an end to the already restricted flying.

The two gleaming white County 110s that awaited me were to have a different role than usual. Instead of being used as chase-and-retrieval vehicles, they were to be used today to tether the Wrangler footwear balloon.

These 110s are kept as clean as possible, but this does not disguise that they are still essential workhorses. Crossing ploughed fields and towing trailers with full loads of passengers are all in a day's work. The only non-standard features on these 200Tdis are the tyres, which are All Terrain Michelins.

The vehicles have less than 100,000 miles on the clocks combined – not bad considering they are eight and ten years old, respectively. Tony intends to take good care of them, as he doesn't consider any lesser 4×4 would meet his needs.

Land Rovers are definitely the vehicles of choice with ballooning enthusiasts, judging by the sheer numbers present at the festival.

For more information on ballooning, contact Tony Pinner at the Ballooning Business Ltd, 4 Back Lane, Hardingstone, Northampton, NN12 6BX, tel: 01604 768617 or log onto www.the-balloon.co.uk

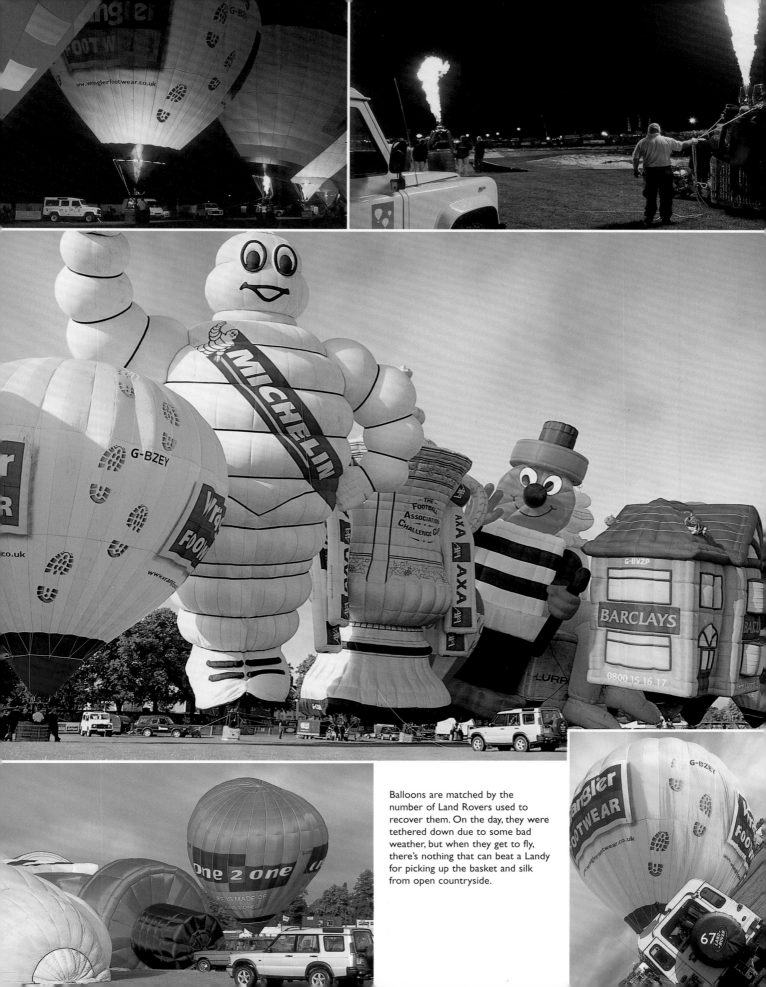

Balloons are matched by the number of Land Rovers used to recover them. On the day, they were tethered down due to some bad weather, but when they get to fly, there's nothing that can beat a Landy for picking up the basket and silk from open countryside.

Big Bucks

There's a wealth of greenlanes just waiting to be discovered in the wide-open spaces of one of Britain's most affluent counties. Dan Stevens came back suitably enriched

Words: Dan Stevens
Photographs: Mark Dixon

'WE'RE RATHER CURIOUS to find out what you're doing,' said the well-spoken woman. Our Land Rovers were scattered across the track as we set up for a picture, and we hadn't noticed the elderly couple coming from behind us.

Here it comes, I thought; the what-the-hell-do-you-think-you're-doing-driving-down-my-track routine. I got ready to offer up the usual line of defence. At least we had a council rights of way officer with us, who knows exactly what's right and wrong, even if he wasn't actually there in an official capacity.

'Well, we're here with a council rights of way officer taking pictures of the track,' said photographer Mark.

True enough, but the woman didn't suddenly start demanding that we get out of her sight and never come back. She was actually genuinely interested and a little intrigued to find out what we were doing – and then she was off across the fields, springer spaniel nipping at her heels.

You'd expect to encounter some hostility to off-roaders in a county like Bucks. It's a well-heeled place, with plenty of money sloshing around. The Prime Minister has his country house – Chequers – here, and the Rothschild estate at Waddesdon Manor is in the heart of the county.

There are a lot of people in Bucks who have paid a lot of money for their own little piece of the English country-side, and it would be a fair assumption that they wouldn't want us driving around on it.

Thing is, that's exactly what *didn't* happen. In two days of driving, we didn't get shouted at, abused or made to feel like lepers even once. In this considerably-richer-than-you corner of England, the locals are most definitely friendly.

Buckinghamshire is another of those satellite counties orbiting around the home planet of London. You're never very far from the capital but – unlike much of Berkshire,

It's not all glamour, you know – Dan gets the gate.

Cruising through the picturesque town of Great Missenden – there's no finer vehicle than the Range Rover to do it in.

say – the county has managed to retain some of its identity. Small villages have stayed small and resisted massive expansion and infilling.

The Chiltern Hills give the county some relief from the flatness that sometimes seems omnipresent in this part of the country: that means there are going to be some good lanes.

We've got something a little special with us – an all-original 1971 Range Rover. It belongs to photographer Mark Dixon, who has spent most of the past week trying to get the vehicle roadworthy after the 31-year-old fuel tank started to fill the fuel system with rust. It's not immaculate, but it's honest and very original.

Mark's becoming something of a serial monogamist with Range Rovers. He's just sold this one and bought an even earlier model, a J-reg in the same Bahama Beige, but in better condition.

For a three-decades-old, unrestored vehicle, this isn't bad. Sure, the plastic seats are patched with gaffer tape and carpet, and the paint has suffered from over-enthusiastic application of touch-up, but the V8 is powerful and sweet, and there's no rust in the (original) rear tailgate. It's original and unmolested, and that's the way these early two-doors should be.

Looks like a stream, but it's also a road used as a public path. We don't recommend driving down here.

We also have an excellent guide in the form of Phil Prigg, who just happens to work as a rights of way officer for Buckinghamshire County Council. He spends most of his working week out on the lanes, and he knows the status, the history and what's around the next corner.

His 300Tdi Defender is more than just a recreational vehicle – it's used regularly to inspect lanes, and as stretched rights of way department budgets don't extend to a fleet of Land Rovers for each member of staff, it's very useful.

I've brought the LRO Defender to fill in if the lanes get tough, because the last thing we want to do is to damage the Range Rover before the new owner takes delivery.

The first lane of the day starts at the unlikely sounding village of Marsh Gibbon. It is – like so many in this part of Bucks – flat, with a solid surface and good drainage.

The even surface has been designed for all users, from walkers to horse riders, so while it doesn't offer much of a challenge to anyone in anything with wheels (that includes prams, wheelchairs, go-karts and shopping trolleys) it does mean that everyone can access the lane.

Bucks doesn't have that many byways, and most of the lanes we're driving are bridleways and footpaths with vehicular rights of way attached.

These signs are still up weeks after the building work that blocked the track has finished.

This is something of a minefield, but basically it goes something like this. The Definitive Map (which we'll call the DM) shows only the conclusive rights of way – so a track that's listed as a footpath definitely has rights for a walker. But it *may* have conclusive vehicular rights as well and, until that's proved otherwise, you can drive down it. Finding out what's legal and what isn't is very difficult, which is why Phil's with us. He knows.

One particular road used as a public path (RUPP), which is less road and more stream, illustrates nicely this clandestine and often bizarre world. It's an old mill race that borders a field at Twyford Mill. Apparently, goods used to be brought down the race to the mill, which is why there's a right of way on it.

In the 21st century, though, the only obvious sign that this is a path of any kind is a gate across the stream. You couldn't drive down it – it's not wide enough and you'd be polluting the watercourse, anyway, not to mention really annoying the new owners of the mill, who may not realise quite what the stream running alongside their property really is.

Right above Whichever way you approach it, the long driveway to Stowe House is an impressive thoroughfare indeed.

Right below This is how much bridge £300,000 buys you – it crosses a railway, and Railtrack were hoping to get away with a cheaper footbridge until they found out there were vehicular rights of way on the track.

Most of the tracks in the north of the county, in the Aylesbury Vale district, are short and simple. It's easy-going laning that takes in some cycle paths and plenty of bridleways. We meander through towns and open countryside, taking in the scent of a county at harvest. Everywhere there's the smell of newly cut wheat; chaff drifting on the air; the bulk of a combine harvester looming over the top of a hedgerow.

The Range Rover is magnificent. Driving this 31-year-old example, you can see why it was such a revelation in 1970. It looks fantastic, uncluttered by the spoilers, black vinyl and side stripes of the later models; a simple, clean design that hasn't dated.

It fits in anywhere, parked outside a row of traditional, timber-framed houses, ambling down a grassy green-lane or barrelling along a busy dual carriageway. It's an aristocratic vehicle without ever coming across as too upmarket.

Off-road, it lollops over bumps and ruts, and where the Defender would leave you reaching for something to grab hold of, the Range Rover cocoons with that soft, pillowy ride. It's not so hot on the road, where it pitches and plunges through corners, but there's always plenty of grip and the traction is superb.

As we pick our way across an uncultivated field, with medieval ridge and furrow plough marks every 30 feet (big ditches that you take in second low, no throttle), the Range Rover just soaks it up. Marvellous.

Further south the terrain changes, and on our second day we're on the edge of the Chiltern Hills. This is where the Ridgeway, Britain's oldest road, starts. It used to run from the Wash down to Dorset, and for thousands of years it provided a dry route for travellers, raised up from the lowlands.

Now it runs from Ivinghoe Beacon, north of Tring, to Avebury in Wiltshire. And this particular bit, near Princes Risborough, is the first section with vehicular rights of way.

We meet a couple of dog walkers on the track, but they seem to be more concerned with not messing up Mark's photography than giving us a hard time. Either they're well used to four-wheel drives using the track (although there doesn't seem to be much evidence in the way of tyre tracks) or they're just not that worried about it.

Quite a lot of the lanes, like so many others in England, cut through farmyards and what appear to be private drives. At one point we drive through the gates to a house, across the gravel in front of the house and through the gates at the other end.

Now, I don't know about you, but I always feel slightly uneasy about this sort of thing – perhaps it's just the English way, feeling that it's wrong to get so close to someone else's property. Of course it's not wrong – it's totally legal and we've every right to do it, but at times

Top Britain's oldest road, The Ridgeway, starts in Buckinghamshire – and this is the first bit with vehicular rights of way. Nice, isn't it?

Middle A typical Buckinghamshire scene – yet again the Range Rover blends in perfectly.

Bottom 'You've owned it for *how* long?' Dan and Phil talk to long-time Series I owner Rex Davies.

Quite tight, some of these lanes — we leave the Range Rover behind and take to the hardy Defender instead.

73

The locals are inquisitive, but not hostile, about what we're up to on the Ridgeway.

like this I'm glad we have only two vehicles, and that they're both fairly low profile.

Pushing on, we cross through newly cut cornfields, and cross the Icknield Line steam railway. There's a sign put up by Sustrans (who have been developing cycle routes through the county), that categorically states only walkers, horse riders and cyclists can use the byway. 'No motor bikes,' it says. Not true – as a byway, the track is open to anyone. As if to prove a point, a Range Rover Vogue rounds the corner. It's the farmer, come to check his combine in the field, and he passes us with a wave and a smile.

Before we get on to the last lanes of the day, we've got a date with some Range Rover manuals.

Actually, it's a lot more interesting than that – we're going to see Rex Davies, long-time Land Rover man and Buckinghamshire born and bred. Rex, now 87, has owned his 1953 80-inch Series I *since new*, and it's always been used for what Rover originally intended it – farm work. Rex's family firm, Wren-Davies Dairies, has only just ceased to be a working dairy, and the Series I has been an integral part of the business for nearly 50 years.

'I was never tempted to trade it in for a newer one, as it always worked so well and did everything I needed it for,'

he says. He's also owned Range Rovers, and has some rare early manuals he has promised to Mark – Rex now uses a Td5 Discovery as a daily driver. But the Series I, which he brought to last year's LRO Show, is still used on the farm.

Phil's taking us to what he describes as his favourite lanes in the county. This is a man who knows almost every lane in Bucks, so they must be good. And they are. We're between Cholesbury and Chesham, which I reckon is one of the prettiest parts of the county, thanks to the Chilterns.

The Range Rover stays in the car park, though – not in deference to its age, but because Mark doesn't want to ruin the paint. We double up in the LRO Defender. Just as well we did leave it behind, because straight away the UCR is very tight and heavily overgrown. The hawthorn is scraping down the sides of the canvas, and it sounds as if there's something trying to get in. The track drops down, trees bordering it on either side, and then begins to climb again. It's a solid surface under the tyres, though, a mixture of rock and earth, and it's well drained – as the wash-outs traced across the hill testify to.

These are the kind of tracks we go laning for. Driving a track bordering a woodland, there are fields to one side and traditional oaks and beeches on the other. In the sunlight, the stark contrast between the dark wood and illuminated fields makes you glad to be in England – you don't get this sort of thing anywhere else. This track is quite muddy, mainly because it never drains out (it's at the bottom of a slope) and the sun never gets to it (those trees get in the way).

Underneath the mud is a solid surface, though, and the Defender's mud tyres clear away the sticky stuff to find something to grip on.

I'm rather reluctant to hand the Range Rover keys back to Mark at the end of the day. I've really enjoyed driving this superb vehicle on- and off-road; and as I swing the huge door open for the last time, I have this urge to go out and start looking for one.

As for Buckinghamshire – well, it's a mixed bag. There isn't a huge amount of lanes, and few byways, but there are some really good ones. But you *do* have to look for them, and most of the ones that we drove are signed as bridleways or footpaths. Reclassification is happening all the time, so make sure you know what you're driving on, and that you're allowed to be there. It is amazing, though, that only 30 miles from London there's still a network of greenlanes that are fun to drive and easily accessible. Get out there and find them.

Superb ride quality means the Range Rover devours off-road terrain with style and ease.

Hert of the Matter

Words: Dan Stevens
Photographs: Fiona Spencer

Within easy reach of the metropolis of London you can explore some of the prettiest lanes – run by some enlightened councils

IT'S A GLORIOUS day, the Hertfordshire countryside basking in the bright late winter sunshine. Our trio of Land Rovers makes its way across the rolling farmland, following a track that winds along the edge of the fields.

We're just 30 miles from the edge of London, but in the stillness of the calm mid-morning air you'd never know it. Strain an ear, and you might be able to discern the faint hum of the A1 to the west, but you'd have to concentrate. With our collective V8, Tdi and 2.25 petrol engines silenced, we can hear only the occasional screech of a startled pheasant, followed by the distant thump of a shotgun.

An idyllic greenlane trip, then. Not quite. Today we won't encounter any irate landowners or angry walkers, because we're here in what could pass as an official capacity. One of our number is a rights of way officer for Hertfordshire County Council.

When Ian Blomeley, who's responsible for the lanes we're currently driving on, called me, I immediately thought he was going to complain about a greenlaning feature. But instead, the voice on the other end of the phone asked if I'd like to go to Hertfordshire and see the work they were doing on rights of way. For many of us, councils are part of the establishment – the people with the power to ruin recreational off-roading. They can close lanes with Traffic Restriction Orders (TROs). They have the power. They are rights of way officers. So it's a bit of a surprise to find myself greenlaning with one.

We've also gathered two enthusiasts with their Land Rovers to join us. John O'Reilly, the Hertfordshire rep for the Greenlane Association (GLASS) has brought along a battered Range Rover, a veteran of many off-road trips. And alongside the LRO Defender, there's a 109-inch ex-military Series IIA run by Lea Valley Land Rover Club member Julian Cotting. It's a great selection of Land Rovers, with the no-nonsense leaf sprung Series, my own ultra-capable 90 and the venerable

Range Rover, which just goes to show that any Land Rover can go greenlaning.

As we potter along the track, Ian tells me about his department's attitude to four-wheel drives on green-lanes. 'Some RoW units don't want four-wheel drives using their roads – Suffolk can be awkward – but that's what the routes are there for. Hertfordshire is one of the better funded councils for rights of way.' Which may help explain the refreshingly liberal attitude to off-road use of the county's byways. The total annual budget for Herts rights of way is £750,000, which may sound extravagant but it equates to £1 per person (based on county population). That's just enough money to lay 30 feet of six-lane motorway, which costs £17.5 million per mile.

Not that you'd ever want to lay even a foot of tarmac across this countryside. Cotton Lane is a section of byway that meanders through ploughed fields, passing through a thicket and taking in a bit of water on the way. Behind a hill to the west is Stevenage, but you can't see so much as the tip of a tower block in the distance. The lane is not taxing, but it is very pretty, especially where it winds up the side of the hill, sinking below the surface of the field where hundreds of years' of use have eroded the surface. When you encounter a lane like this it reminds you that these roads have been in constant use for centuries. Back in the days of horse-drawn coaches, these routes would have been impassable in the winter, and definitely in a worse state than they are now. It's thanks to the work of men like Ian that tracks like this are in good condition, even after a heavy winter and plenty of rain.

We stop off at the Lordship Arms in the village of Benington, where Ian has arranged to meet landowner Richard Bott. His are the fields we've just driven over, and he farms 12,000 acres in the area. There are land-owners who park combine harvesters across tracks, harass off-roaders and stir up trouble. Richard is a rarer breed: 'Nothing that four-wheel drivers do winds me up,' he says. 'I've never known them to leave a gate open.' I think this is going to be a day of overturning prejudices.

Richard's attitude is partly explained by the fact he rides trail bikes off-road, and comes into contact with rights of way users on a regular basis: 'I think many people's attitude to off-roaders is pure nimbyism. In reality the usage by bikes and four-wheel drives is tiny, and most of the legislation governing rights of way is moulded around users on foot.'

He's not precious about his land either. 'The fact I ride trail bikes makes me more sympathetic, but I inherited this land – I didn't buy it. Landowners tend to regard the countryside as a place to kill things, collect subsidies and abuse

Who's going in first? Lots of standing around and poking with sticks ensued.

the peasantry. That's not what it's about for me.' He also reckons that bikers and off-roaders could do a lot more together to improve their lot. 'In reality, four-wheel drive owners and bikers should get together. The Trail Riders Fellowship are adopting RUPPs to look after – we should all get our act together on this.'

We leave Richard to his farming, and head off to find another lane to drive. It's great to meet a man responsible for 12,000 acres of British countryside who has his head screwed on. In his part of England, at least, you won't have to worry about angry men muttering nonsense about taking down your registration number.

Now we're off to a RUPP that leads to something known as the Old Bourne. This seems to be a local favourite with greenlaners – a stream bed which passes as the road. And depending on what the water table is up to, we may not be able to get through it.

With the SIIA leading, we follow the track as it crosses a main road and disappears off into a wood. It's

Get on my land! Pro-off-road driving land owner Richard Bott explains why he doesn't mind Land Rovers crossing his fields.

quite a severe axle-twister for starters, followed by a sharp left-hand turn which means low first and no throttle. Julian eases the 109-inch over the uneven ground, leaf springs stretched almost to their limit as the 35-year old Land Rover finds a way through. Following in the 90, I'm expecting the SIIA to get cross-axled and needing a pull, but with gravity and some careful planning, it sails through. The Range Rover, of course, shrugs off the rough stuff, its supple coils absorbing every inch of the gully.

Then we find our first major obstacle. Water. Not a problem for my Tdi, but for Julian's 2.25-petrol it might prove to be troublesome. He's driven this lane before, and knows that without waterproofing the SIIA will pack up in the middle of the pond. It's about bumper deep, which is just enough to flood an engine bay when the water hits the (fixed, eight-blade) fan. 'It keeps jumping out of second gear as well,' says Julian, 'which means I can't go fast enough to get a proper bow-wave.' If he does stop halfway through, I'll be able to get the 90 close enough to get a rope on the back of the 109-inch.

On the Definitive Map, this RUPP crosses the other side of the hedge, but somehow it has deviated to its present path. And the fact it's a RUPP explains why this big hole full of water is here, and why the correct path has never been reinstated.

'Because of the uncertain status of RUPPs no money has been spent on them for years,' says Ian. 'There's no point in spending £30 per metre on resurfacing a RUPP when it could become a bridleway, when I've got byways in desperate need of work.'

Like so many things, it comes down to money and priority. RUPPs have low priority thanks to the impending wholesale downgrade that may see so many of them losing vehicular rights. This RUPP will probably become a restricted byway under the Countryside and Rights of Way Act, which means no vehicles. A shame, because it's a really good track and it's in fairly good condition.

Not much of a problem for us though. After the time-honoured off-roader's tradition of standing around looking at things we try to drive through it, having figured out that it's quite deep really.

Julian guns the 2.25 and points the Land Rover into the water. Immediately it's up to the wheel hubs, then to the bumper, and water's sluicing out of the gap between the bonnet and the top of the wing. The Land Rover stops.

It's hardly necessary to lift the bonnet to find out why, but somehow it's always the first thing to do when a Land Rover comes to a halt. We all like poring over engines, even when we know full well what's wrong with them. The whole engine bay is caked in filthy water from where it's hit the fan, which has sprayed it all over the engine, liberally dousing the ignition system. John roots around in the back of the Range Rover for some WD40, but by the time he's found it Julian's got the 109-inch fired up. He backs it out and tries again, this time after plenty of water repellent. It goes through in one go, even though the water's pouring out of the bodywork. Although I've seen it countless times before, I'm always amazed that a 30-year-old vehicle, which has come straight off tarmac, can happily plough through deep water with nothing more than a quick squirt of WD40.

The Tdi doesn't falter, and surprisingly, neither does the Range Rover. V8s are not known for their ability to deal with water (too many HT leads) but some basic waterproofing around the distributor means the Range Rover sails through.

There's more water to come though. Last time Julian was up here, which was about two days ago, the Old Bourne was flooded. So flooded, in fact, that they lowered another 109-inch into the water, back end first, to see how deep it was. Just for fun, you understand. Imagine a diagonal line drawn from the rear top edge of the roof to the middle of the sill – that's how far they got it in. So quite what we're going to find next, and how far the two petrol-engined Land Rovers will get, is now entirely dependent on the vagaries of the water table.

But where there was once seven feet of fast-flowing silt and liquid, there's now a rather tame-looking stream. The idea is to drop down into the stream, drive up it following the RUPP, and then exit before the bridge, which is about four feet high. Julian drops in first; the 109-inch

Range Rover's supple coils absorb the rough terrain.

Looks a lot like the village green, but it's actually a byway.

This is the Definitive Map. Not that exciting really, but very useful.

promptly jumps out of gear, lurches down into the stream and stalls. The water's not particularly deep, but there's a dip on the left, and the SIIA's front wheel has dropped into it. We leave it for five minutes to dry out, and walk up the side of the stream bed to check the other end.

'The RUPP actually continues along the stream, under the bridge,' says Ian. Obviously this isn't terribly practical for most users, so the path has moved to one side of the stream, and the height of the bridge means we're not getting any of our Land Rovers through there. A stripped down 80-inch, with a folded windscreen, would probably make it. Our larger, more modern vehicles will take the more obvious route out of the stream – a sharp left turn up the bank, avoiding the concrete piling down the sides.

With the 109-inch started again, Julian trundles down the stream, and flicks the Land Rover to the left to climb the bank. The drop-plate towbar grinds on the stones underneath, and the cross-plys scrabble for grip on the wet earth. Julian hauls the wheel to the right, and as the Land Rover emerges from the climb, the back end gets grip and spins round. It doesn't look like the 109 is going to make it in one, but some deft use of the throttle means it clears the concrete easily.

The 90 makes the turn, and the Range Rover follows suit, the Michelin XCLs biting into the loose surface. The rest of this track has been surfaced recently, using the council's effective method of laying crushed concrete chippings, which results in a smooth, compact surface that blends into the surrounding countryside. It doesn't make for exciting driving, but it does mean that anyone can use this path. It also ensures that it won't deteriorate into a muddy, rutted quagmire, which off-roaders will then get the blame for. At £30 per metre you'll find it's only used selectively – where it's needed, and when it can be paid for.

I get the feeling Ian's quite enjoying this. The RoW unit doesn't have any four-wheel drives of any description, and although it could borrow one if pushed, it's not an ideal situation. Today, Ian's probably getting to see more of his network of byways and RUPPs than he would in a week of normal work. As we drive, he points out areas that have been repaired and those awaiting restoration.

To demonstrate the kind of problems he has to deal with, Ian takes us down the forbidding-sounding Dark Lane. Actually, it's not uninviting at all – it's quite pretty.

There are a couple of large houses at the end of the track – and the occupants are not friendly.

'They've been complaining of mud on the road,' says Ian. 'I took some pictures for evidence' – he hands me the snaps – 'to show that it wasn't that bad.' The pictures reveal that yes, there is definitely some mud on the road. It's hardly enough to count as some sort of biohazard, and you'd either have to be very precious about your footwear or an especially bad driver to get worried about it.

We're very close to a disputed series of four RUPPs near to the village of Great Munden. Many local people want them to be downgraded to a bridleway, and there's a public inquiry into the whole affair in the village hall. We're going to look at the path tomorrow, because the light's fading now, but Ian's about to tell me something rather surprising. 'We use electronic vehicle counters on greenlanes,' he says, 'to assess how many vehicles use the routes. We set one up on the Great Munden RUPP, and discovered there was only one vehicle a day going down there – contrary to the residents' claims of hundreds of Land Rovers pounding down the lane.' So the electronic eyes are out there, watching you. But it's not that sinister. The council wants the RUPPS to become BOATS (byway open to all traffic), and retain the vehicular rights of way, and in this case the counters will prove to be invaluable evidence in the public inquiry. And they help Ian to do his job more efficiently. He's a man who believes that rights of way should be open to everyone, regardless of how they use them.

Mapping the Day

It's 9am, and I'm in the rights of way office looking at that elusive document, the Definitive Map. This is the bible of greenlaners – the only failsafe method of finding out where you can and can't drive. It's a sealed legal document. It is the law.

Hundreds of years of continuous use mean this track has become the stream bed.

Tight fit in among the trees. Left a bit, right a bit, easy does it.

I'd imagined it to be some huge work of cartography, laid out flat in a massive room, maybe with people pushing miniature horses, walkers and Land Rovers across its vast distance with long poles, like a Second World War operations room. Of course, it's nothing so romantic.

The map consists of 91 pieces of laminated A2 paper, showing the entire county at a scale of 1:10,000. The ironic thing is, it's not actually that definitive. Last updated in November 2000, it doesn't show any reclassifications since then or any TROs. To discover what's really going on, you have to cross-refer it to another set of documents, the working map, which shows the changes. This is not a legal document. Confusing, but the good news is that you can order copies of the Definitive Map and the working copy from the department.

Today we've lost the Range Rover and gained another Defender. It's driven by Phil Prigg – and he's another rights of way officer, from Buckinghamshire County Council. He's been into Land Rovers since he was twelve years old, and his tidy 300Tdi boasts Trac Edge tyres, a high-lift and loads of recovery kit. Nice to see a rights of way officer running a Defender.

Our first lane of the day is a BOAT between the villages of Dane End and Levens Green. It crosses open fields, a classic piece of pasture land with the gently sweeping Hertfordshire hills providing a verdant backdrop for the Land Rovers. The countryside isn't dramatic, in the same way that Dartmoor is, but it's very English, with hedgerows criss-crossing the fields. Our track follows the contours of the hill, a well-defined path on solid ground, with the occasional muddy patch to make the tyres squirm a little.

From 4×4 to SUV

JACKING IN A job in the hectic world of advertising sales to sell Land Rovers sounds like a dream job for most of us. Julian Cotting has done just that. 'I took redundancy last year, and decided that I could try and make a living selling Land Rovers to the USA.' He's just established a new company, Global Land Rovers, to export restored vehicles to America.

Which is where the white SIIA that joined us will probably end up. An ex-military machine, it's been through several owners in the Lea Valley Land Rover Club, of which Julian is a member. It's got 1-ton extended spring hangers at the back, and a curious set of Top Cat decals on the rear body. 'They're staying after the new paint job,' says Julian, 'because it's part of the vehicle's identity.'

A sharp right turn means careful power application is necessary.

We can't continue down the byway, because Ian's put a closed sign on the rest of it. Not because he doesn't want people using it, you understand, but because the local water company is laying pipeline there. The prospect of a cyclist or off-roader rounding a corner and colliding with a tracked pipe-laying machine, and then suing someone, isn't worth contemplating.

So we double-back on ourselves to find a byway that starts in the hamlet of Levens Green. It looks like it starts out crossing the village green, and the ruts are testimony to some recent use. It winds past some houses, through some heavy undergrowth and emerges into fields again. The ground's quite wet here, and despite the presence of a drainage ditch on one side of the track, the water's sitting on the surface. 'There's three things you need to know about greenlane maintenance,' says Ian. 'Drainage, drainage and drainage. But the water table has risen so much over the past year it's proving to be very difficult to keep on top of it.' Leaf mulch is another big problem, and years of neglect on some lanes means that most of the mud and gungy stuff you'll encounter is a decade's worth of fallen leaves, rotted down to create a thick, sticky mess that uncharitable types will blame on off-roaders.

'Pull up here,' says Ian. 'I've got something to show you.' He jumps out of the Defender, and delves into the undergrowth, retrieving a piece of barbed wire. 'Last year, this

Defenders and sodden grass don't mix. Our friendly rights of way officer looks on nervously.

was strung across the track at about the right height to catch a trail bike wheel or a horse's shin.' It was deliberately tied round the trees on either side, tight across the track to inflict maximum damage. It could have severely injured someone, or maimed a horse. Such are the sentiments of some of the more unpleasant inhabitants of the English countryside.

Taking in another short RUPP with a neat little ford, we make our way up to the RUPPs at Great Munden. As we pass the village hall, Ian points out the 50-odd cars parked up along the roadside: 'This public inquiry is the biggest thing that's happened here for ages. There's a lot of interest in it.' It's not part of his job to be there today though – the mapping team, who deal with definitions and changes, are dealing with the public enquiry.

The RUPP we drive is in good condition, with minimal damage from vehicles of any kind. It's wet though, and the Defender's Yokohamas are struggling to find any grip on the slippery surface. I almost come to a halt, and I can feel the tyres beginning to spin below me. Backing off the throttle and taking it slowly eases the situation, and the Land Rover makes it to the top of the hill in one go.

There's some tight turns at the end to get through a lot of overhanging trees. It takes concentration and some gritting of teeth to get the 90 through; the branches are very close to the edge of the hard top, and I reckon Julian's going to have trouble squeezing the 109-inch through. I can envisage us getting the SIIA jammed between two trees, the only way out involving chainsaws (which we don't have) or calling in a tree surgeon.

'It'll be fine,' he reassures, 'I've driven this lane many times before.' Sure enough, he gets the long wheelbase through in one go, fighting the wheel to direct it through the only-just-wide-enough gap.

Ian's keen to show us a long piece of byway, which leads to the village of Ardeley. This perfectly illustrates the problems faced by rights of way officers in surfacing and clearing lanes. At the beginning of the lane the byway forks in two directions, one of which passes through an impenetrable thicket and into an overgrown copse. Looking at the sign, you'd think the track went down the drive marked 'Private,' but it doesn't. It goes right through the thicket. 'We've got a bit of clearance to do here,' says Ian.

He's spent a lot of money sorting out the surface on the Ardeley RUPP, but it only goes so far. It's a smooth surface, but not much fun for four-wheel drives. Thing is, it runs out after half a mile, and we're back to mud and ruts. 'Local parents want me to surface the rest of this so their kids can ride to school down the lane, instead of having to battle the traffic on the minor roads,' says Ian.

The lane leads right up to the primary school gates. But it's going to be costly to surface so much byway, and there's another problem further up: Munchers Green, a couple of hundred yards away, is common land and a nature reserve. You can drive across it, but you shouldn't drive off the path or get out and stomp about on the fragile, waterlogged ground.

Trouble is, people have driven on it, and the ground's badly cut up. It needs work to save the surface, and Ian must keep the farmers happy who use the track as access to fields. All users want different things from the land. It's Ian's job to give it to all of them at the same time.

Last lane of the day is out of Ian's patch, but it's been recommended by one of his colleagues. We barrel up the arrow-straight A10, otherwise known as the Roman road Ermine Street, to the village of Therfield. The byway sign points left, so we take the first left and end up at someone's front gate. I can see the track where it runs between two hedges, but the only way of getting to it is by driving across some rather tidy-looking grass.

I hang a left, and immediately the 90 comes to a halt on the boggy surface. The Yokohamas will not grip on this stuff, and I've already cut the beginning of a rut just by being there. I think I've made a mistake, which is confirmed when a woman shoots out of a house opposite and tells us we've gone wrong. Ian's keeping his distance, and I think it's better not to mention that he's from the council.

Surprisingly, the householder's not angry or hostile, she's just saying that in order to get to the byway, we need to drive over the kerb and across what looks like a village green. It doesn't look like the obvious route, but Julian bumps the SIIA over the high grassy kerb and motors over the grass. This bit is much more solid, and he crosses the muddy bit to the other side, hooks a rope up to the 90 and pulls me clear. Easy, and not too much damage done.

There's a good two miles of this byway to cover before it gets dark, so we get a shift on. It's easy going, until we hit a small stream in a big ditch. This requires a bit of assessment, because there's a tight left turn to make directly after exiting the ditch. Julian goes first, and he's doubtful he's going to get round in one.

Slowly dropping into the stream, he opens up the engine when the front tyres contact the other side and the SIIA scrambles up the other side. Luckily, the back end slips neatly round, slewing the rear into line with the front and dispensing with the need to make an 82-point turn (given the 109's less-than-handy turning circle, this could become a reality).

And this is where the lane starts to get really interesting. We'd been warned

Barbed wire is not an unusual sight in the country. Except when it's tied across a lane to catch out bikers, MTB riders and horse riders.

that it got a little tight further up, and it does. We send the 109 in first – if it gets stuck, at least we can drag it out from behind onto safer ground with the Defender. Straight off, the 109's back end slips into a ditch pushing the front round towards a tree. Julian keeps moving though, and manages to avoid the tree by a width. I'm less lucky, and when the 90's back slips down, I slow down. The nearside front slews round and the wing clips the tree. One dent, the first I've added to the 90 in 12 months. I'm not bothered – the paint's not even split – and it's a nice memento of the trip.

It's getting tighter, and to the right is a ditch with a stream. If we put a wheel wrong, we'll end up with a Land Rover in a ditch and no way of getting it out. The 109 comes to a halt up ahead – we can't get any further. The track's washed out completely on one side, and to get a Land Rover in there would involve an angle of 30 degrees and no guarantee of escape at the other end. The 109's certainly not going to make it through.

So we have to reverse. In the Defender this is tricky, but not impossible. In the 109, it's impossible. The back keeps slipping towards the ditch, thanks to a hummock of soil that's lifting the rear up and pushing it off course.

Time for some recovery. Julian breaks out the hi-lift jack, and begins jacking up the back, at an angle, to push the Land Rover further over and away from the ditch. Ian and I push the Land Rover over, off the jack. It kind of works, but we're not making much progress, and the light's failing fast. We try the same trick on the front, but with the added effort of a rope wrapped round the bumper and threaded through the hedge with Ian and me on the other end, pulling the SIIA over. This works, and after we try the same trick on the back the 109 is far enough away from the ditch to risk driving it out. Julian digs some small ruts below the tyres to keep them in place, and drives the vehicle out in one go. Very slowly, but he gets it out with ease, only needing another pull to keep the back end away from that tree that dented my wing. We decide discretion is most certainly the better part of valour, and not really wanting to end up having to abandon a thoroughly-jammed 109-inch in the middle of nowhere, call it a day.

For both Ian and me, it's been a learning experience. He's seen that off-roaders care about greenlanes, and are sensitive to the difficult situation that currently surrounds so much of Britain's rights of way network. And we've seen that rights of way officers are actually nice people. Overworked, under-resourced, and with too many disparate groups to keep happy, they still love what they do, and they're determined to keep routes open. For everyone to use.

Peak Practice

The Discovery Owners Club celebrated its success with a trip into the heart of Derbyshire; LRO rode shotgun with the 34-car cavalcade

Words: Mark Williams
Photographs: David Shepherd

Discos ready for the 'off'.

THE DISCOVERY OWNER'S Club couldn't have picked finer weather to tackle the Derbyshire Peaks.

Its rolling hillsides are lovely all year, but when shafts of sunlight break through thick cloud like theatre spotlights, the pools of gold which drift across the emerald patchwork of a landscape lend it another dimension. A Land Rover Discovery adds another.

You are riding high in every sense, catching glimpses beyond the hedgerows and seeing over the crested hills long before other drivers. Then, just as everyone else has run out of road, you can hang a left and take yourself far off the beaten track.

The Discovery is, by many peoples' reckoning, Land Rover's finest all-rounder, ideally suited to mixed mileage. Having been on the market for eleven years, it's a mystery why it took until April this year for the model to get a dedicated owner's club.

The need for an owner's club was underlined by the response when Steve Goodfellow, John Capewell, Mike Duncalf and Andy Smith launched the Discovery Owner's Club in spring 2000, and the Derbyshire Peaks run underlined the enthusiasm with which it has been embraced; no fewer than 34 Discos turned out at the start point.

Very wisely, organisers Iain Rice and Mike Thompson and sponsors Gordon Lamb of Chesterfield sent the vehicles out a few at a time, led by a fistful of directions and some obscure treasure hunt clues. And within minutes of leaving the hubbub of a Chesterfield trading estate, everyone knew they were going to have a good day.

Steve Goodfellow was going to make the most of the run. Clearly chuffed at the turnout, he set off up the B6051 with a vengeance, daughter Michelle and son Dave watching out for the treasure hunt answers as the 300Tdi made light work of the road through Barlow, Commonside and Millthorpe. Frequently, the Goodfellows were out of the car, counting yew trees and reading bus stop signs. It was slow going.

Things started getting a little wilder along Fox Lane, as we began the steady climb on to the edge of Ramsley Moor, hemmed in by high hedges and woodland until we reached the summit, when the vista suddenly opened out before us, the wild scrub of the moor to the north and the oddly desolate Leash Fen spread out like a grubby picnic blanket to the south.

After a gentle descent, we joined the A621 and took a right to Curbar almost immediately. It's a fairly unspectacular climb to Baslow Edge, with Big Moor rising to the right, so it simply doesn't prepare you for the Curbar Gap, the only pass through the rocky escarpment of Baslow Edge. As we drop in on Curbar, gaps in the houses offer stunning glimpses of the Derwent Valley 600 feet below.

By now I could sense that Steve was getting an itchy transfer box, if you'll pardon the expression. In the bustle of sightseeing traffic which greeted us in Curbar, we were just ordinary tourists, and joining the main road into Baslow put us back in the mainstream.

Rocky roads made the best of the Discovery's ability in low box.

crawling power and Steve forgot about plumbers and fish and got his smile back.

The crossing over the B6001 isn't the best, with limited visibility to the right. The marshalls despatched someone to watch the bend and, with Derbyshire awash with motorcycles, it was a wise move. Once safely over the road, Steve eased the Disco into low ratio second and looked up the steep, broken surface which took the run up to Longstone Moor, with Calver Peak rising to the north. For some of the group's vehicles, this was the first time low ratio had been used in anger.

'The Discovery Owners Club members are all sorts,' said Steve, who has done his fair share of off-roading. 'Some members haven't even got a Disco – they are gearing up to buy one though.'

Up we went, Steve holding the revs at around 3,000 so we ground relentlessly to the top. Or not quite. I spotted our photographer, tendered my thanks for the lift and the company, and asked to be dropped off. Out of the car, I lit up a cigarette and admired the view across Hassop Common.

I hitched a ride with the LRO crew along the top of Longstone Edge, shifting into high box first. From here you can see Chatsworth House, and the Park attributed to Capability Brown. It's a staggering piece of landscaping even from this distance, and for my money, England's finest stately home.

We followed the unclassified road west down from Longstone Edge, into Great Longstone, and turned right towards Monsal Dale car parks. It was lunchtime, and seemed a sensible break to stretch our legs a bit, enjoy what I can only describe as fantastic ice cream from the ice cream van, and meet some more of the Disco owners.

The mystifying clues in the treasure hunt had gathered quite a posse from the DOC at a Baslow church, all discussing fish and plumbing (don't ask) while gazing around with the squint and puzzlement of people who'd just regained their sight. Quizmasters Iain Rice and Mike Thompson are, we all decided, sadists.

But a treat was in store for us on the other side of the Derwent – Bubnell Lane. Following the course of the Derwent north, with superb views of the river, it steadily degenerates, the old asphalt steadily cracking up as it climbs through Bramley Dale. No need for low box, but a strong feeling that your average Ferrari would ground out here and there.

Then came the first test of the Disco's awesome uphill

The crossing isn't the best, with limited visibility to the right. The marshalls despatched someone to watch the bend.

From Monsal Head, the view is superb. At the bottom of the valley, the River Wye twists like a silver party streamer through Upperdale and Cressbrook, flanked on one side by the remnants of the old branch line into Buxton. On the hill opposite, we could see the front runners of our group, the distant Discos climbing at walking pace with the ramblers on the rocky track. Time to move on.

The next section down into Monsal Dale and up Putwell Hill promised to be among the most spectacular of the run. I selected Andy Biggs and his partner Pauline Simister for the dubious honour of giving me a lift, and we set off suitably refreshed. The road into the Dale hides behind the pub. You drive the half mile into Upperdale then take the small bridge on to an incredibly pretty lane lined with ancient hedgerow. It's a low box second kind of hill, punctuated by gates which must all be left closed, regardless of how you find them.

The off-roading element had no fears for Andy and Pauline – Andy having cut his teeth on an old Daihatsu which, by his own admission, he steadily wrecked. This time he was in his gleaming, V-registered Td5.

'The Disco Owners Club came at the right time for us,' said Andy, as Pauline set off to open the umpteenth gate. 'I'd not long bought the Disco.'

We chatted as the Td5 made light work of the firm track but the conversation was frequently stifled by the sheer beauty of the landscape. To our left, the steep, wooded valley of Monsal Dale looked lush and cool, while the pointed peak of Fin Cop rose sharply a mile away. Limestone walls divided the ancient pastures like a web of silver filigree on emerald, the gates flanked by curious standing stones drilled with holes.

There are almost five miles of this greenlaner's bliss, terminating at Priestcliffe. At the T-junction where the track rejoins asphalt lay a curious place – part farm, part MoT centre, with a huge, wartime Diamond T truck among its mechanical debris. We trundled into Priestcliffe and on to the A6 towards Buxton, taking the first track on the left, signposted 'Warning: No Access to Landfill.' It started out as asphalt, rapidly becoming a green-lane which took us past a recycling centre then over the hill towards Chelmorton.

There was a natural break here, brought about by some tricky questions asking the name of a resident horse. Typically, the treasure hunters were foiled by an open stable door, which hid the name plate they were looking for. Andy and Pauline joined other members in trying to puzzle this one out while I felt like another change of chauffeur and left them to it.

Once the flurry of Discos had left the village, I was very much on my own, sitting astride a drystone wall with only the crows for company. Patience wasn't a problem. As I watched the world go by, a tan fox crossed the road ahead, hopped up on a garden wall, and ran along it towards a clump of beech trees. He was instantly mobbed by the birds, and dropped off the wall, out of sight in the long meadow grass. Only the swooping, cawing crows remained to track his progress over the hill.

After half an hour, I cadged a lift with Pete and Viv Johnson, from Manchester, in their 300Tdi. The dog guard should have been a clue but, as I slumped into the rear seat, Martell the border collie let me know he was in on the action by sniffing my right ear – quite alarming when you're not expecting it.

We headed straight for Buxton on the A515, trying to simultaneously follow the erroneous directions, answer the treasure hunt clues, and avoid a collision in the busy tourist traffic. At the top of town on the A6 next to Buxton Golf Course, we pulled over so that Martell could stretch his legs – well, one back leg in particular, fourteen times as it turned out.

It gave us the opportunity to get one more answer on the treasure hunt sheet, before we climbed into the Disco – Martell so reluctantly that Pete had to lift him in. We followed the next directions.

'... don't run over any balls,' said the crib sheet, which pointed us straight across the middle of the golf course. Mike Thompson had warned us that the players might not take kindly to our incursion, but to ignore them. In reality, they ignored us. One even nodded in acknowledgement as we passed.

Pete and Viv are no strangers to what I will term vehicular prejudice. They would, for example, be unwelcome in the Royal Oak at Millthorpe (as the treasure hunt pointed out) because they are occasional motorcyclists. It is odd how some sanctimonious sections of trade and public assume that a crash helmet can transform a civil servant into Attila the Hun, or that environmentalists don't drive 4×4s.

Who'd want a Range Rover? Some emergency repairs as the marshalls wait on the uphill run to Longstone Moor.

Half a mile further on, the directions advised another right turn, and we found ourselves skirting a massive limestone quarry on an otherwise picturesque green-lane. On the right was the ubiquitous drystone wall, on the left one of those concrete-post-and-wire fences only erected by railways and aggregate companies.

A quick call established that the LRO crew were not far behind us, and I wished Pete and Viv all the best before, once again, watching the last of the Landys disappear up the track and hearing the sound of silence.

The quarry warning signs were everywhere. I took advantage of my short stop to answer the call of nature, only to read on the red notice in front of me that beneath my feet was a 10,000-volt cable. Further signs warned us to dive for cover on weekdays if we heard a siren – blasting had deposited a boulder the size of an engine block on the track. I couldn't help thinking that the energy of anti-off-roaders would be better spent stopping stone companies shipping Derbyshire away by the lorry-load.

The LRO crew hove into view, and I climbed aboard. By now, we'd been on road or track all day, and the end game – a pint and sandwich in the Plough in Flagg – had become an oasis-like mirage. But just as we mentally quaffed an ale, we rounded a bend in the

track and the green chasm of Woo Dale beckoned us in.

Three heifers watched with curiosity as we opened the gate. They were quickly joined by a dozen more, which cantered over to see what all the fuss was about like women at the January sales. As we shut the gate, I made a crummy joke about the dale being named for the first comment people make when they see it. A minute later a 'Wooooo' escaped my lips involuntarily.

Woo Dale is the oddest landmark, which just happens to have a right of way running through it. It's not the biggest dale, but strangely quiet and peaceful; a private place which begs you to switch off the engine and sprawl on its grass for fifteen minutes. We succumbed, snapping a few pictures in the process. Eventually, the tail-end Charlies trickled past us and reaching the pub became a matter of urgency. When we arrived 20 minutes later, we were greeted by a few ripe comments, such as 'Did you get lost?' and 'Td5 break down then?'

Personally, I would have been happy to have drifted even more languidly through the back roads of Derbyshire's Peaks. We'd just spent eight hours driving 50 miles, but the combination of the scenery and low box driving had made both figures a complete irrelevance. You should try it some time.

91

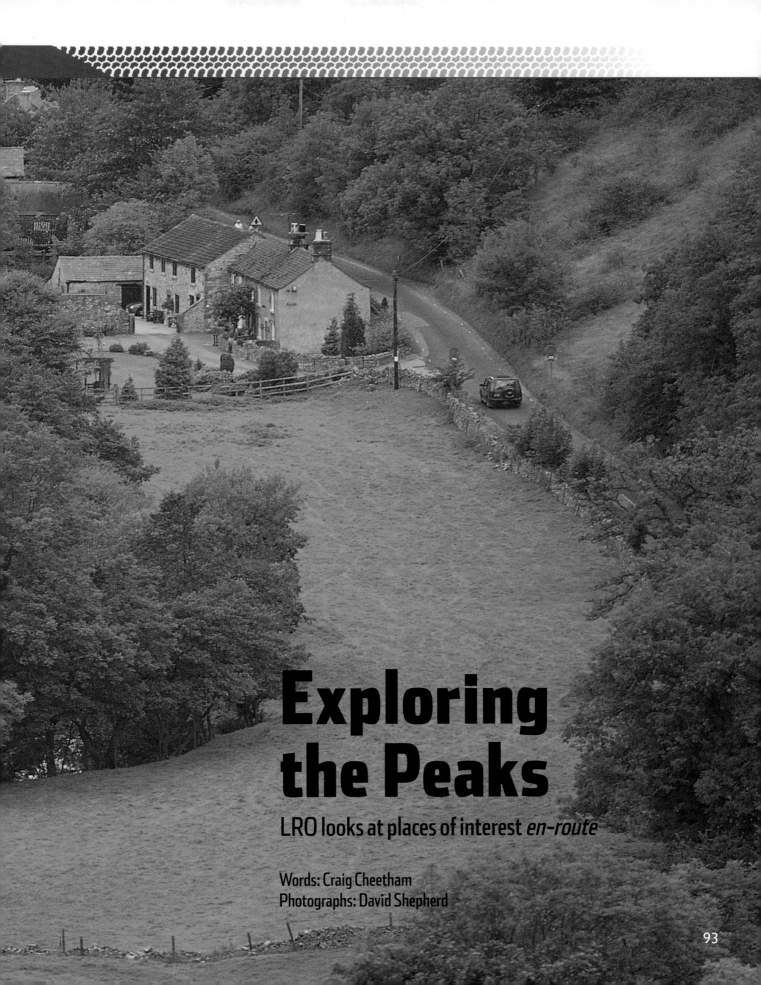

Exploring the Peaks

LRO looks at places of interest *en-route*

Words: Craig Cheetham
Photographs: David Shepherd

IF YOU'RE THINKING of trying out the route yourself, why not make a whole day of it and explore some of Derbyshire's greatest beauty spots for yourself?

Starting in the shadow of Chesterfield's crooked spire, the first place of historical interest you reach is Baslow; a small but fascinating town on the edge of the vast Tideswell Moor. Depending on your time in Baslow, you can either walk three miles along Baslow Edge, a grit-stone outcrop offering stunning views up into the Peaks themselves, or you can explore the historic town itself.

The River Derwent meanders its way through Baslow, but its most interesting feature is the old limestone bridge on Bubwell Lane – it may only be ten feet high, but the bridge is a remarkable feat of achievement given its 18th century origins.

The old mill overlooking the town on the lead up to Baslow Edge is also of interest – its architecture may be in stark contrast to the quaint stone buildings of the town itself, but the building found fame in the television series Colditz, where it played the role of Colditz Castle itself.

If you get chance, a slight deviation from the route takes you to the spectacular grounds of Chatsworth House, ancestral home of the Duke of Devonshire. Its original owner famously lost the house and gardens in a card game, but today the stakes are somewhat lower – a small fee will allow you to explore what has to be the archetypal British stately home. And such is the beauty of Chatsworth that you'll want to visit it more than once. On Sundays, though, the house gets very busy and parking can be a nightmare, so you may want to stick with the original route.

Our route took us through the village of Bubwell and up the first greenlane, High Rake. Parts of high Rake are better suited to four-wheel drive vehicles, but that doesn't stop the annual Derbyshire Drystone Rally using the course as a special stage. Give it enough momentum and an Opel Manta will find its way over the Rake, but only going the opposite way to our Land Rovers. The wide and gritty quarry tracks might lend themselves well to rally cars, but the loose, rocky ascent that took us up there would certainly not be passable in anything other than low ratio and four-wheel drive.

The end of High Rake brings you out at Longstone Edge, with spectacular views across the Derbyshire dales and into the grounds of Chatsworth, before swinging up into one of Derbyshire's most beautiful hamlets: Monsal Head. The Head is an Area of Outstanding Natural Beauty and boasts a magnificent view over Monsal Dale and the Wye Valley. The River Wye runs through the valley and at one point the underlying rock is so hard that the river is forced to carve its way through a limestone ridge, before meeting the River Derwent at the bottom of the dale.

The route of the former Midland Railway reaches across the valley in the form of a spectacular five-arch viaduct which culminates in a tunnel straight through Monsal Head. When it was built in the 1870s, locals complained that the viaduct and tunnel were unsightly and damaged the natural lie of the land, but today both are spectacular

Chatsworth: probably England's finest stately home open to visitors, and a snip at the entry charge for both house and the superb gardens, attributed to Capability Brown.

aspects of an already stunning landscape. The viaduct no longer carries trains, but is a regular source of human traffic as a popular walking route across the dale.

It's also possible to see Putwell Hill meandering up the face of the far peak. From here it looks intimidating, but as our group proved, it is well within the reaches of a Land Rover Discovery.

The next place where it is safe to stop is the ancient spa town of Buxton. With a population of 75,000, Buxton is the highest town of its size in England and sits some 300 metres above sea level.

Now internationally renowned for its mineral water, Buxton has a thriving tourist industry. But it's only tourists who will buy Buxton water in Buxton, for all the locals know that St Ann's well in the town centre has been there since the middle ages, and it is perfectly simple to draw your own water from the Spring. Even though it comes naturally from the Peaks, the water here is clean enough to drink without purification.

One of the most dominant features of Buxton is the impressive Crescent – a huge building originally commissioned by the 5th Duke of Devonshire in 1780. The Crescent was in danger of demolition until just two years ago. Until the late 80s it had been a desirable five star hotel, a temporary home to many wealthy or famous tourists. But in 1989 the structure started to collapse, and it has taken ten years and millions of pounds to

Over the River Wye at Monsal Dale, as Disco owners prepare for what was, for some, the first low ratio climb of their lives.

secure its long-term future. Today, the Crescent still stands empty, but the restoration work is expected to be completed later this year.

If you get chance, have a wander round the spectacular Pavilion Gardens, where tropical plants and flowers grow in temperature-controlled environments. Buxton Opera House is situated within the gardens and is top billing for many stars, while a special international operatic festival takes place in July and August.

Our route takes you north out of Buxton and through the idyllic meadow of Woo Dale, before dropping into the village of Taddington. The village is built entirely from limestone – its main industry – and sits over 1,000 feet above sea level. Taddington's history dates back to the 1640s and among its many attributes is Five Wells Tumulus, one of the oldest surviving burial plots in the country.

But hopefully that won't spoil your appetite, for the route we have described here ends at the 18th Century Plough Inn, in the picturesque Village of Flagg. As well as a tasty and hugely welcome range of local ales, the Plough boasts curry-filled giant Yorkshire Puddings among its specialities. These are a great way to end your tour!

Lincs

with the Past

North Lincolnshire
is steeped in history,
with glorious unspoilt
countryside, coastline ...
and greenlanes galore

Words: Dave Phillips
Photographs: Peter Gathercole and Dave Phillips

Driver Profiles

FRANK CHAMPION'S 1990 Range Rover is the first he's owned, but the secretary of the Lincolnshire Land Rover Club has owned and enjoyed several Series IIAs and IIIs since 1983.

He bought it five months ago, when the original VM diesel had just been replaced by a 200Tdi unit, which Frank, from Gainsborough, reckons has plenty of torque as well as returning 35 mpg. The only modification he has made so far is to fit side steps to make access easier for his eight-year-old son.

CARL DAVIS is a trials scrutineer and competition secretary for the Lincolnshire Land Rover Club, so he knows what to look for in a vehicle.

He found it in the shape of this 1984 90, which is all but a Defender 90 in name, as it has been fitted with a 300Tdi engine to replace the original, naturally aspirated diesel – not to mention a new galvanised chassis, plus body panels from a mid-'90s Defender. 'There's not much of the original left,' he admits.

PAUL SMITH, from Caistor, drove his father David's 1990 Defender 90, which is still running on its original 200Tdi engine. 'Dad's had it six years and it's been no trouble – just a new clutch fitted,' he says. 'It's a real workhorse that all the family drives.'

KAREN NOBLE, from Doncaster, borrowed husband John's diesel-powered Series IIA for the day. Work commitments meant John couldn't make it, but that didn't stop Karen from getting behind the wheel, with her uncle Des in the passenger seat.

The vehicle's a real mystery. The logbook shows that it was built in 1971, but wasn't registered for the road until 1976 – hence the R-reg plate and Series III grille.

THE BEACH IS deserted, the row of beach huts locked up for the winter. They look tired, their bright paintwork blasted away by the fine sand borne on the wind off the sea. If I stay long enough, that same wind will soon fetch the paintwork off the Discovery.

I've parked it on the edge of the beach at Mablethorpe on the Lincolnshire coast, but I won't be dallying here long. The North Sea looks grey and sullen, like molten lead, with the menacing wind hurling enormous breakers up the sand and shingle.

There's something strangely exhilarating about the British coastline in winter, when the hamburger stands and souvenir stalls are closed and the crowds have departed.

But there's a real danger lurking here, too. Many hundreds of people lost their lives – and thousands were made homeless – along this stretch of the east coast 50 years ago when a great storm sent a huge tidal surge flooding into the North Sea, which then totally overwhelmed the sea defences. It's a sobering thought.

It's time to head inland to explore the greenlanes and unspoilt scenery of the Lincolnshire Wolds – and even there the sea still has had an influence. The uplands are the remains of a great chalk plateau that was, millions of years ago, part of the seabed.

Ghost coast: rows of deserted beach huts in Mablethorpe typify seaside resorts in winter.

Above All Land Rover life is here: Defender leads the way, followed in line astern by Discoverys old and new and a Range Rover Classic.

Left top Shapes of things to come ... not the prettiest structures ever, but there's no shortage of raw material to keep them turning.

Left bottom Bracing is not the word for the Lincolnshire coast in winter; bone-chillingly freezing would be a bit nearer the mark.

A great upheaval of the earth's crust saw what is now Lincolnshire rise up out of the waves. Then successive ice ages gouged and carved the present landscape. Only 10,000 years ago, this region was gripped in Arctic conditions and roamed by long-extinct woolly mammoth, rhino and sabre-toothed tiger.

Who knows what the future will bring? I drive inland, past two massive wind turbines that stand sentinel behind the sand dunes, harnessing the raw energy of the biting wind. They're modern monuments to Man's ingenuity, but nothing's permanent. With rising sea levels caused by global warming, who knows when the waves will return to reclaim a part of the world that has a very tenuous hold on terra firma?

Global warming? Listen, you wouldn't believe such a thing even existed right now. The field drains beside

the road that slices across this stretch of wind-chilled marshland are frozen solid. I stop to photograph a pair of very puzzled-looking swans, skating on the ice and wondering what on earth has happened to their (normally) watery domain.

My air of melancholy fades, though, as I near Louth, on the edge of the Wolds. Nestling below me and dominated by a vast Gothic church spire, it breathes permanence and continuity in a way that only an old English market town can. Its prosperity was for centuries based upon the famous herds of Red Lincoln cattle that waxed fat on the rich pastures hereabouts.

In fact, the town and its livestock were so important that in 1770 the Louth Navigation was built – a canal that allowed ocean-going vessels of 30 tons to sail inland twelve miles from the coast to collect the precious cargo. It thrived until 1848, when the railways arrived.

The rolling landscape unfolds before me as I head for Market Rasen. In places, snow is piled high along the roadside where the snow ploughs have been through. The sky's bright at the moment, but a menacing black cloud is skidding in over the landscape from the north-east.

It almost goes without saying that the self-same cloud arrives at Market Rasen just as I do – and I'm soon enveloped in a blizzard.

My rendezvous is franchised dealer Duckworth Land Rover, situated opposite the racecourse for which the town is best known. A meeting is held here on the first Tuesday of every month but today's has been cancelled due to the icy conditions. Just as well … there wouldn't be an awful lot for the spectators to see in this white-out.

But it will take more than the merest touch of winter weather to put off our mission. I'm meeting up with a varied collection of Land Rovers and their owners for some winter fun in the Wolds. They range from early examples of Solihull workhorses through to the very latest Td5 Discovery, driven by Ben Duckworth. Ben, a keen off-roader, is reassured by the return of the centre-locking diff that had been omitted on earlier Series II Discos. The odds are that he'll need it for some extra traction before the day is through.

Frank Champion, chairman of the Lincolnshire Land Rover Club, has turned up in his well-abused Range Rover Classic. Fellow club members, Carl Davis and Paul Smith, are both driving 90s, while Karen Noble is behind the wheel of a tidy – and very late-registered – 88-inch Series IIA.

Left to right Taking a breather while we get some photos in the can. Carl Davis takes pole position in his 'not much left of the original' 90.

Doesn't that Disco gleam? Just as well most of the lanes we drove had width on their side.

One of this area's big attractions is the genuine 'get away from it all' atmosphere it serves up.

The three-mile-long RUPP south of Goulceby, along the route of an old Roman road, is a highlight. Great views of the Wolds from on high.

Main picture Big sky … an ever-present feature round here.

What we all have in common is a sense of fun and a longing to get out there to explore, knowing that our Land Rovers will excel in conditions that will be persuading drivers of other vehicles just to stay at home. We've a veritable cast of thousands today, so we split into two groups after agreeing a rendezvous location for the photographs.

Only a mile outside Market Rasen, our group is already getting a taste of mud under the wheels as we leave the tarmac behind and follow a byway through Willingham Woods. It's principally a conifer plantation, but it also has substantial stands of mixed deciduous trees, including thickets of silver birch.

The lanes are firm and easy-going as we head off through Linwood Warren and skirt Legsby Wood *en route* to Linwood village.

The verges of the lane are a tangle of wild honeysuckle, suggesting this would be a pleasant and fragrant route to take on a summer's evening. But although the blizzard has now passed, it's still freezing up here and it will be a couple of months before the dormant buds of the woodbine burst to herald spring.

We're back on tarmac very briefly, heading north through Market Rasen to Hamilton Hill, where another byway starts opposite yet another picturesque wood. After a short drive across open ground, we enter Willingham Forest before crossing a railway line and taking a drive through Middle Rasen Plantation.

From here, it's a short hop along a metalled country lane to Walesby, where we pick up yet another byway to Claxby Hill, shadowing the Viking Way long-distance footpath.

As its name suggests, this was a route across the high ground, once traversed by the Vikings. They, along with the Danes, knew this area well. Many of the towns and villages in this area date back to those times when the fearsome warriors from across the North Sea arrived in their longboats, then raped and pillaged their way across this region.

They weren't the first invaders here, though. Lincolnshire was of great strategic importance to the Romans, who built great towns, including Horncastle, Caistor and, of course, Lincoln itself.

Minutes later, we can see Lincoln – or rather the triple towers of its cathedral – more than 20 miles away. That's because we're now at the top of Claxby Hill, the third-highest point in Lincolnshire. It's a murky sort of day, but the view is breathtaking.

Besides Lincoln, we can also make out the cooling towers of the power stations on the tidal River Trent above Gainsborough and the gaunt cranes of Grimsby and Immingham, on the mouth of the Humber.

The county town of Lincoln was an important city for the Romans, who built a fort here and called it Lindum. But they weren't the first – the Celts had built a wooden hill fort here on the limestone plateau 200 feet above the River Witham.

Our friends from Rome weren't the last occupiers, either. William the Conqueror built the castle here in 1068 and much of it still stands today. He also ordered the building of the great cathedral, which began in 1072

'Maybe we'd get on a bit better if we had something other than a map of Belgium.'

and was completed 20 years later. It's the third biggest in England – smaller only than York Minster and St Paul's – covering an area of 57,000 square feet. A special place indeed.

But there's even more to see from this unique vantage point in deepest Lincs. Ben Duckworth tells us that on a clear day you can even see Sheffield and the Peaks of Derbyshire away in the distance. He should know; he spends a lot of time here.

Unlike some Land Rover main dealers, Duckworth's takes off-roading seriously. So much so, they acquired this site in order to give their customers a taste of mud.

All buyers of new Land Rovers these days are entitled to a free session with one of the nine Driving Experience centres in the UK. But Duckworth's reckoned this was unfair on buyers of used Land Rovers, so they took on Claxby to put it right.

Here, you will certainly get an immediate impression of what your vehicle is capable of, as some of these climbs and ascents are very steep. Today, with a generous coating of ice, they're treacherous, too.

But nobody suffers any mishaps. After all, I'm in good, experienced company. The Lincs club members are all very keen off-roaders who know this site well, having staged countless trials here.

More than 20 years separate Ben's 2003 Discovery and Frank's 1990 Range Rover, but they have a lot in common today: both are equipped with road-biased tyres, yet they effortlessly handle everything their drivers hurl them at.

It's all terrific fun, but after three hours it's time to head off again, this time down a couple of miles of country lanes to the village, where two fords cross the little River Rase. One is about 100 yards long, briefly following the course of the river itself across a hard, stony bottom.

The clouds are gathering now and dusk won't be long, but there's still time to explore a little more. There's an even better, longer ford at Little Cawthorpe, south of Louth. But rather than drive straight there, we make a detour to explore another green-lane, this time a RUPP (road used as a public path) nearly three miles long that follows the course of an old Roman road south of Goulceby. This time we're on high ground, with more great views across the rolling hills of the Wolds.

The oak and ash trees that line the lane are bare, huddled against the snow-laden fields in their winter livery. It's picture-postcard pretty, but stepping out of the vehicles into a sub-zero world, with a significant wind-chill factor on top, is enough to take your breath away.

It's no warmer when we eventually arrive at Little Cawthorpe. Sadly, meltwater from the snow that has thawed over the past few days has sent a flash flood rushing down the little stream. There's enough brown, swirling water to send waves up over the bonnets and, although we're all driving diesel-powered Land Rovers, we don't want to risk a mishap at such a late stage in the day. Instead, in the gathering twilight, we drive off into Louth to find a warm, welcoming hostelry where we can enjoy some sandwiches, chips and a swift half.

It's been a very long day, but a good 'un. After swapping countless tales of off-roading tales past and present, we depart, the best of friends. But Land Rovering is like that, isn't it?

You Can Do It Too

Lincolnshire Land Rover Club runs regular green-lane trips for members through the Lincolnshire Wolds, as well as trials on off-road sites. Contact the membership secretary David Summerfield on 01472 398428.

We stayed at The Kenwick Park Hotel at Louth, set in 300 acres of landscaped grounds with health and leisure facilities including an indoor heated swimming pool and 18-hole golf course. The friendly staff are very helpful and have good local knowledge.

In Lincolnshire we drove a mixture of byways and RUPPs (roads used as public paths). There were also many other greenlanes, including UCRs (unclassified roads) that we did not have time to try. Most are largely unrutted and can be driven throughout the year without risking damage to your Land Rover, thanks to the hard underlying chalk strata, but some are across clay and should be avoided in winter and during prolonged wet spells. All the tracks we drove were wide, with little danger of scratching paintwork. Well worth a couple of days of your time.

The Kenwick Park Hotel in Louth.

Words: Dave Phillips
Photographs: Fiona Spencer
Helpers: John Pearson, Michelle Carn,
Phil Wicks and Guy Bailey

WELCOME TO THE
COUNTY OF
LINCOLNSHIRE

Wolds Apart

From the dramatic open spaces of the Fens to the rolling
uplands of the Wolds, Lincolnshire is never flat and boring.
LRO heads east to explore the ever-changing terrain of
Britain's second-biggest county

AUTUMN ARRIVES EARLY here in Lincolnshire. Huddled
on the telephone lines along every empty lane are flocks
of swallows and house martins, about to escape the east
coast for their annual migration to north Africa.

Right now, we wish we could wing it to balmier climes
too. We're also huddled — behind the sea wall that separates the North Sea from the low-lying fields. There's a
near-gale blowing onshore, straight from the Arctic and
gusting so fast that it hasn't had time to warm up before
it got here.

We're just north of Skegness — the seaside town that the
pre-war railway posters used to describe as 'bracing'. We
take in the view of the storm-tossed turgid waves without
saying a word: we daren't open our mouths in case the
wind rocks our teeth out of their sockets.

We all love to be beside the seaside, but it's still a
relief to escape back to the shelter of our convoy of Land

Rovers. They may be draughty — and three of the five
vehicles boast only virtual heaters — but they're more
fun than a beach hut.

It's early on the second day of our two-day tour
around Britain's second-biggest county and, considering the adventure we've already had, we can't wait to
get driving again and explore some more.

It all started yesterday, in the very south of the
county. The Fenland village of Maxey is our starting
point and we all feel slightly guilty that we haven't done
this trip before.

Lincolnshire is, after all, near enough on the doorstep
of the LRO offices in Peterborough. Our only excuse is
that it has a reputation for being flat and boring ... but
today we aim to disprove that.

Not at first, though. The level black fields stretch for
eternity, with scarcely a tree to break the monotony. The

Above Our convoy traverses the track along a typical Fenland drain.

Right Big skies typify the rural Lincolnshire scene.

Below and opposite (left to right) A herd of cattle spies on our antics.
Rights of way are clearly marked.
This greenlane has been ploughed up by the farmer.

isolated farm buildings cling to the horizon, as if afraid of being blown to oblivion when the wind rakes across these flatlands. But this raw scene has its compensations – not least in the huge skies that stretch unbroken from horizon to horizon and which, at present, are illuminated by the watery colours of a September dawn. It's like driving across a Turner painting.

The peat soil here is as deep and rich as you get, which makes this among the most valuable arable land in the country. Carrots, celery, potatoes, cereal crops and, oddly, tulips all jostle for root space in these fields, but it wasn't always so.

Not much more than 200 years ago, this was the wildest wetland wilderness in the UK – a malaria-plagued swamp where freshwater floods from the uplands met the relentless tides of the North Sea and created a near-uninhabitable morass. But Man's ingenuity drained these watery wastes with a series of drainage channels and pumping engines that lifted the excess water from the low-lying land and hurried it to sea.

It's along those drains that we drive now as we explore a network of UCRs (unclassified roads – aka farm tracks) between Bourne and Spalding.

Our convoy consists of five vehicles. At present I'm leading the way in my Td5 90 Station Wagon, followed by the Project Discovery (300Tdi) piloted by LRO's photographer, Fiona Spencer, and senior designer, Michelle Carn. Also riding the rutted tracks is advertising manager Phil Wicks, in his Td5 Series II Discovery, along with editor-in-chief John Pearson in the 2.25 petrol/LPG Series III Project Lightweight, and our friend Guy Bailey in his ex-military 90, powered by a 2.5 naturally-apsirated diesel.

The latter is a tad underpowered on the tarmac, but it makes no difference out here on the soft Fenland soil, where its low-down torque is no disadvantage.

It's early in the day, but we've encountered our first problem: the Lightweight's brake lights have failed. The

switch under the bonnet has corroded badly and John can't budge it. He elects to drive on regardless (and carefully). Hopefully, we'll be able to pick up another switch from a town *en route*.

Leaving the Fens, we head west through the bleak villages of Morton and Stainfield before splashing through a ford at Bulby Hall, where our antics are watched impassively by a herd of inquisitive cattle, crowded against a nearby farm gate. Happily, the devastation of Foot-and-Mouth disease didn't reach these parts last winter; we hope it doesn't in the coming months as the cold, wet weather closes in.

But there's a rare hint of autumn sunshine now as we cross the A1 and, keeping to country lanes, head west of Grantham and the Leicestershire border to explore an interesting-looking series of greenlanes around Belvoir Castle, the imposing ancestral home of the Dukes of Rutland.

Near here, in the garden of Woolsthorpe Manor, Sir Isaac Newton wrote the Laws of Gravity after watching an apple fall from a tree. Legend has it that the very same

Above left   John eventually finds LPG in Newark.

Left   This overgrown lane hasn't seen traffic for months.

Below   Another lane dug up by a farmer.

108

Above and right The rolling Lincs countryside offers exciting greenlaning with panoramic views.

tree still stands, three centuries on, but it's more likely that it's one of its offspring.

The UCRs and RUPPs (roads used as public paths) live up to their promise, but inevitably our Ordnance Survey maps are out of date and some of the greenlanes have recently been reclassified. Guy, accompanied by Michelle, inadvertently drives one, only to discover that it now diminishes into a bridleway immediately after a narrow bridge over a canal. It necessitates an umpteen-point turn in a very narrow, overgrown section of the track barely wider than the 90 – and in the middle of this tricky manoeuvre he stalls the engine. And it won't re-start.

Every turn of the ignition key is met with the depressing muffled click of the starter solenoid. And here we are, stuck on a bridleway where we're not supposed to be, at right-angles to the track in a position where it would be near-impossible to effect a recovery. Nice one.

Luckily, a sharp tap with a hammer freed the stuck starter and we were able to beat a hasty retreat. 'It's the first time it's ever done that ...' Guy assures us. '... and it's the first time I've ever given Michelle a lift.' Our senior designer, now renamed The Jinx, is unceremoniously ejected from the 90 and travels again in the Discovery. And Guy's starter motor doesn't give him any more problems. Spooky, eh?

We head north now, following a route picked out by Fiona that includes plenty of greenlanes, as well as minor country roads. At Allington we drive a byway that leads to

Skegness

SKEGNESS WAS A small fishing village until the 19th century, when it was 'discovered' by the poet Tennyson. It became one of his favourite haunts and he did more than anyone to popularise it. But it was to his own detriment, because this coincided with the Victorian fashion for seaside holidays.

The advent of steam railway travel had made it possible for families from the major towns and

cities to reach the coast easily and soon Skegness, like so many other unspoilt seaside settlements, had changed beyond recognition. Hotels, guest houses and the inevitable pier soon sprung up and Skegness became the seaside capital of the east coast of northern England. And, in its prime, it was considered rather genteel by the new middle classes who could afford to holiday here.

But that was to change. After the second world war, entrepeneur Billy Butlin built his very first holiday camp here, and 'Skeggy' thus led the way for affordable seaside holidays for the masses. The amusement arcades, funfair rides, and kiss-me-quick hats followed – but only for a couple of decades. Package holidays on the sun-kissed coastline of Spain were a very tempting prospect to a generation used to those famous 'bracing' winds of the east coast and Skegness, like so many other British seaside towns, slipped into decline.

the A1, and the convoy gingerly filters out into the heavy traffic and follows the dual carriageway for about four miles before we exit at Long Bennington. We head east again along the lanes, enjoying some excellent greenlaning around Hough-on-the-Hill before coming unstuck a couple of miles later, near Normanton, where a farmer has kindly decided to plough up a RUPP. This is a public right of way and we could legally drive on across his handiwork – and a field of sugar beet – but there's plenty of room here to turn around and head instead for another greenlane near Bassingham.

By now, it's early afternoon and the Lightweight has run out of LPG. It is still suffering from mixture problems on petrol, and running rough, so John elects to make a detour to the nearest gas supplier, in Newark. Foolishly, the rest of the convoy follows him, and we all get hopelessly lost and separated in the town centre. It's an hour later before we all finally regroup and continue along our route, across the chalk uplands of the Wolds, taking in greenlanes near Metheringham and Belchford before arriving at Skegness for our overnight stop.

The hotel we stay at is smack-bang on the seafront and, in the Edwardian tradition, boasts an imposing facade that hints of grandeur within. In its time, I'm sure it was, but today the flaking ballroom is divided up into smaller partitions of flimsy chipboard and the pound-shop plastic-framed prints on the wall have faded to blue.

Left top The gale-lashed beach doesn't look very inviting.

Left bottom Where next? We gather round to discuss where we're going.

John (*left*) has got his Lightweight stuck (*above top*), but Guy is on hand (*above middle*) to dig out and effect a recovery in his 90, after which he pushes John's head under (*above bottom*) and tells him never to do it again. Or is he just washing his newly-painted military shovel … ?

Below left   Mike makes good his escape anyway, roaring through deep mud at a speed that shouldn't be possible with a naturally-aspirated diesel.

Below   Dirty driving – Phil's Td5 Discovery combines comfort with excellent off-road ability.

Above   On the level – this branch line railway crossing is still manned.

Right   Michelle in her 300 Tdi Discovery takes the splash, followed by Phil in his Td5 Disco, Dave in the Td5 90 and John in the SIII Lightweight.

But it's clean, the rooms are comfortable and bed and breakfast is dirt cheap.

We continue the cheap-and-cheerful theme with a fish and chips supper on the promenade, shivering cheerfully in the teeth of an onshore gale.

The wind drops a little overnight and we're up bright and early the next morning to head north along the coast. But this is no scenic drive: just mile after depressing mile of caravan sites and amusement parks.

I keep expecting to see a sign for Billing-next-to-the-Sea, but instead there are a multitude of villages ending in 'thorpe' – Winthorpe, Addlethorpe, Hogsthorpe, Authorpe and Trusthorpe ... all the way to Mablethorpe. This means they were all settlements founded by the invading Danes, who must have struck some fear into the locals when they came ashore in their longboats. Well over a thousand years on, the Danish influence lives on in this part of the world – well, they eat a lot of bacon butties and drink lager.

Even when the worst of the tacky stuff is shrinking into the distance in the rear view mirror, this still isn't a classic coast road cruise. For starters, you don't actually get to see the sea unless you park up and climb the high bank that separates the angry North Sea from the low-lying land. And having made that effort, into the teeth of the freezing wind, you get to see storm-tossed muddy water breaking onto a flat expanse of mud and sand. And then you drive off in search of something interesting.

We find it at Manby, a few miles inland on the way to Louth (self-proclaimed Capital of the Wolds). Here, the former RAF base now boasts an off-road course, owned

Lincoln green – we explore the picturesque tracks through Willington Woods.

by Motorplex (run by CSMA, the Civil Service Motorists' Association) .

It's a custom-built course with plenty of challenges and varied terrain – including gravel, sand ... and lots of mud, glorious mud. This is the end of summer and the weather has been fairly dry, but the mud is tricky enough in places to give us a few problems. John comes a cropper in the Lightweight, when he gets out of shape while negotiating a carefully-chosen route through some deep, muddy ruts. Soon he's stuck up to the axles and the only way out involves a lot of shovelling and a recovery by Guy's 90.

There's also a great water section on the course – too deep for most of the vehicles, but Guy and I can't resist putting our 90s through. We both end up with wet carpets for our troubles, as we wade in beyond the bottom of the doors, but it's good. If you really love mud, then this will be the place to head for this winter. It will be like the Somme.

Despite devoting most of the morning to playing in the goo, we still haven't had quite enough off-roading. There are some excellent greenlanes on the way home, so we head for Market Rasen and Willingham Woods, where the tracks through the mixed woodland make a change

from the wide open scenery. Then it's a short hop to Lissington, and yet more lanes to explore.

We enliven the return journey at Rowston, where there's another ford to splash some of the mud away. The Land Rovers have behaved themselves, by and large, and we've enjoyed another brilliant two-day British break. Who ever said Lincolnshire was boring?

Notts Landing

Words: Rachel Burkitt
Photographs: Mark Williams and Newark and Sherwood District Counil

DEATH HAS GOT its dates mixed up. It's spring, yet instead of new life, gloom hangs in the air.

A pall of smoke from burning pyres hangs over the landscape like a shroud, and the smell of hay is tainted with the odour of disinfectant. The devastation faced by farmers and the tourist industry puts into perspective the fact that, for Land Rover owners, Britain's green and pleasant lanes are closed for business. Yes, greenlaning is off the agenda.

But we're a resourceful lot here at LRO. Faced with our favourite pastime being off-limits, we decided to do some lateral thinking. If greenlaning in the countryside is on hold, what can you do to satisfy that mud-slinging urge?

Magnificent Southwell Minster – this Norman cathedral is one of Nottinghamshire's finest gems.

LRO heads to the mid Shires, in search of muddy adventure ...

Try the Big One – a 100-foot hill climb and descent on a 30-degree incline to refine your braking skills.

Simple. Find yourself a professional off-road driving centre close to other attractions, and have yourself a great family day out. That's what we did when we visited Lee James 4×4 Professional Off-Road Driving Training and Events, near Nottingham.

A quick call to the Nottinghamshire Tourist Board identified a variety of attractions in the immediate area. We liked the sound of Boughton Pumping Station near Newark and the Laxton Visitor Centre and Village. It was time to surf the internet to see if they were worth visiting.

Boughton Pumping Station looked promising. A picture showed an impressive Edwardian Grade II listed building with a 200 foot high chimney. Thanks to the combined efforts of the community, government and private sector funding, it has been transformed into a visitor centre with an exhibition on renewable energy, restaurant and gift shop.

Laxton provided a complete contrast from Boughton's industrial landscape. Just a short drive away, the village – which is mentioned in the Domesday Book – possesses England's last open-field village system dating back 700 years.

It was time to hit the road. The Lee James Off-Road Centre is on the A617 and A614 junction, between Nottingham and Worksop. Preventative measures, advised by MAFF to combat Foot-and-Mouth, were in operation. All vehicles entering or leaving the site use one entrance, and are sprayed with disinfectant. People

working with, or in close proximity to rural livestock, including horses, are asked not to enter.

The 26 acres of natural wooded hillsides and open grassland offer challenging off-road terrain including mud, water, hills, ditches, gravity-defying side slopes and woodland trails, which are currently being graded. Special stages include the Rolling Road, the Moguls, the Roller Coaster, the Black Hole and the Big One – a 100-foot hill climb and descent. Other attractions on the site – available to pre-booked groups – include quad biking and target and tactical activities.

Lee James and chief instructor Dave Gallop came to meet us as we pulled up at the new clubhouse. Lee took us through the different courses on offer, from a one or two-hour taster session to experience the thrill of off-roading, to the 4×4 two-hour owner sessions.

Lee explained his approach to off-roading as we climbed into one of two Defenders used on site: 'My main message is that people can bring their own Land Rover if they want to and we can show them how the systems work. But more importantly, we demonstrate the limitations of off-roading to give them an idea about how they can go about it, without damaging expensive vehicles.'

First stop was the Rolling Road, an ex-heavy-duty commercial conveyor belt – without the belt – set into the ground. It cleverly demonstrates our 90's systems. As soon as our front axle hits the road in first gear without the diff lock, we are stranded, with power spinning out to a single wheel. Then with diff lock engaged we drove on to it only to find we came to a standstill again, with the drive being lost to one wheel on each axle. For novice

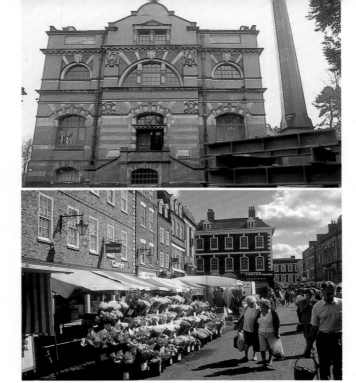

Above Boughton Pumping Station has plenty of interest both inside and outside; the grounds are open for picnics.

Below Newark market with its wide selection of stalls. The town's castle is also well worth a visit.

drivers it's a useful, practical demonstration for the limitations of a standard 4×4-drive system. Lee pointed out that the Rolling Road would be no obstacle for a vehicle with traction control, such as a Freelander: 'This would be explained as part of the demonstration, plus the knowledge and techniques required by a standard 4×4 – increased momentum in a higher gear. As a practical demonstration it's a lot easier for drivers to understand.'

The Freelander would have struggled for clearance on the Axle Twister; an uneven downhill track designed to test axle articulation. Drivers can choose whether to use their own vehicles or the Defenders provided by the centre.

Dave, who spent twelve years as a Land Rover mechanic in the RAF, said the course was designed to test vehicles to the limit. He was driving his 110 at an angle through an impressive side slope.

We finished the course with a drive down the Big One – a 100-foot descent down a 30-degree incline back to base. For Lee it's an opportunity to teach cadence braking and advanced power braking. Using first gear and diff lock as we descended, he explained the need to feed in the gas on slippery areas. 'The objective with feeding the gas in is to keep the wheels turning; in most cases you will manage to keep directional control and prevent the wheels from locking.'

Deputy editor Mark and myself were impressed with the centre's layout. It's a well-designed course with plenty of variation and good ground for Landys. The woodland drive will be a great territory when it's ready.

Leaving behind the dual carriageway we made our way to Laxton. Here, hedge-framed open fields lined the route as we drove into the attractive brick-built village. Its unique medieval field system is a fascinating anachronism that has survived thanks to a series of events, including a dispute between two land-owning Earls and an agricultural depression during the 1880s. By 1906 there came a move from enclosing the unique field system to preservation. Since September 1981 the Crown Estate Commissioners has been Lords of the Manor of Laxton, which includes fourteen farms, each between 93 and 148 acres, with around 80 acres of enclosed land and another 30 in open fields.

The visitor centre revealed more interesting facts, including the continued operation of a form of manorial government that has survived since medieval times. It has met for centuries in the adjacent Dovecote Inn to control the cultivation of the open fields. Foot-and-Mouth restrictions bar visitors from the bridleways that lead to the fields and remains of a castle. But the village is still worth visiting for its concentration of farms, clusters of cottages, impressive church, and pinfold on the Kneesall Road.

Leaving Laxton, we headed towards the A616 and motored through a series of ugly conurbations towards Ollerton, a grim reminder of the industrial legacy of coal mining, with a lack of vegetation and a surfeit of depressing architecture. But when we reached Boughton Pumping Station it was worth it. The building was built at the beginning of the century to supply Nottingham with clean water. In 1905, it supplied water to 1.5 million homes. But by the end of the 1970s it became redundant and the impressive triple expansion steam engines, which had pumped water for more than 60 years, were removed. By 1995, after 20 years of neglect and vandalism, the Station was saved for posterity by a regeneration project that has transformed it into an award-winning complex for visitors, business and the local community. Energetica – The Future of Power, is an interactive exhibition that illustrates life after fossil fuels, demonstrating new ideas for energy production and conservation, including solar energy and how to harness power from landfill sites. Other attractions include a 40-foot high water feature, a 120-foot deep well and a heritage exhibition that illustrates the centre's history from its original design to present day.

Our day was a success after all. We managed to get our off-road thrill, combining it with a fascinating glimpse of Nottinghamshire's history. Without the Foot-and-Mouth epidemic we would have gone greenlaning, but missed out on some of the historical sites we visited. It just goes to show that, with a touch of ingenuity and imagination, you can still get out into the countryside for some off-roading.

Shropshire probably has more greenlanes than any other British county. Dave Phillips couldn't resist taking his Discovery to the Welsh borderlands to explore them – and, boy, is he glad he did

Words: Dave Phillips
Photographs: Fiona Richardson

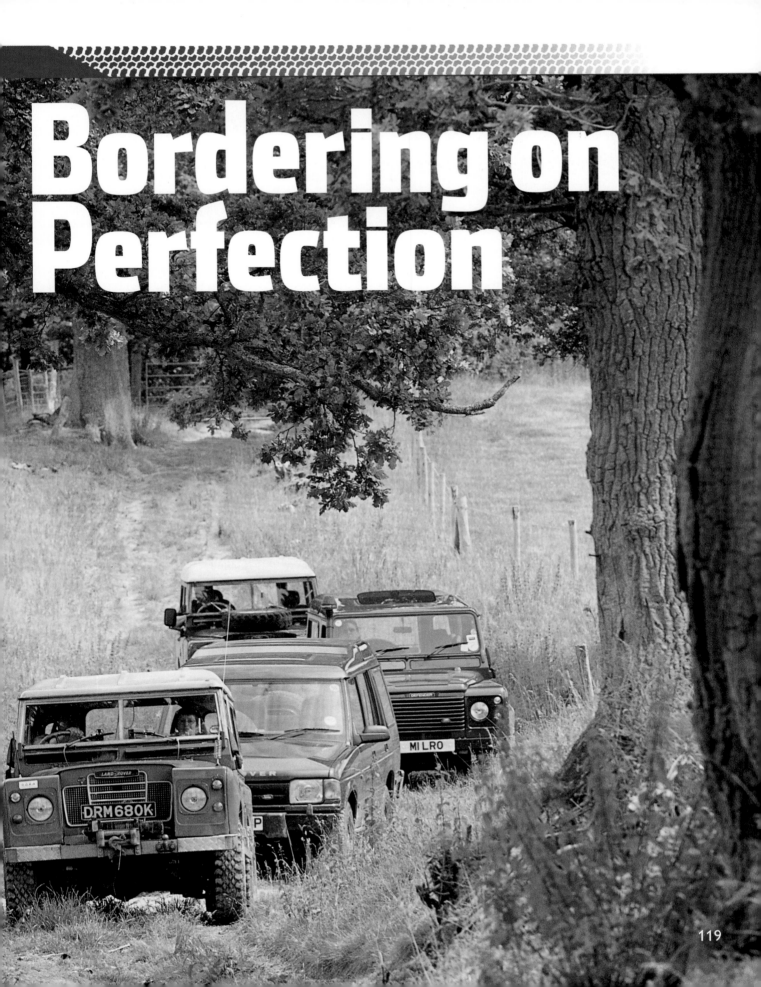

Bordering on Perfection

Happy explorers – Paul, John, Steve and Judy, Dave.

OUR LAND ROVERS brush against rampant wild honeysuckle, filling the cabs with an almost overpowering sweet scent as we edge our way through the overgrown lane, the hedgerows a riot of colour and greenery.

Here in Shropshire, in a quiet backwater of the English countryside bordering Wales, we seem to have found Heaven on Earth – for greenlaning fans, at least.

The Ordnance Survey map unfolded on the passenger seat is a kaleidoscope of fluorescent colours from all the marker pen lines we've drawn to trace the maze of lanes we can drive legally. For once, we're spoilt for choice. Can it *really* be this good?

It seems sort of unfair that here, in such a sparsely populated area of the country, there are so many greenlanes with so few drivers to enjoy them. But our fellow travellers from the local Land Rover club aren't complaining – they're grinning from ear to ear in a display of happiness bordering on smugness. And so would you if you had this on your doorstep.

Suddenly, there's a flurry of feathers and foliage ahead as a buzzard bursts through the towering foxgloves and flaps furiously to get airborne. The big bird of prey looks as ungainly as a jumbo jet but, like the 747, it's devastatingly efficient at the job it was designed for – amply demonstrated by the sight of the unfortunate young rabbit it's carrying in its talons.

Once aloft, it spreads its huge wings and lets the warm air currents do the job of carrying it back home to its lair in the cluster of tall pine trees on the towering hillside across the valley.

We're headed in that direction, too, but it'll take us rather longer under Land Rover power. Not that we're complaining, of course; we're all savouring every moment as we press on at barely walking pace.

Leading the way, at the wheel of his well-abused 88-inch Series III, is the man who knows these lanes better than anyone.

Steve Mainwaring, rights of way officer for the Staffordshire and Shropshire Land Rover Club, has driven every inch of these byways and unclassified country roads many times over. His exhaustive research means he can drive them safe in the watertight knowledge that he has every legal right to do so – and he has even uncovered evidence to get some other lanes upgraded to byway status.

In the passenger seat is his wife, Judy, acting as official gate-opener for the trip. Gate-closer is Paul Forsyth, a fellow Staffordshire and Shropshire member, at the rear of our four-vehicle convoy in his 88-inch Series IIA. Sandwiched between is LRO gaffer, John Pearson, in his Td5 Defender 90 and me in the 300Tdi Project Discovery.

As usual, LRO photographer Fiona hops from vehicle to vehicle to get the best shots, as the stunning scenery unfolds before our windscreens.

There's a surprise around every corner, because the terrain is just so varied. Early on the first day we begin our adventure close to the attractive market town of Much Wenlock, on the sharp, natural escarpment known as Wenlock Edge.

We drive up a track over Hepmoor Hill before following a minor road that runs parallel to the River Corve to Hungerford, where a densely overgrown byway suddenly veers up and over a bank, shadowing a tree-covered hill known as Big Wood.

From here, we explore another short stretch of byway before heading to Glenburrell and a river crossing that entails a steep drop in, as well as a slippery climb out. We all make it without mishap – in my case in first gear/low box, with diff lock engaged to cope with the slippery, boulder-strewn river bed.

From this lush, green valley we head south-west, climbing as we go, to the Welsh border. Only the narrow upper reaches of the River Teme separates us from Powys. A tributary of the Teme, the River Redlake, is easily forded before we tackle a byway up a steep gradient and turn on to a UCR (unclassified country road) that runs through the gloomy conifer plantations of Bucknell Wood.

We're making good progress, but not for long. This is very much a working wood and its owners, the Forestry Commission, are felling hundreds of acres of mature fir trees. Unfortunately, they have dumped a huge pile of stripped trunks across the path – which we can neither climb nor drive around.

Not to worry: Steve's out of the SIII in a flash and chatting to the foresters who, minutes later, arrive with a lorry and huge grab to move the offending objects clear of the path. This man has the gift of the gab. He's tactful and a great negotiator – valuable skills indeed for a rights of way officer.

By now we're less than half a mile from Herefordshire, where our maps reveal many more miles of enticing-looking byways, ripe for exploration, but we stay within the Shropshire border, heading along the valley of the River Corve, where two more byways meander across the meadows. Grazing sheep and cows are the only witnesses

Above   Almost can't see the Landys for the trees.

Left   The older Land Rovers on our trip show what they were designed to do – Steve Mainwaring's SIII takes its turn fording a narrow stream.

Below   Paul Forsyth's SIIA gets its feet wet.

Driver Profile

NAME	Paul Forsyth
VEHICLE	1963 Series IIA

LOOK – HE'S STILL SMILING, even though a dropped conrod has just knocked this lump of cast iron off his engine block in the middle of our trip.

His 1963 Series IIA started life with the former East Shropshire Water Board – very appropriate, as Paul likes nothing better than wading through water deep enough to send it flooding in through the door bottoms.

'I like driving across rivers when there's been a bit of rain and there's a fair old current, but I do get just a bit twitchy when the back starts to float off,' he admits.

He bought the SIIA a year ago from the widow of its previous owner. It had been standing, undriven, under a tree for the previous ten years, but the bulkhead and chassis were in remarkable condition.

When he bought it, there was a 2.5 BMC diesel under the bonnet with a cracked block, which Paul replaced with the 2.25 diesel from a Series III. Now he's faced with the dilemma of which engine to drop in next.

to our passage as we negotiate the deserted, overgrown lanes. Listen, this is the life …

The lanes are lovely to drive through, but that heavy growth of vegetation is giving Steve some grounds for concern. The Foot-and-Mouth outbreak of 2000-2001 meant they saw no traffic for a year and, with little attention from 4×4s since, they are in danger of becoming nigh-on impassable – not just to Land Rovers, but to horse riders, cyclists and, eventually, even ramblers.

What the anti-greenlaning lobby forgets (or simply doesn't realise) is that it is motor traffic that keeps the vegetation on and along these lanes within manageable bounds. This is one of Steve Mainwaring's hobby horses, on which he can argue long and hard – and does so with gusto whenever his beloved greenlanes come under threat.

Our final lane of the day is part of an old Roman road, close to the village of Shipton. Like most of the lanes

Top to bottom Big country, wide skies.

There's a lane in here somewhere – honest.

Lack of traffic means the byways are badly overgrown.

An open byway at the back of the Long Mynd.

we've driven today, the surface is excellent, comprising mainly stone. But the final half-mile is in a poor state, due to much of the stone surface being surreptitiously carted away to be used as building material elsewhere. As a result, there are now some very deep ruts – ones that I decide would be unwise to drive into in the Discovery, so I make a detour along the tarmac lanes to meet the other three vehicles at the far end.

Steve had predicted the rest of the convoy would be safely through before I got there; but in fact I arrive to the unmistakable sound of a hard-revving diesel engine.

Paul has inadvertently dropped his SIIA into a deep hole that Steve and John managed to skirt around, and now he's having trouble extracting himself, despite his mud tyres.

The extra strain is clearly too much for the veteran 88-inch. Within a few hundred yards there's an almighty clanging and banging as the abused 2.25-litre diesel drops a conrod, taking out a sizeable lump of the engine block in the process.

Despite this setback, Paul is still smiling as we tow it to a farmer's gateway for collection later. We're finishing the day with a spot of off-roading and he doesn't want to miss a moment of the fun. 'Ah, well ... I was thinking of converting it to petrol, anyway,' he says, philosophically.

Driver Profile

NAME	Steve Mainwaring
VEHICLE	1972 Series II

STEVE, PICTURED HERE with his wife, Judy, has owned his 1972 Series III for three years. One of the first jobs he did after buying it was to convert the 2.25 petrol engine to run on LPG – a job he did himself.

'Fitting it was pretty straightforward, but I had it checked out at a specialist just to make sure,' he says. 'I did it for economy. It has halved the cost of fuel bills, which is especially useful at weekends when I go exploring the lanes.'

Other additions Steve has made include a Milemarker hydraulic winch, which is powered by a power steering pump that began life in a Leyland DAF van. To withstand the rigours of bleak Shropshire winters, Steve has converted the notoriously inefficient Land Rover heater by fitting the matrix from a Ford Fiesta Mk3. 'It's transformed it and it's like a sauna now,' he smiles. Finally, for maximum off-road efficiency, Steve has fitted seven-leaf Lightweight springs all round. 'They greatly increase the wheel articulation when driving in ruts or on uneven surfaces,' he says.

Top   The strain is clearly too much for the veteran 88-inch.

Middle   A rare stop.

Bottom   Fun and games at Buildwas Leisure Motor Track.

While the weather on our first day had been dull but pleasant, the second day dawns even duller and very unpleasant, with showers of heavy rain and low clouds enveloping the high peaks of Long Mynd, our destination for the morning.

But we carry on regardless and, once we reach Church Stretton, the weather gods smile on us and the clouds open for shafts of sunlight to pick out the rocky summits we're about to drive to.

'You see that big pile of rocks away up there?' says Steve, pointing to a particularly bleak crag. 'That's known as the Devil's Chair and it's said that when it's shrouded in fog it means he's in residence.'

Sounds like so much superstition, but Paul insists he knew a man who dared to venture to the top one summer's day when the summit was shrouded in black clouds. 'Suddenly he was caught a huge thunderstorm and struck by lightning, which killed him on the spot. Blew him right out of his shoes,' he says.

Yes, that sudden change in the weather is indeed very welcome.

Up on the high ground, there are views for miles around – right across to the misty, purple peaks of the Welsh mountains in the distance. Gone now is the lush vegetation of the lowland valleys. It is a treeless moor, with heather the only plant able to withstand the bleak winters, for snow lies on these hills for months on end each year.

Today, even though it's midsummer, we need fleeces when we step out of the vehicles. Apart from gate-opening duties, stops are rare, with mile upon mile of uninterrupted driving along unclassified roads, some of which form part of the Shropshire Way long-distance footpath.

However, we meet neither rambler, rider nor driver all morning – we have these magnificent views all to ourselves, sharing them only with the hardy upland sheep, the occasional rabbit and the inevitable buzzards, soaring high above us (bad news for those occasional rabbits).

Eventually, our run of luck with the weather ends and the clouds gather. There are many more miles of lanes to explore, but with the rain teeming down and visibility down to a matter of yards now, we reluctantly call it a day.

At LRO, we love greenlaning and get enthusiastic about *all* the places we explore, but Shropshire really does live up to the well-worn 'neglected corner of England' tag. I can't think of any area of the country I've driven where there is such a wealth of lanes to drive.

Forget the Devil in his chair. This place really is a greenlane paradise.

Drive on the Wild Side
Leisure Motor Track, Buildwas

ALTHOUGH SHROPSHIRE is probably blessed with more greenlanes than any other area of the country, it is a very different matter when it comes to off-road sites. In such a lowly populated area, there are inevitably fewer drivers – and therefore less demand.

But Steve and Paul still managed to come up with a cracker at Buildwas, where we sampled the Leisure Motor Track owned by Jenny Morgan.

There are 47 acres of mixed terrain to explore here, including dense woodland, sections of very deep mud, water splashes and plenty of hill climbs and descents – including what must be the tallest hill for miles around, offering magnificent views of all the surrounding countryside (and, oddly, the pink cooling towers of the nearby power station, situated on the banks of the adjacent River Severn).

Wildlife here includes wild deer, countless rabbits and the inevitable buzzards – none of which seem to mind the rumble of 4×4s at play.

Although individuals can drive here by booking in advance, the owner prefers organised clubs and groups. Contact Jenny Morgan on 07831 398763.

Words: Craig Cheetham
Photographs: Mark Williams
and Newark and Sherwood
District Council

Forest Recommissioned

The Cannock Chase is once again open to organised 4×4 expeditions. LRO goes exploring ...

IF YOU GO down to the woods today, you're sure of a big surprise. You see, until eighteen months ago the Cannock Chase was out of bounds to Land Rover owners who wanted to investigate its muddier areas.

But thanks to the careful organisation and dedication of one man, Land Rovers can once again get into low box and get their tyres dirty playing in the dense forests.

The man to thank is Jim Sampson whose company, Overlander Training, organises marshalled routes through 720 acres of the Chase. Three years ago, the Forestry Commission closed the Chase to four-wheel drives after irresponsible drivers damaged the land, driving in areas they shouldn't have and using lanes so churned up that should have been left to recover.

Thanks to Jim's hard work and dedication, repairing tracks, planning organised routes and convincing the powers that be that he would treat the forests with the respect they deserve, he's now allowed to take parties of overland adventurers through the Chase every weekend.

'It's taken a lot of hard work,' says Jim as he casually hands me the keys to his silver Range Rover. 'Indeed, even now I have to spend a lot of time here in mid-week, making sure that the routes we use are kept in tip-top condition and deciding which tracks can be driven at which time of year.'

'I tend to use different tracks each weekend, so they have time to recover after being used. That way, the Forestry Commission is kept happy. In fact, it's been very supportive of my actions, and even promotes my trips in its forest shops and literature.'

Jim hops into the passenger seat of the Range Rover, seemingly unflustered by the fact that I am about to take his pride and joy down rocky slopes, through mud baths and within inches of resolute conifers and dense, stump-concealing foliage.

It's understandable that, first, he wants to make sure I can drive.

'I want you to stop halfway up here and turn the engine off,' he says as we approach an unbelievably steep hillclimb. I'm facing the clouds, engine dead, and my mind is rooting through its disorganised filing system back to the off-road training – I'm not very good at thinking on Sundays. Remarkably, the theory of failed hillclimbs comes flooding back to me. It's a good job, because later on I'll need it for real.

But now I slot the Range Rover into reverse, cross my fingers, cross my legs and turn the key. The Rover lurches into motion, then cruises sedately down the hill. It's the first time I've tried the theory of getting down from a failed hillclimb and I'm amazed at how controllable the Range Rover feels.

Jim, too, looks rather relieved. As does LRO's deputy editor Mark Williams, standing at the bottom of the slope with a camera as more than two tons of metal rumbles towards him. He confesses later that he was getting ready to run off into the forest as fast as his little legs (watch it, Tank – MW) would carry him, and I try my best to assure him there is no reason to be scared. He doesn't believe me.

Before we set off into the forest, the rest of the crews that have joined us have a go on what Jim calls his 'nursery slope'. We've got a diverse turn-out of vehicles. As well as Jim's Range Rover there is a Td5 Discovery, a 300Tdi Discovery, a Series IIA 109 Station Wagon and a mightily impressive 101 GS, recently rebuilt by its owner, Bob Willets.

Training over, we pull away from our meeting place into the forest. At the head of the convoy is Jim's Range Rover, navigating the maze of tracks and lanes in Cannock Chase with the help of its owner's huge knowledge.

I ask Jim if he needs a map to get around.

'Not any more,' he replies. 'I've spent the best part of two years scouring the area, looking for usable lanes and tracks, and now they're all engraved on my memory.' And Jim must have a mightily impressive memory, with hundreds of acres of forest to remember and over 150 different routes to choose from.

Our first track is a gentle warm-up. Nothing more than a water splash, a mild hillclimb and a rocky descent, but little do I know what Jim has got in store for us.

The fantastic forest scenery is not only nice to look at, it makes the off-road tracks seem even more extensive. The tall pines and conifers conceal the actual climbs and descents, so it is only when you come to a clearing that you realise you are 1,000 feet above sea level, with views across Staffordshire as far as Stoke-on-Trent and Congleton to the north, Cannock and Wolverhampton to the south.

The Cannock Chase sits in Staffordshire's industrial heartland – an oasis of pretty, if cultivated, recreation. Indeed, in 1958 it was one of the first places in the country to be recognised as an Area of Outstanding Natural Beauty by the National Parks Commission, and it remains the only one of its kind to be situated within a green belt. When you're up in the forests, it's hard to believe that three million people live within 20 miles, but part of the Chase's attraction is its accessibility as a weekend retreat.

An off-roader's dream – signs to warn walkers that 4×4s might be playing in the woods – and that they're perfectly entitled to.

I swing the Range Rover down a rocky path and drop into low-ratio second. The track is getting steeper as we descend and the surface beneath the wheels is little more than loose gravel. Suddenly, the road seems to disappear over the Range Rover's bonnet to a sheer drop. I stop and select low-ratio first, looking desperately at Jim for guidance. Instead, he just grins with a steely reserve.

A quick glance down the track confirms the footing is good and there's little chance of losing control of the vehicle, so I take my feet off the pedals and hold on for dear life. The Range Rover cruises undramatically down the slope towards a ditch, which I exit at angle to avoid thumping the towbar on the ground.

I look at Jim. 'That was easy,' I say grinning. Jim just grins back. He knows what the next descent is like, and he knows what we have to drive over to get there.

Our convoy weaves its way through thick woodland. In places, colonies of ferns have sprung up in just two weeks and it's almost impossible to see the track – we really are at one with nature.

So far, the only wildlife we have seen are flies and midges, clustering on the windscreen in a bid to join us in the comfort of the Range Rover. As we drive deeper into the forest, two fallow deer does bound across our path. We stop and kill our engines in the hope they'll be followed by their fawns, but none appear. I blame the 101 – it even scares me when I see it coming my way, such is its intimidating height and snorting exhaust note.

We continue to climb into the forest, our track weaving in and out of conifers, sometimes with just inches to spare either side.

Our progress is halted slightly by log-and-soil jumps erected by mountain bikers looking to 'catch big air', but who shouldn't have been using the tracks. Jim is understandably livid, particularly as we have to dismantle them by hand before progressing.

Another delay is caused by one of the wettest Julys on record. Although the sun is shining, the previous week had seen torrential rain and the ground is soft underfoot.

I turn the Range Rover up another steep climb, along a tricky path with diff-snagging tree stumps. Using momentum to get through is impossible as we have to pick our route carefully. It's no surprise when the Range Rover buries itself into the soft peat with all four wheels spinning.

I swap seats with Jim in the hope that his experience and local knowledge will help the vehicle up the track, but it's going nowhere. Instead we drop down the slope slowly and send Colin Farrell in his SIIA up first.

Driver Profile

NAME   Dawn Cleaver
VEHICLE   1996 Discovery 300Tdi

DAWN CLEAVER HAD never driven her Discovery off-road until earlier this year, but these days you can't keep her away from the Cannock Chase.

'I was probably like a lot of Discovery owners,' she says. 'I bought mine because I wanted a big, safe vehicle which I could use just for normal driving. I never took it off-road and the thought had never even crossed my mind until I heard about the Chase being reopened.

'One day, I just thought "what the heck" and booked myself on a one-to-one driver training course with Overlander Training.

'I couldn't believe how much fun it was. I had been missing out on so much just using my Discovery for trips round town and to the supermarket, but these days I spend most weekends up to my axles in mud. If you've got a vehicle that can do it, you're daft not to!'

'I've only got road tyres on the Range Rover,' says Jim. 'Since this course is used by a lot of first-time off-roaders, I think it's important to prove that these vehicles don't need mud-plugging tyres to be impressive. And with these tyres on, if I can do it, I know they can.'

Colin's Rover is running on slightly more aggressive tyres which we hope will carve a route through the soft ground, but his attempts are to no avail. The track is impassable and we don't want to cause any damage to the ground, so instead we turn around and seek an alternative route, zigzagging through the woodland and out on to a ridge at the top of the forest.

After spending a couple of hours in the shade of tall pines, it takes our eyes some time to adjust as we break out into the open to stop for a breather and enjoy the view. Our vantage point looks out across the top of the forest and puts a real perspective on how far up we have climbed.

Jim indicates the route down with a pointed finger and a grin. A few hundred yards down the track there's a break in the trees and an old logging track takes an almost direct route to the Chase's lower reaches.

The surface here is light and sandy – easily kicked away with your foot. Quite how it will support two tons of Range Rover, or indeed a gargantuan 101, is anybody's guess, but Jim is confident. He's

Ali Khan and crew don't mind bringing their fairly new Discovery out to play in the forest – vehicle damage is unlikely.

Dawn Cleaver and her Discovery cope admirably with a steep descent.

been down here several times before and he knows that the descent is nothing for a Land Rover. Instead, it all hinges on the ability of the driver. Bizarre then, that the first to attempt it is yours truly.

I engage low-ratio first and creep towards the edge of the drop. Deputy editor Mark, on the back seat, pretends to look relaxed. Jim, in the passenger seat, doesn't seem to have a care in the world. As for me, I don't consult the mirror to find out what I look like, but I certainly wish I hadn't just eaten my sandwiches. It's a long way down to the bottom of the hill, and I've just spied a cruel-looking axle-twister halfway down.

'That's just evil,' I moan. As usual, Jim sits there and grins. 'No problem at all,' he mutters.

I tentatively edge the Range Rover over the lip of the slope, glad that Jim's is such a capable and comfortable vehicle.

And I needn't have worried. The Range Rover appears to relish the challenge, crawling down the hill with a gurgle, like a contented baby.

We are only travelling slowly, but as we approach the axle-twister I see firm rock on the ground, which allows

Driver Profile

| NAME | Colin Farrell |
| VEHICLE | 1967 Series IIA Diesel |

COLIN BECAME HOOKED on Land Rovers when he bought his Series IIA twelve years ago.

'I bought it because I needed a large vehicle to use every day,' he says. 'I never desperately wanted one, but once I'd got it I knew it was something special. It certainly wasn't long before I was going out and learning all about off-road driving.

'I've personalised my IIA in lots of ways, there are loads of dials on the dashboard, it's got a brilliant Ford Granada heater and I've just had the interior fully re-trimmed.

'I bought myself a secondhand Discovery a couple of years ago and I no longer needed the IIA as daily transport, so I put it up for sale. When it came to the crunch, though, I just couldn't go through with it. It's strange how you get attached to a Land Rover ...'

me to shave just a small amount of speed off with the brakes and pick my route through, dipping the wheels into the wash-out one at a time and praising the Range Rover's superb axle articulation – the undulations are soaked up as easily as a car passing over a sleeping policeman, with no drama and no chance of grounding the vehicle.

'I told you it was easy,' says Jim. I wonder what his definition of difficult is. We stop away from the bottom of the slope and wander back to guide the other vehicles down.

The Discoverys cope much in the same way as the Range Rover, absorbing the bumps like sponges in puddles.

It's a different story for the two leaf-sprung vehicles. The 101 kicks a rear wheel up just as Mark snaps away, while Colin in the Series IIA reckons he'll still be vibrating three hours after coming down the hill. But we're all down safely and heading down one of the Chase's less taxing tracks.

The variations in terrain and scenery are the Chase's greatest assets. Within a mile you can experience driving over peat, rocks and sandstone, while views range from stunning vantage points to dark, intimidating lanes shadowed by a tunnel of great trees.

There was a lot of mining and quarrying in the Chase earlier in the century, and much of the terrain is man-made. But erosion and neglect has left many once-passable tracks only suitable for the world's toughest vehicles. Of course, Land Rovers find them a doddle.

We've been out in the Chase for several hours, and Jim is planning his grand finale. A 20-minute run through easy forest lanes and over well-maintained tracks takes us to the east of the Cannock Forest, where a man-made lane has been cut through the valley.

To the right, the forest rises steeply to at least a couple of hundred feet above our heads. We turn right across a rickety bridge, and face our final challenge.

A steep, rock-strewn path climbs all the way to the top. The surface is both damp and loose, and despite my best efforts to keep the Range Rover within the correct power band, it loses traction a couple of hundred yards up. I now know why Jim was making sure everyone was confident with failed hillclimbs, as I let the Range Rover rumble backwards against engine braking.

Jim suggests two options for reaching the top. The first is to put the Range Rover into low-ratio third and floor it. The second is to engage low-ratio first and try to guide it up the hill at 1,400 rpm precisely, giving a little throttle if the revs drop. I choose the latter option and, for once, I've made the right decision. The Range Rover creeps grindingly up the hill – it just keeps going to the top. Once again, the sheer ability of even standard Land Rover vehicles has proven itself, and all but Colin's Series IIA makes it to the top without incident.

Colin's leaf springs seem to work against him, the bounce denying him traction, so instead he stays at the

Dense forests and rocky valleys are part of the appeal of the Cannock Chase.

bottom – taking the sensible option of catching up with us on the way to the pub.

After a day's thrilling off-roading there is no better way than to round off with a quick beer, but even with such an incentive ahead it is with great regret that I leave the Cannock Chase.

Here, just 20 minutes away from Birmingham, is some of Britain's most stunning off-roading, and suitable for first-timers, weekenders and career mud-pluggers. It can be technically challenging, but with Jim to select appropriate routes, there is little chance of damaging your road-going vehicle.

Thanks to Jim's hard work and dedication, not to mention the bridges he has built between off-roaders and the Forestry Commission, this wonderful woodland is once again available for the enjoyment of responsible Land Rover owners.

Brilliant driving, brilliant scenery and brilliant company. What are you waiting for?

The Cannock Chase – its heritage and history

THE CANNOCK CHASE as it is today is very much a 20th century creation, with most of the development and tree-planting taking place after the First World War. However, the area is steeped in history. The earliest records of the area date back to Norman times. The Chase was part of the King's Forest of Cannock, established by William the Conqueror for the private use of his estate. The forest remained in royal ownership until 1290, when hunting rights were passed to the Bishop of Lichfield, who renamed it the Bishop's Chase of Cannock.

In those days, the Chase was largely covered by oak and elm trees, but most of these were lost in the 15th and 16th centuries as they were destroyed for charcoal. The industrial revolution of the 19th century nearly saw the death of Cannock Chase. Coal was king, and Cannock had plenty of it. Much of the Chase was mined and many of its fauna were destroyed.

But it was its natural hills and contours that saved the Chase. It played a large role in the First World War, housing two large military training camps, a hospital and a German prisoner of war camp. Indeed, there is still a large German cemetery within the Chase where the bodies of dead prisoners were buried.

After the War, the Chase was divided into two areas. To the west was vast heathland, still used for military exercises and manoeuvres. To the east, the Cannock Forest was planted, with large evergreens soon springing up from its fertile land, while the RAF Hednesford air base was built in the Chase's southern reaches. After the Second World War, the Earl of Lichfield granted the heathlands to the County Council, and it is this area which is the main part of today's Cannock Chase Country Park.

It might be a man-made phenomenon, but the Cannock Chase is incredibly beautiful. So much so that it became

Give a Range Rover a hill and you just can't keep it on its lead!

one of the first places in England to be dedicated an Area of Outstanding Natural Beauty by the National Parks Commission in 1958.

Today, its beauty is well-preserved and it offers a wide array of outdoor pursuits. The Chase is managed and maintained by the Forestry Commission, and using it for off-road driving is only made possible through properly organised trips with Overlander Training.

Trainer Profile

NAME	Jim Sampson, Overlander Training
VEHICLE	1988 Range Rover VM Diesel

JIM SET UP Overlander Training two years ago, after winning over the Forestry Commission for use of the Cannock Chase.

He is the only operator allowed in the Chase and champions responsible off-road driving.

'I am very strict on the safety of both drivers and the environment,' he says, 'but that doesn't mean the Chase doesn't offer challenging off-roading.'

Indeed it doesn't, as we found out for ourselves. Jim's Range Rover, Bertha, is also something of an oddity. It was first registered to Land Rover as an experimental vehicle and was used as a development testbed for three years.

When it finally left the factory in 1991, it had the same specification as a current model, despite being registered three years earlier.

Hidden Heart

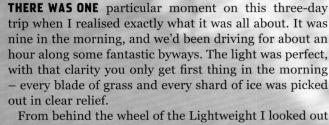

LRO explores the heart of middle England – a rural paradise in Warwickshire where leafy lanes provide a stunning backdrop to an afternoon's off-roading

Words: Dave Phillips
Photographs: Fiona Richardson

THERE WAS ONE particular moment on this three-day trip when I realised exactly what it was all about. It was nine in the morning, and we'd been driving for about an hour along some fantastic byways. The light was perfect, with that clarity you only get first thing in the morning – every blade of grass and every shard of ice was picked out in clear relief.

From behind the wheel of the Lightweight I looked out over a landscape that hadn't changed for centuries. Or if it had, it didn't matter. What counted is that it felt old, and remote. There were no houses, no metalled roads, no pylons or telephone wires, no roadworks or double glazing. Just a soft, green road lined with old oaks to create an elegant avenue, bordered by uncultivated grazing fields, covered in hillocks and rough grass.

And this was all within half an hour of Land Rover's Solihull factory, in the heartland of that congested part of the country known as the Midlands. If I'd climbed one of those oaks, I could have caught a glimpse of some industrial estate in the distance, chimneys belching smoke.

This is one of the great hidden truths about England – that you can venture just a little way from civilisation and suddenly find yourself in another world. Warwickshire proves this. Stuck in the middle of England, it gets dismissed as 'being near Birmingham'. But this neck of the woods is also known as the Heart of England – an altogether nicer term – and driving along that byway, I really felt that I was in the centre of something very English.

Warwickshire is also where the LRO Show is held at the Royal Agricultural Showground near the pretty village of Stoneleigh, which is why we took the LRO Lightweight, Discovery and Defender 90 to this beautiful county to investigate what there is to see and do in the area. We liked what we found.

We weren't setting out to do a greenlaning trip – heavy rain meant the ground was saturated, and we didn't want

133

Above Our Disco and 90 amble along a non-challenging but beautiful byway. Risk of damage is zero!

Left Attack of the hungry sheep! The farmer who feeds them must be a Land Rover owner.

common sight in the rough grazing fields, and there's a wealth of pretty little villages to stop in for lunch.

During many hours of driving we encountered one trail biker, and he was having his lunch. That was it. Granted, it was midweek, but it was still great to be able to get away from the busy roads of the West Midlands and take off into the fields and woods of England. Coming off the end of one of the lanes, we emerged into a small village. Even after just 40 minutes of driving, it felt slightly odd to be surrounded by houses and driving on tarmac, despite the fact that this was more of a hamlet than a village.

Gated roads are also a feature of the area. These are little-used, hard-surfaced roads with no fencing, allowing livestock to roam across the road. The gates are situated at intervals along the roads to keep the animals in specific fields, and you have to watch out for sheep and cows. We almost got held to ransom by a large flock of very determined sheep who had decided we were bringing them food. They blocked the road, and when we

to do any damage. But we did want to see what the county had to offer. We brought along the OS maps and found plenty of greenlanes – proving yet again that you can locate some cracking byway driving without too much effort.

These lanes pass through stunning, classically English countryside, all gently rolling hills and old woodlands. Saxon barrows – the raised mounds of earth covering the graves of long-dead noblemen and warriors – are a

Super Stoneleigh

THE ROYAL SHOWGROUND at Stoneleigh has everything – and that includes a brilliant off-road course. It's a well-constructed route that includes plenty of different terrain, from muddy uphill climbs to gentle slopes, with diversions to allow for people getting stuck, or for drivers who don't want to risk their vehicle through the more treacherous parts. This means that should somebody get stuck or have a mechanical problem, the course can keep running without holding everyone else up.

Taking LRO's 90 and the Discovery round the course shows up the parts different vehicles can and can't reach. The weather had been very wet in the weeks leading up to our visit, and the Disco, running on road tyres, struggled with muddy sections that the 90 breezed through. But, having said that, there's enough elements to the course to allow a vehicle on road-bias tyres to have a good time.

The variation in the ground, from wooded sections to steep hills, makes it an interesting place to put any Land Rover through its paces. One moment you can be descending a steep downhill, and the next be tackling a series of fierce humpback ridges. On one side is the open parkland of the Stoneleigh estate, with herons fishing on the Warwickshire Avon river that runs through it, and on the other is the showground. You start out at the hilly end of the course, working your way through the twisty sections to the water. Out of this you meet an uphill section through trees, and emerge at the top to come down at the furthest edge of the route. There's spectator seating around the course that provides great views of the site.

Essentially it's a non-damaging course. There's nothing that will snap halfshafts, blow diffs or drown a vehicle. Of course, this depends on individual driving style, but you can expect some serious excitement without destroying your vehicle. There's also a milder off-road course, allowing you to drive through the beautiful Stoneleigh estate and take in the surroundings, without having to deal with water obstacles and low-box descents. It's your choice.

Above None of the lanes we drove are particularly hard work – perfect for a morning's light off-roading.

Below Scenes we met on the lanes around Stoneleigh.

finally managed to push through them, they followed us down the track, expecting food. I'd wager that the farmer who feeds them drives a Land Rover.

Creeping over the county border into Northamptonshire, we managed to trace some neglected stretches of Watling Street, the Roman road that runs north from London – or should that be Londinium?

Today, the A5 London–Holyhead trunk road follows this route, but search and you'll find little scraps of the original, where a layer of soil and turf covers the Roman paving beneath. Many Roman roads remain public rights of way and are classified as byways – they're easy to recognise due to their arrow straight course, and their tendency to go over obstacles (such as hills) rather than round them. But, as ever, some are being lost through reclassification by county highways departments, intent upon turning them into bridleways.

Driving a short unclassified country road (UCR) near the village of Crick, we passed beneath a bridge carrying the thundering traffic on the M1 – the contrast was notable. Trouble is, we couldn't get on to Watling Street, which here runs parallel to the motorway, due to a locked gate at the end – presumably to deter joyriders (who had thoughtfully left a burnt-out Fiesta slewn across another gateway on the lane). The old Roman highway looked

137

beautiful in the pale sunlight, carpeted with thick, lush grass. Another one of those unexpected back-in-time moments, just 400 yards from the roaring motorway traffic.

None of the lanes we drove are particularly hard work, they're mostly non-damaging and they're not too long – perfect for a morning's light off-roading. The worst you'll encounter is overhanging trees that could scratch your paintwork.

Back in Warwickshire, we found one very tight and under-used UCR with high hedges and plenty of under-growth waiting to spring out on us. Getting the convoy through was tricky, and involved a fair bit of manoeuvring in reverse to avoid some awkwardly-placed branches, with the roof of the Defender one inch from the over-hanging foliage. Wing mirrors tucked in and windows wound up, I eased the 90 through at a crawling pace.

Water drained from the fields had created deep pools on the lane and, when these were combined with a tight bend, some concentration was required. We were careful and, although the water had soaked the ground, under-neath the going was firm gravel, preventing any damage from the vehicles.

The lane straightens up and carries on for about two miles, sloping slightly downhill. Underfoot, the mud is thick and sucks at the tyres, making it more difficult than it looks. It had that very fertile smell that some mud

possesses, the kind of smell that hangs around for a few days afterwards.

The 90's Yokohamas have a habit of trying to pull the vehicle out of the ruts, which is not what's needed when you really want to stay in them. It tried the same trick crossing a byway that ran through the middle of a ploughed field, consistently attempting to haul itself onto the higher ground. It proves the Yokohama's side cleats do their job very well, but when you want to stay in the ruts, it's hard work battling the wheel.

That lane – a winding strip of green grass bordered by ploughed earth – is another real scenic one. Because

Mud sucks at the tyres through this lane – it's far more difficult than it looks.

Above left   Up to the axle in water on this lane.

Above right   The Discovery copes well on greenlanes but, with road-bias tyres, the going was tough on Stoneleigh's rain-soaked off-road course.

Left top   Canals criss-cross the West Midlands as a reminder of the area's industrial heritage.

Left middle   Warwick Castle is a popular local attraction.

Left bottom   Take a step back in time in quaint villages.

it's open, driving it in the sun is a great experience, and you're not hemmed in by branches and high hedges. We found a disused railway line to play on, complete with embankment to drive up (and down). The railway line continues for a fair way – the track disappeared years ago, but the route is still driveable with no surprises. We had to watch out for dumped rubbish though – steel cord from discarded tyres could have put paid to our trip, and mattress frames proved another real hazard.

Sadly the lane itself didn't go anywhere in particular, turning into a farm track that led back on to the main road. It's at the foot of Borough Hill, the site of a Roman settlement.

The Lightweight provided plenty of fun, in its inimitable back-to-basics way. It's at its best on greenlanes and country roads, where it seems to blend in to the surroundings better than the more modern Land Rover. The simplicity of the design, and the fact it looks standard gives it that classic old Land Rover feel. You can hear every stone that hits the floor, every drop of water that splashes under the tyres – you feel connected with the surface you're driving on. And trundling along at low speeds feels a lot better than vainly trying to keep up with traffic on the M1. If it's possible for a car to feel organic, then the Lightweight certainly does. It was in its element on these lovely lanes.

Completely standard, aside from 7.50×16 Hi-Milers, it went almost everywhere the 90 did, only getting caught in one particularly muddy rut. This was really down to the tyres, so I reversed back up the lane to a turning spot – no drama. It did develop a tendency not to start when it was hot; and the only cure was leaving it for 30

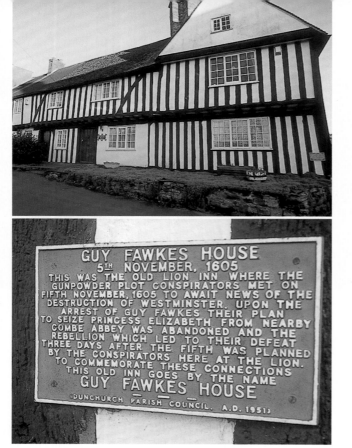

The Old Lion Inn in Dunchurch, where Guy Fawkes conceived the Gunpowder Plot.

High Drama in Shakespeare Country

EVERYONE KNOWS WILLIAM Shakespeare came from Stratford-upon-Avon, about eight miles from Warwick. It's a pretty market town right in the heart of England, and the river runs through the town – the name Stratford means street-ford, and the town has always been one of the main crossing points over the Avon.

Shakespeare's birthplace is in the town centre, and it's been recreated as it would have been, at the time of his birth. There are tour buses that run regularly through Stratford, allowing you to see the historical sights of the town.

The cottage of Anne Hathaway – Shakespeare's lover – is one mile from Stratford in the hamlet of Shottery, and you can walk there along a path that Shakespeare may well have used. There's a pond nearby strewn with lilies, and it's claimed these flowers were the inspiration for the image of Ophelia (in Hamlet) floating down the river, just after she'd killed herself. Shakespeare and Anne Hathaway are buried in Holy Trinity Church in Stratford.

minutes to cool, and then it fired first time. But otherwise it didn't miss a beat, and the next time you read about it, the problem will have been sorted. It sounds like a fuel delivery fault – the Zenith carb can be a law unto itself – but the timing isn't spot-on either. It's running-on even on engine shut off.

The Lightweight may not have the mud tyres and a locking centre diff, but it does have one great advantage over the Defender – you can take the roof off in five minutes. On a day as nice as the one we had, this had to be done. Result: exposure to beautiful, crisp spring weather, surrounded by glorious countryside. Idyllic. Even after the very wet, liquid mud covering the Lightweight had begun to be thrown over the windscreen and into my hair, I kept the roof off. I think I'd be prepared to drive a roofless Land Rover in just about any weather, because it's such an enjoyable experience. This is what Land Rovering is all about.

The 90 is proving to be a very capable machine, providing a stress- free off-road experience. It seems to go just about anywhere it's pointed with ease, despite being fitted with road bias suspension. Over the Stoneleigh off-road course it was fun, safe and competent and always felt capable of taking on more demanding terrain.

There's plenty of history woven into the Warwickshire countryside. In the village of Dunchurch you'll find the old Lion Inn, where the Gunpowder plot conspirators waited for news of Guy Fawkes' attempt to blow up the Palace of Westminster. Both Warwick and Stratford-upon-Avon are steeped in medieval history, from Shakespeare to the magnificence of Warwick Castle. The ruin of Kenilworth Castle – once the finest and largest in England – is a stone's throw from the NAC Showground. And, if you really want to become a pilgrim to the birthplace of your

Land Rover, Lode Lane is easily accessible, although there's not really a lot to see. The factory entrance is quite low key, and the only clue to what goes on behind the gates is a Land Rover

sign, and an expedition-prepared 130 parked up on the verge outside.

Warwickshire is an area worth exploring properly, and to get the best out of it you'll need to leave the obvious routes and get into the heart of England. There's something very satisfying about getting away from the hectic traffic to discover what the countryside is really made of.

In a Land Rover you've got a much better chance of being able to do this, and you'll see some very rural, rather wonderful, unspoilt countryside. In a few days we found some real surprises, without really trying very hard.

You'd be hard-pushed to find a better place than Warwickshire for some relaxing laning and fascinating history.

Psst! Ever heard of Rockingham Forest?
Not a lot of people have, but it's a
greenlaning heaven

Can You Keep a Secret?

Words: Dave Phillips
Photographs: Fiona Spencer

PETE'S PINK AND perspiring, and it's through worry, not toil. Our normally unflappable art director is in a right old flap – and no wonder. His immaculate Series IIA is at the mercy of gravity, poised at a precarious angle on the edge of an all-engulfing rut.

'So much for a spot of gentle greenlaning,' he grimaces, tiptoeing around his pride and joy, fearful that a heavy step might send it tumbling onto its side. He's regretting bringing it now.

We're navigating a tree-canopied greenlane deep in Rockingham Forest. Never heard of it? Well, not many people have, because it's one of England's best-kept little secrets. But here at LRO we know it well, because it's right on our doorstep. In my case, I live right in the middle of what was once one of the biggest forests in the British Isles, stretching across most of Northamptonshire, as well as parts of neighbouring Leicestershire, Rutland and Huntingdonshire.

Like most of the country's native oak woodlands, much of it disappeared from the Middle Ages onwards as our ancestors felled the giant trees to build houses, churches and warships. This area suffered particularly badly, because it sits on ferrous-rich ironstone – and the medieval smelters needed vast quantities of timber to fuel their furnaces.

Yet quite extensive fragments of the old broadleaf forest remain, augmented during the last century by plantations of conifers, in their regimented rows. It covers 200 square miles in all. Between the woods there are the rolling hills and open farmland of the Nene valley, punctuated by picturesque stone villages and, of course, some terrific greenlanes.

We'd started today on the banks of the Nene, meeting at the Haycock Hotel at Wansford-in-England for a coffee and briefing. Behind the name of both pub and village there's a colourful story.

It concerns a village ne'er-do-well named Barnaby who, several hundred years ago, decided to sleep off the effects of an night's hard drinking atop a stack of hay in a meadow beside the river.

Overnight, a flash flood carried off the haycock, along with its unconscious occupant, only to wedge itself against an arch of the village's stone bridge. When Barnaby finally awoke at daybreak, he looked up to see dozens of giggling folk peering down at him from the parapet. 'Where am I?' he groaned, fearing he had been swept downstream and out to sea.

Top left   We're spoilt for choice on where to drive next, so it's time to get out the Ordnance Survey maps and decide which of the many Rockingham Forest byways to explore.

Above   Stuck in a deep, muddy rut, but the rest of the team get together to push, pull and heave Pete Comely's SIIA to safety. It's good to have a 101 Forward Control handy.

Left   Making a splash through a ford at Nassington.

'In Wansford!' laughed the crowd.

'What, Wansford in England?' was his reply.

In days gone by, the Haycock was an important coaching inn, for the old Great North Road ran through the centre of the village. It's rumoured that the infamous highwayman Dick Turpin frequented its dim, smoky bar.

Ghosts of Turpin and his bloody accomplices may still haunt its panelled corridors at dead of night, but right now it's bright and early and we're poring over Ordnance Survey maps. John Pearson and I are swapping notes on our favourite lanes and planning our route for the day. Along the way, we'll be meeting various Land Rovering friends, each sparing an hour or two to join the gang and have some fun.

We head off up the valley, shadowing the river, for our first port of call, near the village of Yarwell. This is a lane

that JP and friends drove just a few days ago, when the going was easy, but there has been a lot of rain in the past few days and it's much muddier and more slippery than usual.

And this is where Pete and his 1969 88-inch come unstuck. To avoid scraping his diff along the ridge between the deep ruts, LRO's art director tries to straddle them, but the Avon Rangemaster tyres haven't got enough grip in the conditions and two wheels slide off into oblivion, leaving the Series IIA tottering sideways at a 45-degree angle.

There's only one answer – call in the cavalry – and on this occasion the horsepower is provided by JP's mate, Neil Marsland, and his 101 Forward Control. The 1976 lump of ex-military might is suffering from poor traction from its inadequade bar grip tyres, but its superior ground clearance allows it to shrug off the deep ruts threatening to engulf the rest of the convoy. With recovery rope attached, Neil's soon pulling Pete's stricken SIIA to safety.

Luckily, not all the lanes we plan to drive are so difficult. The next, a mile or so up the road at Nassington, is in fine fettle. The biggest difficulty here is negotiating the concrete chicane placed at the entrance by the county council to deter travellers, both gypsy and new-age, from setting up illegal camps along its leafy verges. It takes a lot of

Left top Land Rovers are often blamed for deep ruts, but wet weather and farm machinery caused the damage to this lane.

Left middle Dan Breen's Series III is a reliable greenlaner, but it did blow a head gasket when overstressed on the off-road course.

Left bottom 101 Forward Control negotiates a tricky chicane placed by the local council to deter travellers from setting up camp here.

Left top 101 Forward Control, Series III, Series IIA, and a trio of Defenders – all excellent greenlaning machines.

Left bottom It's on this UCR that Pete discovers his 4WD selector has failed – so it's 101 Forward Control to the rescue … again.

What to do in Northamptonshire

NORTHAMPTONSHIRE IS ONE of those Midlands counties that most folk rush through on the way to somewhere else. But they don't know what they're missing. As you enter the county, brown signs erected by the county council say 'Welcome to Northamptonshire, Rose of the Shires' … which means nothing. For centuries, Northamptonshire has been known as the county of spires and squires, which is much more appropriate. Great country houses abound, including Althorpe, home of the Spencer family, where the late Diana, Princess of Wales, was raised, and is now laid to rest.

Towns within the Rockingham Forest include Oundle, famous for its public school and magnificent stone buildings. The Talbot Hotel in the town centre is said to be built from stone and timber salvaged from Fotheringhay Castle. Market day is on Thursdays. The area abounds with cosy, thatched country pubs, most offering real ales and good food, plus traditional Northamptonshire skittles, played on a table. Try the 16th century King's Head on the banks of the River Nene at Wadenhoe for a taste of all three.

The Rockingham Forest area is a popular destination for former American servicemen and their descendents, as the US 8th Airforce operated from many airfields in the area between 1942 and 1945. Although most are now disused, some have stone memorials to those who lost their lives in the Second World War – Polebrook Airfield alone saw the loss of 175 B17 Flying Fortresses.

Rockingham Forest is famous for its wildlife, including the red kite – a magnificent bird of prey which had been extinct in England for 100 years until re-introduced to the area a decade ago. Today they are commonplace – especially at Fineshade Wood, where there is a viewing centre complete with live video links. If you want to watch something more adrenalin-inducing, pay a visit to the Santa Pod Raceway, near Wellingborough, to watch the drag racers, high-speed cars and bikes.

Defender at the gate ... the Norman gatehouse at Rockingham Castle to be exact.

shuffling and shunting to get Neil's 101 through, followed closely by the shining 110-inch Defender twin cab, which has just turned up with Nick Curtis, who works for franchise dealers Marshalls of Peterborough, at the wheel.

This is a lovely lane, thanks no doubt to the underlying limestone that prevents surface damage in the form of deep ruts. We drive through splendid open countryside, under a disused railway bridge and through a sizeable ford, before briefly hitting tarmac and then tackling a longer stretch of very driveable byway.

We're close to Fotheringhay now – a small village that's big on history. A king of England was born here and a queen of Scotland died here, in a once-great castle of which, today, only a great mound and a few fragments of masonry remain. It was in the great hall of this castle that Mary Queen of Scots was executed, on the orders of her cousin, Queen Elizabeth I.

It's worth getting out of the Land Rover here and making the short walk to the top of the mound, from which you'll get a commanding view of the broad, fertile valley below, where the meandering River Nene slithers like a silver snake through the flood meadows. And before you climb down, note the Scotch thistles, which grow with wild abandon on this blood-stained mound, yet nowhere else for miles around. Pretty spooky stuff, eh?

The oldest vehicle in our convoy is Dan Breen's Series III. Dating back to 1971, and bearing chassis number 194,

it's one of the earliest of the Threes. In August 2000 he replaced the original and sluggish 2.25-litre diesel with a 2.5-litre petrol, culled from an early 90. That tad of extra power, and the traction afforded by mud remoulds, makes it ideal for greenlaning.

That's about to be put to the test as we head for a rather sticky UCR (unclassified road) the far side of the market town of Oundle. To reach it, we pass through another fragment of the old Rockingham Forest, known as Bearshanks Wood. Local legend has it that dozens of Scottish prisoners of war were massacred here following the Jacobite Rebellion of the 18th century, and their ghosts are said to haunt it. Today, in broad daylight, it is strangely cold and silent as we hasten past the cottage and barn-cum-studio on the edge of the wood where former punk band The Stranglers recorded some of their most haunting hits of the 1980s. Coincidence? Maybe.

Beyond the wood is the UCR, which is situated on a moderate hill. In dry weather it's an easy passage in either direction, but today the wet and slippery clay surface means we'll be going downhill to avoid spinning wheels and surface damage. It should have been plain sailing, but Pete's SIIA gets stuck again and needs to be towed out. At this stage he discovers that the four-wheel drive selector has jammed and he's been on rear-wheel drive only for most of the morning.

But we all get through unscathed, before tackling our final greenlane of the day, which heads back to the Oundle–Brigstock road. We're treading gently and the driving is easy, yet we still get accosted by a Frontera-driving 'local' who rants and raves at 'outsiders' turning up and damaging 'his' lanes. It turns out that I live closer than he does. He won't talk reason, so to avoid confrontation we break for lunch.

The weather has closed in now and the rain is again sheeting down, so we abandon plans to drive some lanes through the woods at Ashton (venue for the annual World Conker Championships, no less). Instead, we all head off to Rockingham Castle, on the outskirts of the former steel town of Corby, where LRO Adventure Club leader Vince Cobley has created a new off-road course.

It's great fun, but the heavy rain has made the grassland so greasy that even the most gentle slopes are slippery. Dan manages to blow a head gasket on his SIII while trying to power up one incline, while the conditions provide a graphic illustration of the importance of picking the right tyres for off-roading. JP and I are driving near-identical Td5 90s, but his is striding across terrain that's leaving me scrabbling for grip, because his is shod with BFG mud terrains, while I'm on all-terrain rubber. The difference is startling.

The Rockingham course is nothing short of spectacular, with every sort of off-road challenge you could hope for, set in fantastic scenery. This place is going to be a real favourite once it's properly up and running.

The day ends on a happy note, despite Neil damaging a brake hose on his 101, leaving him with only half of the dual-circuit braking system. It's a monster of a truck to pilot home with reduced braking power, but he cheerily sets about the task, as does Dan in the stricken SIII. It's been the sort of day where you find yourself driving along with a broad grin on your face.

But greenlaning and being out in the best of the British countryside gets you like that, doesn't it?

Top   JP tackles a steep rocky slopes on the exciting new off-road course at Rockingham.

Above   Trying to power up the slippery slopes blows the SIII head gasket.

Below   Pete's stricken SIIA gets another helping hand – this time by Vince Cobley in a Defender 110.

The County Set

Northamptonshire, Leicestershire, Rutland ... we're collecting counties as we explore the biscuit-tin-beautiful countryside and villages of the Welland Valley

COUNTY BOUNDARIES CAN be useful, but they're of little use to us today. That's because we're taking our Land Rovers off to explore the byways, tracks and winding country lanes of the exceptionally pretty Welland Valley, which rather unhelpfully ignores local authority borders as it wends its picturesque path through Northamptonshire, Leicestershire and Britain's smallest county, Rutland.

We're looking forward to putting our chosen routes to the test. Also on trial is Land Rover's latest – a 2003 model Defender 110. It has air con, electronic traction control and leather seats, but we're more interested in how it performs in the mud. Editor John Pearson is at the wheel, putting it through its paces.

Leading the way in his well-travelled Td5 Discovery is LRO Adventure Club leader, Vince Cobley, who has been driving these lanes for more than a quarter of a century. Years ago he used to work as a lorry driver, delivering to local farms, so he knows the local agricultural community and, more importantly, which UCRs (unclassified country roads) we're welcome on.

Above Into the valley – Discovery Td5, new Defender 110 and rebuilt Series IIA pick-up were our chosen steeds.

Below Battle stations – The Victorian monument on the left commemorates Naseby; the more recent one (right) trumps it by being in the right place.

Words and Photographs: Dave Phillips

151

To ensure that we remain welcome, we're working on the principle that small is also beautiful when it comes to greenlaning convoys, so we're restricting our team to three vehicles. Bringing up the rear is art editor, Pete Comely, in his pristine Series IIA. He lives a little further down the Welland valley and he's keen to get off the beaten track in this area.

Our adventure starts on the Northamptonshire border, where we take an unclassified country road through to Naseby. Today it's a sleepy settlement of quaint stone cottages, but in 1645 it was the epicentre of a seismic event in British history. The Battle of Naseby saw thousands of troops massacred in these fields as Oliver Cromwell's Roundheads defeated the Royalists in the English Civil War.

To commemorate this defining moment in history, a monument was erected just outside the village in 1823. In the grandiose manner so beloved of the Victorians, they decided that a 60-foot replica of Cleopatra's Needle would fit the bill nicely. And so it did – the only problem being that they managed to erect it a mile from the battlefield.

Above The 2003 Defender – Land Rover has improved the Defender without taking away any of its strengths, a real winner that's a joy to drive on and off-road.

Below Bog standard – The 2003 Defender shows that, straight out of the crate, it's capable of taking on deep wading duties.

Above Vince and John discuss the rules of Pooh Sticks by a ford across the River Welland.

Below Pete enjoys an entirely different game in the SIIA.

This was put right in 1936, when local historians built a more modest monument in what they considered to be the right spot, on a bleak ridge overlooking the killing fields, from where Cromwell himself is said to have led the cavalry charge.

Both monuments still stand, but some Naseby residents would claim that the real marker to history lies buried nine feet below the ground. Local legend has it that Cromwell's dying wish in 1658 was that he should be buried at the scene of his finest hour. His body was duly smuggled out of London by his loyal supporters and, it is said, secretly laid to rest at Naseby.

Besides being a watershed in British history, this hillside is also something of a watershed in geographical terms. From its porous limestone bubbles the sources of Shakespeare's Avon, Oxford's Cherwell and, of course, the River Welland.

It's absolutely pouring with rain right now and you can't help but wonder at how three raindrops, falling just a few feet apart on this ridge, will eventually end up in the Bristol Channel, the Thames estuary and the Wash, respectively.

The rain is making it hard going, so we're careful not to cause damage as we take another greenlane through to Sibbertoft. Here we get a respite from the mud in a sand quarry that's long been a favourite of Vince. It's owned by farmer Jasper Hart, a natural joker who grinned from ear to ear a few years back when he rescued me and a stricken Discovery with his tractor. I'd got it stuck in pack ice while driving across a frozen pool on a very frosty December morning.

But today there's no ice and we all have fun wading through that same pool. The Defender's traction control chatters away nicely to get editor Pearson up an improbably steep, slippery ridge. Unsurprisingly, he seems happy with the way it's performing.

After Sibbertoft we take another UCR, this time splashing through the Welland via a delightful ford. The river here is just a tiny brook, twisting through the countryside like a silver-grey ribbon. It has a big, broad valley for a river so small, but it didn't carve it itself, of course – it's the handiwork of a huge glacier more than 10,000 years ago during the last Ice Age.

The glacier was also responsible for the mixed terrain of this valley. It brought with it deposits of rock, clay, sand and gravel, which it duly mixed up and dropped at will. And we're driving them now. It's a sobering and humbling thought.

But the River Welland isn't the only waterway of significance in this area. Soon we're at the Grand Union Canal. Or, to be more precise, the Leicester arm of the Grand Union. It's amazing to think that excavation began as far back as 1793 to connect the East Midlands to London, via a canal from Leicester's River Soar to connect with the existing London–Birmingham canal at Braunston, Northamptonshire.

The biggest obstacle along the 22-mile route was a big hill at Foxton, which rises to 412 feet above sea level. But this didn't deter the determined engineers, who in 1810 built Foxton Locks – a flight of ten lock chambers which, like a giant staircase, carries long canal boats up the 75-feet incline.

At the time it was built, the canal network was the freight network of Britain. Barges laden with coal from Nottinghamshire and Derbyshire would have queued at these locks, which took 45 minutes to negotiate.

Later in the 19th century, the canals were all but superseded by the new-fangled railways, but small volumes of freight were still carried by barge until 40 years ago. The final death knell of the network was the great freeze of 1963, when barges were iced-in for weeks on end.

Today, the canals are enjoying a new lease of life as a watery playground for pleasure boaters. Pottering along in a canal boat at walking pace makes for a relaxing holiday – a bit like greenlaning, really.

And it's greenlaning that we're doing again now, as we shadow the infant river downstream, witnessing it growing in stature as every mile passes. For

No go – we chose not to drive this overgrown greenlane near Foxton. The hedge had become overgrown and encroached across the track.

much of its length it marks the boundary between Northants and Leicestershire, later dividing Rutland and Northamptonshire.

Finally, much further downstream after it has flowed under the old Great North Road (the modern A1), it becomes the border between Lincolnshire and Cambridgeshire.

The boundary between Rutland and Leicestershire is the Eye Brook, a tributary of the Welland which we cross in its upper reaches close to Uppingham, Rutland's seond-biggest town and home to a famous public school, which was founded more than 400 years ago.

Foxton Locks, near Market Harborough (*left*), were built to help the early wheels of industry turn quicker. Canal traffic these days (*right*) is leisure-orientated.

For a county with so much history, it's curious to reflect today that it didn't even exist a few years back. Rutland was Britain's smallest county until the politicians moved in (what use was a county *that* small … ?).

It was duly annexed in the local government reorganisation of 1974 and disappeared to become part of neighbouring Leicestershire.

At least that's what the bureaucrats of Whitehall thought. The Rutlanders were having none of it and fought bitterly for more than 20 years until it was finally reinstated.

Rutland's capital is a few miles further north of Uppingham. The market town of Oakham was once a Norman stronghold, and a great castle was built here in 1185 during the reign of Henry II. Today only its great hall remains, but it is said to be the finest example of domestic Norman architecture to survive in Britain.

Oakham overlooks mighty Rutland Water, at 3100 acres the biggest lake in southern Britain. It was formed in the early 1970s by flooding the valley of the River Gwash. We're sorely tempted to make a detour to drive its picturesque shores, but the shortening winter's day instead sees us heading for another reservoir, Eyebrook. As its name suggests, this was built by damming the Eye Brook in 1935, to supply the neighbouring steel town of Corby with water.

But within a few years it had a much greater claim to fame, when it was used by the 617 Dambusters Squadron

Above River crossing – shallow reaches of the upper Welland are easily forded in a diesel Defender.

Below Traditional values – a fine example of the hedgelayer's art in Rutland.

from RAF Scampton, Lincolnshire, for practise runs before they attacked the dams of Germany's industrial heartland, the Ruhr, during rhe Second World War.

Today we're treated to an altogether different aerial display when we get a glimpse of a magnificent osprey soaring high above the steely waters, hoping for a trout supper. It may be out of luck, though, for every perching post around the lake is occupied by flocks of hungry cormorants.

There are more greenlanes to explore now as we head off across country to Wakerley Woods. Wildlife abounds in these parts, including red kites, which have been successfully reintroduced in the past decade after an absence of more than a century. Today, these spectacular birds of prey are commonplace.

Sunset is fast approaching on this dismal grey day, so we continue along the valley, stopping to admire a tremendous feat of Victorian engineering at Harringworth, where a railway viaduct three-quarters of a mile long and 85 feet high strides across the valley over 82 brick arches. It was built to carry the former London, Midland and Scottish branch line from Oakham to Kettering and is still in use today for freight traffic.

In the centre of the village lies a cosy pub, the White Swan Inn, which dates back to the 15th century. But there's no time to enjoy a pint in front of a log fire, not

Top left An eyeful of Eyebrook – we also enjoyed a good view of an osprey searching for a fish supper.

Above top This byway boasts commanding views across the Welland valley.

Above bottom Underneath the arches – there are plenty of them at Harringworth, 82 to be precise.

Below Riders appreciate being given a wide berth to pass by on a narrow lane.

Above left   Some off-road fun at Tixover Quarry put the seal on a fine British Break.

Above right   A quiet lane near Duddington.

Below   An impressive relic of a former age – the 11th century water mill at Duddington.

today; we head instead to Duddington, where an even older building stands on the river. The watermill dates back to 1086, earning a mention in the Domesday Book.

The fine, stone-arched bridge on which I'm standing to photograph it dates back to the 14th century.

However, even that is a mere youngster compared to the remains of one that was discovered a few years back by archaeologists. The timber remains they found sunk into the banks of the River Welland at Tixover were put there by the Romans, more than 2,000 years ago.

We're heading for Tixover Quarry now. It's a place we all know well – after all, it's where Vince runs regular LRO Adventure Club driving and training days, and is also a venue used in the tough Ultimate Challenge. Nothing so extreme for us today, though: we settle for an hour or so of off-road fun before the sun finally sets on our adventure.

The 2003 Defender has performed admirably, but so too has the Td5 Discovery and, of course, Pete's ever-green SIIA. Our vehicles and ourselves are cold, wet and muddy ... but can you think of a better way of putting a smile on your face on a miserable winter's day?

Freelanders on Trial

Words: Dave Phillips
Photographs: Fiona Richardson

Four different versions, scores of testing roads, two demanding days, two coastlines ... and one amazing trip

IT'S EARLY MORNING as a quartet of Freelanders assembles in a McDonald's car park. Nothing remarkable about that – there'll be dozens of 'em in and out of here today, disgorging families for their fixes of fast food – but for most of them the day's adventure won't go much further than the supermarket car park up the road.

Our party of Freelanders is different. We're on the edge of the North Sea in Lowestoft, the most easterly point of the British Isles, about to head west to the Welsh coast and the shores of the Irish Sea. And to get there, we're going to avoid motorways, dual carriageways and most main roads. Our plan is to cover most of the journey along country lanes and byways.

And along the way, we'll be assessing the merits of Freelander's four different engines – the original 1.8 petrol and 2.0 diesel, plus the latest V6 petrol and Td4 diesel.

East to west ... which is best? We're about to find out.

I'm at the wheel of a gleaming V6 Station Wagon version which, with just 7,000 miles on the clock, is barely run in. It's an ex-demonstrator, on loan to LRO from franchised dealers, Marshalls of Bedford.

To help me in my coast-to-coast quest, I'm joined by eager volunteers from the Freelander Club. Julian Read, the club chairman, is supposed to be here with his tricked-up ex-Camel Trophy support vehicle, powered by the original 2.0-litre diesel engine, but sod's law dictated that late last night, of all nights, was the one it chose to break down for the first time – on the side of the M11 as Julian and his pal, Steve Smith, headed north from Southampton.

Driver briefing – 'We go out of here, head west, and stop when we get to the Irish Sea … simple'.

Freelanders on top – we were quite happy to leave the dual carriageways to White Van Man.

The problem turned out to be only a knackered fan belt tensioner, but Land Rover Assist was unable to fix it at the side of the motorway, and took the stricken vehicle to the local franchised dealer for urgent attention the next morning.

Well, next morning has dawned and there's still no sign of Julian. A frantic mobile phone call reveals the dealer hasn't got the parts in stock, but is lending him a courtesy car (a standard diesel Freelander) instead. With time marching on, we decide to start our epic journey without him and arrange to meet in an hour's time, in Norfolk.

Julian's elder brother, Alastair, and his fiancée, Sue Faber, are driving Sue's Td4 three-door, barely a month old and with just 1,500 miles on the clock. Fellow Freelander Club member, Alan Gibson, is at the wheel of his 1.8-litre EXi petrol – a 1999 five-door Station Wagon which has covered 39,000 miles.

These are going to be our four Freelanders on trial. But also joining us for the first stage of the journey is yet another club member, Michael Palmer, just coming along for the ride in his 1.8 S three-door. He joins us for the photocall on the sea front, where the normally murky-brown North Sea is, for once, shining blue under the cloudless summer sky. A good omen? We hope so, as we head west.

I lead the convoy, with LRO photographer Fiona in the passenger seat, performing the dual duties of navigating and looking for photo opportunities as we purr along the delightful lanes of the Waveney Valley on the Norfolk–Suffolk border.

Here, not far from the bustling madness and uniform rows of holiday homes of Great Yarmouth, lies a far more agreeable pastoral landscape that time appears to have forgotten. The lush meadows are so deep in grass, the contented cows appear to be wading up to their bellies in a sea of green. They look up only briefly as our convoy cruises past: they're used to seeing Land Rovers in these parts. And proper Land Rovers they are – make no mistake about that. Like all Solihull products, Freelander is a no-compromise creation, where off-road ability is imperative.

The birth of the so-called 'baby' Land Rover was greeted by suspicion in some quarters back in 1997, but

in the subsequent five years it has grown up fast in the reputation stakes.

The old 'hairdresser's car' jokes are stale now; in fact, they went flat very early on: once you've witnessed a Freelander's traction control-assisted performance on slippery surfaces, you're sure to be impressed.

It's no coincidence at all that the Freelander is Europe's biggest-selling 4×4 – now setting out to conquer the world in general and the USA in particular. The new 2.5-litre V6 power plant and auto box were introduced last year with that market in mind.

And there's a distinctly American atmosphere to the countryside now as we head further west, into the sandy heathland between Bury St Edmunds and Thetford. Jet aircraft thunder across the skies, a noisy reminder of the big USAF bases nearby. On the roads around here you're as likely to meet Corporal Ken from Kansas behind the wheel of a Jeep as you are farmer Fred and his trusty Defender.

But we're leaving tarmac behind us now and, for the next twelve miles, we don't meet another vehicle at all.

The timeless stone villages of rural Northamptonshire bask in late afternoon sunshine.

We're exploring a wonderful complex of byways, across open fields and through lonely conifer plantations.

Because of the dry, stony soil they are barely rutted and certainly very Freelander-friendly. The lower ground clearance compared to other Land Rovers isn't a problem here. But the occasional muddy patch, usually lurking under the dense shadow of trees, is enough to make things more interesting for us.

Michael leaves us now, heading back to King's Lynn in Norfolk, where he works as a fireman. But Julian has joined us in his courtesy car. Like his beloved Camel, it is a Station Wagon powered by the original 2.0-litre diesel,

A typical dusty byway on the Norfolk–Suffolk border.

but it turns out to be a very different beast.

Without the Camel's roll cage and off-road body protection it is noticeably lighter, he says – and the suspension feels a lot stiffer.

The scenery changes as we cross into the Fens of Cambridgeshire. The big horizons of this flat, treeless landscape shimmer in the heat-haze of the blistering sunshine. The unmistakable smell of onions hangs in the still air, as farmers harvest their crops while the good weather lasts.

We press on, over the busy A1(M), where the roaring multi-lanes of HGVs, sales reps and holiday traffic are at such odds with our quiet country lanes. It's the same story over the A14, M1 and M40. The landscape is changing yet again, with the rolling hills and honey-stoned villages of Northamptonshire blending into the peaceful tranquillity of rural Bedfordshire and the northern tip of Oxfordshire. By the time we reach Warwickshire and the Avon valley, we're halfway across the country – and we've encountered little traffic. This really is a stress-free antidote to the frenzy of modern road travel.

We've all refuelled by now and, although we haven't got out the calculators to work out the figures, it's clear that all four vehicles are enjoying remarkably good fuel economy. Pottering around the lanes, seldom exceeding 50 mph, is clearly working wonders on the mpg front.

It's been a lovely day so far and we're all grinning from ear to ear as we head west into a glorious sunset, through Worcestershire and the valley of the River Teme.

Then we veer north and shadow Britain's longest river, the mighty Severn, towards Shrewsbury.

Above Playtime – the brothers Read can't resist a spin in the mud.

Left Most of the lanes we drove were well signposted.

Below Vroom with a view – mirror image of a convoy wends through the British countryside.

It's just outside the county town, in the village of Harley, that we're staying overnight before completing the final leg through Wales tomorrow. We're all looking forward to a hearty meal at the *Plume of Feathers*.

In fact, we're just 20 minutes from a well-deserved rest when disaster strikes. Alan, at the rear of the convoy, suffers a sneezing fit just as the rest of us brake at a junction. Losing concentration for a moment is enough to see him piling into the back of the stationary Td4 driven by Alastair and Sue. The impact is severe and, although both vehicles can still be driven, the crumpled bonnet of Alan's Freelander is stuck closed – as is the back door of the Td4. Nobody's smiling now, as we retire to our base for the night.

The next morning, we're all up bright and early for the last stint. Everybody's in brighter spirits today, but Alan reluctantly decides not to drive the last leg, but instead wend his way home to Billericay, Essex, in his damaged vehicle. He says his farewells as the three remaining Freelanders continue westward.

The lanes south of Shrewsbury, across the hills of the Long Mynd, are narrow, banked and topped by steep hedges – reminiscent of Devon, in fact. But they're great fun to explore by Freelander as we continue upstream along the Severn valley to Welshpool and the Welsh border.

Now the scenery becomes more dramatic at every twist and turn in the road, as we head into the mountainous terrain of Snowdonia. There are lots of UCRs (unclassified roads) in this area, begging to be explored, but some

An impressive line-up – Freelanders on parade as the drivers stop for a well-earned snack *en route*.

of them are quite rocky and rutted; not particularly inviting to Freelanders. Rather than risk any further mishaps, we press on towards our destination – the southern shore of Barmouth Bay, north of the spectacular Cadair Idris. It just happens to be due west of yesterday's starting point, Lowestoft.

To get there, we need to negotiate the sleepy, small market town of Dolgellau ... which we do in a matter of minutes, continuing our journey.

'These mountains are all very impressive, but after a while they all look the same to me,' I remark to Fiona. 'This is just like the bit we drove half an hour ago.'

Fiona goes silent for a moment, then says: 'Er, it is. I think we're heading back the way we came ...'

Sure enough, we were. How we managed to get it wrong, in a tiny town with only two choices of direction, will always be a mystery.

But, mistake rectified, we continued the journey without mishap, enjoying spectacular views from the mountain and across the estuary before finally descending down to Fairbourne, where the waters of the Afon Mawddach mingle with the steely-grey waves of a choppy Irish Sea.

The weather has turned now, but we hardly notice the cold drizzle as we celebrate our arrival – 370 miles and nearly two days after we left Suffolk.

Now comes the difficult bit, though: choosing a winner. The ride quality and comfort of all four vehicles was, unsurprisingly, near enough identical to make no difference. The only area where they were at variance with each other was under the bonnet – allowing us to compare the differences between the four engines.

As I'd suspected, fuel consumption figures were mightily impressive. The 24 mpg from the V6 was pretty amazing, after all the tales we've heard of owners returning figures in their teens. But I deliberately didn't use

sports mode on the Steptronic gearbox, which probably helped us achieve the frugal final figure.

In truth, though, it's obvious that the style of motoring was largely responsible for the fine economy we enjoyed on our run. Pottering around the lanes – a task ideally suited to the Freelander – is clearly beneficial to your bank balance. All four Freelanders performed this task admirably, but we all agreed that the winner just had to be the splendid Td4 diesel. Its performance is much zippier than that of the really rather lacklustre early 2.0-litre diesel version – and comparable to the 1.8 petrol. With a return of 38 mpg, it was also the most economical to drive.

With the extra power, we rated the V6 second. Yes, it's thirstier, but it's the one to go for if you're a petrol fan. And, as the 1.8 petrol's mpg return wasn't far off that of the 2.0-litre diesel, we marked them third and fourth, respectively.

But there weren't any real winners and losers in this shoot-out. The one thing that's clear is that all Freelanders are great, fun vehicles that are ideal for exploring our wonderful British countryside.

If you own one, you really should get out more.

Here at last – it's been a gruelling 370 miles, but our arrival on the beautiful Welsh coast makes it all worthwhile.

Topless on the Beach

For so many, this is what owning a Land Rover is all about – wind in the hair, lungfuls of sea air … and feeding chips to the gulls; Suffolk, here we come

Words: Dave Phillips
Photographs: Fiona Richardson

THE SUN'S BEATING down and the wind in our hair is laden with salt. This is motoring with a smile – and we're certainly grinning as we turn on to yet another greenlane. We can see the gulls wheeling overhead, but we can't hear their cries. Nor the crashing of the waves breaking on the shingle.

All Land Rovers are equal – but some are more equal than others when that meteorological myth known as an English summer finally becomes reality. Here and now, on a hot day by the stunning Suffolk coast, it's essential to go topless, we reckon.

We're driving an eclectic mix of Land Rovers: Series III Lightweight, Defender 90 and three-door Freelander. But they've all got something in common – they've got their tops off for the lads. And we're having fun, fun, fun just like any Beach Boy should.

One of the greatest writers of the 20th century used to frequent this coastline. George Orwell, who lived in Southwold, had a healthy distrust of governments – all governments. His most famous book, *Nineteen Eighty-Four*, first published in 1949, was his prophesy of a thoroughly grim future for mankind.

Happily for us, 1984 wasn't as bad as Orwell predicted. In that year, Series III production was petering out … and the LRO Lightweight rolled off the Solihull production line. After years of abuse at the hands of squaddies, it eventually ended up getting more abuse at the hands of LRO staff members.

Today, editor-in-chief John Pearson and myself are sharing the driving duties and getting a tan in the process. It's not a comfortable experience: our backs are soaked with sweat from the hot (and very unpadded) vinyl seats and it's too noisy to hold a conversation in.

But that's not the point: sometimes you have to suffer a little to enjoy a lot. And today the enjoyment of open-top motoring is an adrenalin overdose. We carry on grinning inanely as this heritage coastline unfolds before our split windscreen.

Right top Our convoy tackles a typically gentle Suffolk greenlane.

Right bottom Replacing a Freelander roof isn't quite as easy as it should be.

Below When the boat comes in – there are quite a few working Discoverys in the Southwold area.

I don't know whether George Orwell (known to his friends as Eric Arthur Blair) would have appreciated this sort of frivolity. He was a very serious-minded sort of chap; a socialist with a conscience who, despite ill health, volunteered to fight against fascism in the Spanish Civil War and got shot in the neck for his trouble. For a while, he lived among the poverty-stricken mining communities of Lancashire to gather the material to write his landmark documentary book, *The Road to Wigan Pier*, in 1936.

Orwell is unlikely to have known the joys of driving Land Rovers. He died of tuberculosis, aged 46, in 1950, when the original Land Rover was a mere infant – still considered a farm workhorse rather than a passport to fun. The post-war years were austere times and it's a shame Orwell didn't live to see that the future didn't turn out quite as bad as he'd feared.

Today, we're on the road to Southwold Pier. We're leading the way in the Lightweight, with Dan Stevens following in the LRO Defender 90, recently converted into a full-tilt softie.

Going topless in the Lightweight and 90 was pretty easy: undo a buckle or two here, a strap or three there, and it's off with the canvas in minutes. Not so the Freelander, whose annoying little plastic canopy takes

three men, a step-by-step handbook and endless frustration to put on and off.

The brand-new Td4 is making its off-road debut here, with LRO's publishing director, Ian Richardson, at the wheel. It's not a case of Big Brother coming along to watch over us – he's here to join in the fun, too. And he's clearly doing so, judging by the grin on his face.

Luckily, the lanes we are driving are very Freelander-friendly. The heathland bordering the Suffolk coast is dry and sandy and, despite heavy use, the tracks don't get rutted.

Did I say 'heavy use'? I wasn't joking. Around a corner appears a hard-working Discovery, with a 'Wide Load' sign affixed across the front grille. Actually, it's a very *long* load – it's towing the business end of a combine harvester on a trailer. The harvest is in full swing; and for the local farmers, it's a case of all hands to the pumps. The countryside is at work.

We meet other users at every turn, including ramblers, joggers, cyclists and horse riders – all happily sharing these lovely rights of way. We even come across a family in a well-laden hatchback, the driver gingerly picking his way along the potholed lane, no doubt looking for a nice picnic spot away from the tourist hordes. Well, good for him.

Above Blot on the landscape – nobody has yet invented a picturesque nuclear power station – Sizewell pretty much proves it.

Below The enjoyment of open-top motoring is a real adrenalin overdose.

Above The LRO chaps discuss the merits of a holiday in the Martello Tower. This restored Landmark Trust property will set you back nearly £1000 a week at peak times.

Right Let's get serious – not all Land Rovers play all day.

Guiding us along the byways is local expert, Peter Catton, a member of the 200-strong Suffolk Land Rover Owners' Club. He normally explores them a Discovery, but today he has hitched a ride with us. Nobody wants a roof over their heads in this weather.

Peter bought his 300Tdi Disco brand-new in 1996, when he retired from his job with British Gas. It now has 104,000 miles on the clock – trouble-free apart from a few leaking seals and gaskets over the years. It sounds as good as new; and only a few hairline scratches on the bodywork, sustained from close encounters with bushes and brambles on his greenlaning forays, betray the hard life it's led.

The best lanes lie between Southwold and Aldeburgh, a stretch of coastline unspoilt apart from one very significant blot on the landscape – Sizewell nuclear power station. There is something decidedly Orwellian about the way it broods over the countryside, a landmark for miles around.

Offshore, there are two structures that look like oil rigs but are in fact towers housing the inlet and outlet for the reactor's cooling water. As a result, it is said that sea temperatures here are two degrees higher than anywhere else on this coastline.

More welcome landmarks include the famous House in the Clouds, at Thorpeness – a seven-storey structure with unrivalled views along the coast. Nearby is a white-painted wooden windmill in full working order.

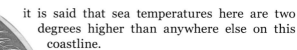

A spot of Orwell reading in Orwell country.

Fancy a beach hut in Southwold? It'll cost you.

Above   Through the undergrowth, in the forest west of Southwold.

Left top   A chat on the beach.

Left bottom   They'll still have a roof over their heads even if global warming does its worst – the House in the Clouds at Thorpeness.

The Martello Tower south of Aldeburgh was built in the 19th century as a precaution against an invasion by the French under Napoleon and it still stands today, which is hardly surprising considering the walls, consisting of more than a million bricks, are reputed to be all of twelve feet thick.

But nothing can be considered *really* permanent in these parts. Winter storms erode the fragile coastline and whole communities are at risk of disappearing – just as one town already has. Dunwich was already a major settlement by the time William the Conqueror invaded England in 1066. By the 14th century it was one of the biggest fishing ports in England and a thriving market town with nine churches.

The soft clay cliffs upon which most of the town stood gradually eroded away over the centuries, leaving Dunwich today as nothing more than a tiny hamlet.

Those same destructive storms also uncover a semi-precious treasure – nuggets of amber that are washed up on the shoreline and collected eagerly by beachcombers, who find a ready market in the local jewellery shops. Amber is the fossilised resin of pine trees that grew tens

169

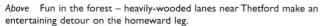

Above Fun in the forest – heavily-wooded lanes near Thetford make an entertaining detour on the homeward leg.

Right A vote of confidence for the off-road course at Bures, used for LRO Adventure Club driving days – a big thumbs-up from our willing testers.

of thousands of years ago before sea levels rose and the North Sea flooded in. Today, Southwold is famous for its amber trinkets.

It's also famous for Adnams real ales, colourful wooden beach huts and, of course, *that* pier. But before we get down to exploring the town, we can't resist taking the rough track south to the mouth of the River Blyth and the local fishing fleet.

In among the shantytown of creosoted rough huts is a tiny fish and chip shop, where fresh-caught cod and plaice are cooked to order. It's probably the slowest service in the world – we pay our money and wait a full 45 minutes – but it's well worth it, we reckon, as we scoff them hot from the paper wrappers with lashings of salt and vinegar. They've never tasted better.

As the summer sun sets over the saltings, and the tourists return to their guest houses, we venture into the near-deserted town to explore.

We park up by the beach huts – which, believe it or not, can fetch as much as £60,000 – and set off on foot for the wooden pier, which has been restored to its former glory under private ownership.

Built in 1899, it was damaged by storms in 1934 and a stray sea mine during the Second World War. Storms in 1955 and 1978 reduced it to just 100 feet long ... hardly reaching the water, in fact.

Chris and Helen Iredale purchased the sorry, derelict structure in 1987 and set to work, replacing the rotten wooden pilings and rebuilding the all-timber structure so that it again stretched 623 feet into the waves. It reopened in February 2002 – an event marked by a visit from Britain's only sea-going paddle steamer, the PS *Waverley*, which normally plies its trade on the Clyde.

It's been a long, hot day, which we finish in style with a couple of pints of Adnams' finest, anticipating what the second day of our break will bring.

What it does bring is a long drive south to the Essex border, to sample the thrills of one of Britain's most famous off-road venues. At 59 acres, Bures is one of the biggest sites used by the LRO Adventure Club. This former quarry, abandoned more than 20 years ago, has been gradually reclaimed by mother nature and now boasts dense woodlands as well as mud, sand, deep water ... in fact, every sort of challenging terrain you would ever want to throw a Land Rover at.

It's great fun for all to drive and Freelander driver Ian is particularly pleased that the site organiser, Peter Graves, has created plenty of non-damaging but exciting tracks

where drivers of all Land Rovers can enjoy risk-free off-roading. What a brilliant site – no wonder it is so popular when the LRO Adventure Club holds its driving days on the third Sunday of every month. Well recommended.

After an action-packed morning, we leave Bures to head north through the delightful Suffolk countryside, driving through towns and villages where time seems to have stood still. Distinctive, pink-painted, half-timbered cottages predominate in a rolling, pastoral landscape that was immortalised by the great British artist, John Constable.

We end our Suffolk trip just south of the Norfolk border, between Thetford and Bury St Edmunds, where we revisit a maze of brilliant greenlanes that photographer Fiona Richardson and I had discovered just a couple of weeks earlier on our East–West Freelander marathon.

A fortnight ago, we barely had time to scratch the surface of the potential of these byways; and today we again run out of time well before we run out of lanes. They're all sandy, virtually unrutted and very Freelander-friendly.

With the tops still down, we head for home – very dusty, a bit sunburnt, but happy as, er, sandboys. The road to and from Southwold Pier has been a very pleasurable one.

The road to Southwold Pier ends here. The inset picture shows how it looked in 1899.

171

Big Country

Cumbria has some of the greatest scenery this side of the Scottish border;
LRO goes greenlaning in England's finest (and biggest) wide open spaces

Words: Dan Stevens
Photographs: Bob Atkins

YOU MIGHT HAVE seen those Victorian paintings of the Lake District, all brooding mountains, dangerous skies and stormy waters. It all looks so *Lord of the Rings* that it's tempting to think there's a fair bit of artistic license at work and that, in real life, it couldn't possibly live up to that.

Well, it *does*. This scenery delivers, and you can't get away from it. The mountains are always there, towering over everything else, reducing the efforts of humans (roads, cars, houses) to meaningless specks. Even in the overcrowded, claustrophobic tourist season, the size and majesty of the geology means that, for most people, the Lakes *are* Cumbria. It's a big place, though, so let's see if we can find some splendid isolation.

We've managed to miss the chaos that engulfs the Lakes in high season, by paying a crafty visit after most of the trippers have packed up and gone home. It's early autumn, just before the trees really start shedding their leaves, but the first hint of browns and burnt oranges is beginning to spread across the landscape.

The sky, however, insists on staying resolutely grey and as we sit in our B&B in Hawkshead waiting for our guide to pitch up, we're feeling just a little subdued by the total lack of *any* weather. The sky is all the same colour and tone ... it's perfectly calm and the temperature can best be described as run-of-the-mill.

Still, we have a huge amount of countryside to get out into and explore. A vast amount of Cumbria is the Lake District National Park and unlike, say, Dartmoor, there are enough vehicular rights of way to keep the most demanding greenlaner occupied for a weekend. And because you're covering a fair amount of road miles between different areas, there are actually more than enough routes.

Our guide is Steve Beck, owner of one of the limited edition Tomb Raider Defenders, and a real greenlaning enthusiast. Steve's been scouting the area for possible LRO Adventure Club visits, and he's already successfully arranged and guided one trip.

We're keeping our convoy down to two vehicles – Steve's 90 and my borrowed 90 Station Wagon, which is standard apart from a set of General Super All Grip tyres to increase the ground clearance and give it more of a chance when I have to follow where the Tomb Raider's BF Goodrich Mud Terrains have been.

The pressures of tourism on the area mean that minimal impact is a vital part of *any* outing to Cumbria, whether you're in a Land Rover or on foot – and keeping greenlaning trips down to as few vehicles as possible is good practice.

We'll be reduced to just one vehicle for some of these tracks, because I'm under strict orders not to damage the pristine Montpelier Red paintwork of the Defender, and Steve says a couple of the tracks are rather overgrown.

He doesn't seem at all bothered by the prospect of scratching the metallic Bonatti Grey on his 90, though. It may be desirable, under a year old and his principal mode of transport, but he's nevertheless determined to use it properly. Good man.

Our first track of the trip isn't of the paintwork-threatening variety, so the 300Tdi follows the Tomb Raider through a wood and over rocky tracks, with the Furness Fells ringing the natural arena. This byway is part of the Cumbria Way and, like many trails in the area, it's made up of rocks and boulders, with washouts on the bends.

You've got to concentrate on the ground, because you need to steer round the bigger boulders – but it's hard when the backdrop is so beautiful. The Fells aren't huge mountains, but perhaps that's why they're so lovely – the scale isn't quite so daunting – and the colours are phenomenal. Somehow, it doesn't feel like England in autumn, more like Canada in summer.

If and when you follow in our tyre tracks, kill the engine, get out and spend a minute taking in the silence and the serenity of the mountains.

We ditch the 300Tdi by the road and head off for Grizedale Forest, sandwiched between Coniston Water and Windermere. There's a maze of tracks criss-crossing the plantation, all unclassified roads (UCRs). Incredibly, they're all signed with little pictures of Land Rovers and trail bikes.

Working closely with the Land Access and Recreation Association, the Lake District National Park Authority (LDNPA) has come up with a scheme that grades routes according to their sustainability and suitability. These neat little signs indicate routes you can drive, and everything else is graded accordingly. It all sounds like a marvellous idea; and when you're actually driving the tracks it adds a feeling of increased legitimacy to your presence.

Only problem is, it doesn't seem to have been much of a success, with user groups and the LDNPA falling out

Excellent, clear signs make it very easy to understand where you can drive – shame the access scheme never worked out.

over the gritty details. That's a shame because, for once, it seemed like everybody might just be able to get on with each other.

The forest is fairly empty today, and we have the stony tracks to ourselves as we wend our way through conifer plantations and more traditional English woodlands. We're diverted off the path we want to take by a 'road closed' sign, which says there's forestry work taking place further down and, when I ring the number on the sign to enquire, the helpful lady on the end confirms this.

I've become so used to finding out-of-date 'road closed' signs on greenlanes that I've given up taking any real notice of them, but this one checks out; and when we get round to the other end, sure enough – there's a mighty forestry tractor loading up enormous tree trunks.

Steve is adamant that I drive along the next track, because there's an interesting rock step at the beginning that normally requires a couple of goes to get up – which is all very well, but first of all we have to get round the fallen tree.

It's turning into a bit of an adventure, this. The tree is more felled than fallen, cut down and carelessly left lying straight across the track. By local standards it's not a very big tree, and if it was lying flat across the ground we could easily drive over it, but it's bridging the track. It needs moving. And we've got a winch.

Sadly, that turns out not to be the best way of shifting fallen trees. The tree is wedged between two others and, when we try to drag it round, it just jams between them.

Dragging it out backwards is no use because there's nothing to wrap a strop around, and reducing it to kindling is just not an option. The Forestry Commission

'If only I'd paid more attention at Scouts' – Dan desperately tries to remember how to tie a double-shank half-hitch.

174

owns the tree, and it's not ours to chop up.

So we tackle it from the other direction, encountering a school trip complete with children who have difficulty staying on either side of the track, scattering like nervous antelope when I (slowly) round the corner in the Td5. It's steep and rocky, and I back off the throttle to avoid sending any stones spinning out from under the tyres.

The rock steps are really more of a deep washout and, as is always the way with these things, when you walk down them beforehand they don't seem to be too severe.

Drive down them, though (in the full knowledge that you have to go back up afterwards), and it suddenly becomes a lot trickier.

The Land Rover lurches down the first drop, brakes creaking and groaning as I ease it down on the pedals. Forget all that feet-off, let-the-engine-do-the-work training; for these precipices you want the vehicle to be hardly moving at all, holding it on the brakes and slowly – *very* slowly – trickling it down the rocks.

It's exhilarating stuff, and we haven't left so much as a rock out of place to show we've been there.

There's that unnerving, suspended moment when a tyre leaves the ground and the rear of the Land Rover rocks in space, followed by the relative security when it thumps back down on the solid rock.

Going down is straightforward, but coming up is harder – and I manage to bring the Land Rover to a total halt by getting it cross-axled and jamming the sill bar against the rock.

It's happy to go backwards, though, so I try again and this time pick a better line that doesn't involve stuffing the driver's side into the rocks.

This strategy works and, with tyres scrabbling for purchase (none of yer fancy traction control here, thank you very much), the Td5 hauls itself to the top. It's exhilarating stuff, and we haven't left so much as a rock out of place to show we've been there.

On the way back down we pass a couple of genteel ladies of a certain age, who are so friendly and chatty I have to keep checking with myself to confirm that I've never actually met them before.

'We saw you go up the track ...' says the taller, well-spoken one, '... and we thought we should hitch a lift from

'Ooh, young man!' Cheerful ladies come over all enthusiastic about the Tomb Raider.

175

you,' giggles the shorter one with a stick. The prospect of being trapped in a short-wheelbase Land Rover with three sweaty blokes would fill me with a certain kind of fear, but this game pair seem to think it would be a right old laugh.

A late lunch in Hawkshead sees us encountering the traditional English virtue of closing the kitchens at 2.30, even when there are coachloads of tourists clogging up the village centre. Next time, we'll remember to pack a picnic and please ourselves.

Just to demonstrate the variety of lanes in Cumbria, the next one is very different. Steve calls it Leafy Lane because it has lots of trees (he's got a right way with words, has our Steve). You can see what he means: hazel and silver birch form a mile-long arch down its length. This could quickly get out of hand and, if it hadn't been for the LRO Adventure Club advance party cutting back the invasive undergrowth, you'd have difficulty walking down here, never mind easing a Land Rover past it.

As it is, it's just accommodating enough for Steve's Defender, although the roofrack catches on a few branches, sending clanging noises through the whole vehicle that sound like a submarine's hull breaking up.

There's no spectacular Lakeland sunset that evening, thanks to the aforementioned static weather that makes this morning look like this evening, so we settle into a bar in Keswick instead of searching for photo opportunities. Cheers ...

Next morning brings the same skies, but the slight haze in the air makes the mountains look far more spectacu-

lar than we've seen thus far. The further away they are, the lighter they become, making a beautiful contrast between the dark greys in the foreground and the pale blues away in the distance.

You certainly notice it driving down the old coach road that meanders between Matterdale and Threkeld Commons, with the mighty Skiddaw – one of only four mountains in England that manage to make it above 3,000 feet – dominating everything.

Below us is the A66 between Keswick and Penrith, traffic rushing from point A to point B, but up here it's calm and quiet. It's pretty easy going, and you hardly

If it hadn't been for the LRO Adventure Club advance party cutting back the undergrowth, you'd have difficulty walking down here.

need four-wheel drive, but low range and ground clearance are useful to avoid crashing over the rocks.

It's just as well the track is here, because on either side is fearsome-looking bog. Steve says one part of the track had to be closed because the bog encroached on to it, making it impassable for anybody.

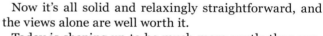

When the going is as easy as this, there's more time to admire the scenery – which is a bit of all right, wouldn't you say?

Now it's all solid and relaxingly straightforward, and the views alone are well worth it.

Today is shaping up to be much more gentle than yesterday, and we take in a couple of UCRs that still have a layer of broken, grass-infested tarmac over the top. The bonus point here comes when we descend from Mosser Fell and drive parallel to Lowes Water – one of the smaller lakes, but still big enough to give that unique contrast between glassy water and craggy mountain.

As we make for the coast, Sellafield rises from between the mountains like something out of *Star Wars*. It's intrusive, but somehow – in the fuzzy, vague light – it seems to fit in with its surroundings, another vast structure in this big landscape. The tall cooling towers and the sci-fi chimneys look almost mythical. Some of the effect is lost when you get close up and it very much becomes the great, big nuclear reprocessing plant that it is.

Leaving the glow-in-the-dark coast behind us, we head inland for Bootle Fell to sample even more of the wind-blown high country that Cumbria does so well.

This is a UCR that climbs from the village of Bootle, and when you get to the top you can see the Irish Sea behind you. On such a grey day the sea and the sky blend into one steely-blue haze. It's getting colder as well and, for the first time since last winter, I can see my breath as it condenses on the air.

Cumbria is a big county and covering distance takes time, but take a weekend out and go try it. It's best to avoid the crowds of high season, giving you some space to enjoy this very special place.

Manx for

Everything

For the Land Rover owner seeking greenlane excitement, the Isle of Man has it all: high peaks, hidden tracks, barren moorland and a unique charm that left Dan Stevens captivated

Words: Dan Stevens
Photographs: Peter Gathercole

IT'S A TINY place, the Isle of Man. So small, in fact, that the whole thing manages to fit on to one Ordnance Survey map. Stand on top of one of the highest hills in the middle of the island and you have a near 360-degree panoramic vision, the Irish Sea surrounding you.

Sitting out there between Great Britain and Ireland, with its hybrid Gaelic/English culture, the Isle of Man would be a splendid anomaly if it hadn't prospered, and always remained fiercely independent of the UK. Nowhere on the island is more than an hour's drive away, and you'll see the same car twice on the same day, at opposite ends of the island. The trains are steam and electric, and they've been running the same trams for 100 years.

179

It looks like the geological offspring of a liaison between Cumbria and Ireland, with fells rising out of moorland that gives way to farmland, which in turn slips into the sea.

There's nothing unusual in that – the British Isles are full of places with similar geographical make-up. The really astonishing thing about the Isle of Man, though, is that you can venture from sea level to a height of 2,000 feet in about 20 minutes, from anywhere on the island.

So you can imagine the possibilities for a greenlane excursion. With this kind of terrain all crammed into such a small place, we'll be able to cover a lot of different ground without really having to go too far.

We've hooked up with Discovery driver and secretary of the Isle of Man Four-Wheel-Drive Club, Richard Crane, who is going to guide us around the area. Although he's not Manx-born, he's pretty much Manx-bred, having moved here with his parents when he was twelve. He's lived on the island ever since, and discovered off-roading through a succession of beaten-up Suzuki SJs.

To make up our contingent we've got David Llewellyn in his 90 turbo-diesel, and I'm enjoying the relative luxury of editor John Pearson's 2001 Td5 Defender.

By some incredible piece of luck, the atrocious weather that's afflicting most of the rest of the British Isles (never describe the Isle of Man as being part of the UK, because it isn't) is just missing the Irish Sea.

Leaving Douglas to track down our first greenlanes, I can see squalls blowing out towards the Lancashire coast and curtains of grey drizzle hanging above the sea. But on the island it's dry, calm and still.

Our first track is typical of what you can expect to find on the island. It's rocky, up the side of a hill (the attractively named Honeyhill) and with spectacular views. Stunning views are something you get used to quite quickly on the island, because just about everywhere you go you can see either the sea or mountains, both of which are equally fantastic.

Like many tracks on the island, Honeyhill suffers a drainage problem. There's a distinct lack of the angled hillside channels that are designed to divert water away from the track and into a field.

Erosion and washouts are big problems here; what was once an easy-going surface is now littered with potholes. That's not going to stop my Defender, Richard's Discovery and David's 90, but it's the kind of damage that can only get worse if some maintenance isn't sorted out soon.

Honeyhill ends up on one of the TT course's famous corners – Creg-ny-Baa. There's a long straight coming down from the mountains, and the Creg is a tight (well, it is if you're doing 180 mph) corner leading into another straight.

A bunch of diesel Land Rovers isn't ideally suited for tackling the world's most famous motor cycle road race course, even if there is a total absence of speed limits outside built-up areas, so we restrain ourselves and head south.

You can split the island in two halves, north and south, along the valley that runs from Douglas in the east, to Peel on the west coast.

It's strange that such a small place should have a north–south divide, but there it is, on the signposts that direct you to *The North* or *The South*. It's really more

Stormy, brooding skies and lonely rugged terrain lend an air of drama to the Manx landscape.

of a geographical divide than a cultural one, even if the south has the airport, the ferry terminals and most of the towns.

The island's rights of way set-up is different to the UK's. On an OS map you'll see byways, but they're not signed as such. Many of these are classified as Greenway Roads, and you'll need a permit to drive them.

This means applying to the Department of Forestry and Fisheries (DAFF), which will give them only to responsible groups. The Isle of Man Four-Wheel-Drive Club is considered a responsible group so, thanks to Richard, we've got a permit to drive the Greenway Roads.

It's a system that seems to work fairly well, and DAFF has a warden patrolling the area to enforce it. Many of these routes run through sensitive areas, so even a small amount of bad driving can easily destroy the fragile moorland.

Inevitably, some people ignore the restrictions, which ends up giving all off-roaders a bad name.

'The idea is to keep the impact of vehicles down to a minimum,' says Richard, 'but a minority of people, mostly motor cyclists, drive the tracks regardless.'

We turn off the twisty Port St Mary to Peel road, and double back on ourselves down the grassy, damp track.

This is open moorland, with thick bracken on either side of the Land Rovers and peaty, black soil under the tyres.

The ground's wet, so I'm trundling along in low third, keeping the speed constant and avoiding any really wet areas. I'm not so concerned about getting stuck; rather I'm trying to avoid chewing up the soft ground. It's one of those tracks that doesn't look too challenging, but if I veer off course and make a mess of it, it'll be hard to get out. It's worth the risk, though, because you're treated to a superb view of the Calf of Man, a small, uninhabited island off the southern tip.

There has been little conflict between rights of way users on the island, and Richard says there are very few problems with off-roaders clashing with everyone else.

'The club has set up a working committee for all users – from walkers to horse riders – to get better signs for the lanes, and it's working. We all tend to get along. We've never encountered conflict in the past, though some have started to voice their concerns.'

Luckily, the club has an excellent and constructive relationship with the authorities and all the team members are very proactive. 'Very few people go off-roading without the club, so we are seen as a responsible force.'

By the time we've had lunch and driven north to find the byway at Doarlish-Cashen, it's starting to get dark. It gives the island a brooding, wild feel, but it's not much use for our photographer. The gloomy sky makes driving the rutted, boggy track difficult and it's difficult to spot the big holes full of water.

Four-wheel drives or tractors don't cause the ruts – they're from motor bikes. Compared to a trail bike, a Defender with aired-down tyres causes little damage, because it tends to float over the ground rather than dig down to keep moving. These multiple, narrow ruts are everywhere on the island, often more than a foot deep: you really have to concentrate on negotiating your Land Rover through so that it doesn't slip into one.

As the autumn sun slips further below the cloud line, we make our way across the island to Douglas, via some easy-driving lanes. Quite a lot of these are covered in broken tar. Richard says these were regularly used roads at one time. Lack of use and neglect has meant that they're now damaged and overgrown and, although the roads have retained their status as highways, they're now only suitable for four-wheel drives. Great news for us, then.

Tarmac gives way to rocks when we reach Nab. Here, we're greeted by a byway that descends into woodland, bordered by a stone wall that meanders precariously down the side of the hill. Gnarled, wind-blown trees arch over the track, creating a natural canopy through which we can see stars in the night sky. We're all eager for a pint of Bushy's, the local brew, but suddenly Richard starts swerving all over the road. He stops, and winds down the window.

'I've got a stone trapped in the brake disc,' he says. 'Should be able to shake it out.' He belts off up the road, and then stops suddenly, the brakes emitting a horrendous

scraping noise. It's not coming out, so we have to remove the wheel and borrow a helpful dog-walker's torch to find the stone and extract it. It's typical of Land Rovers – there always seems to be one last job to do before they'll let you have a beer.

Next morning we start on the TT course, driving the numerous tracks that weave in and out of the tarmac roads as we make our way north.

Heading towards the village of Laxey, we turn off the main road at Windy Corner. This is another track that starts out as broken tar, and then changes to gravel followed by rocks, which eventually turn into washouts. From up here, you can see the way the landscape changes really quickly – from moorland to heath, and then to farmland before reaching the coast – all in about 20 minutes. This is one of the most striking things about the island, journeying from beach to mountainside within minutes.

Making our way down the track, we stop to open (and close) a gate, as two trail bikes appear round the corner. They're moving fast, faster than you ever could in a four-wheel drive, but they slow right down when they see three Land Rovers in the way. The riders, each with a brief nod of the head in a gesture of thanks for doing the gate, scoot past our vehicles and shoot off up the track.

'They go really fast,' says Richard, 'so quickly that we once had a bike jammed underneath the front of a Land Rover. The rider couldn't stop in time, bailed out and his bike skidded under the front of the 90.'

The small village of Laxey is home to the world's largest water wheel. It's a massive testament to Victorian ingenuity

Have spade, will cut drainage channels.

Abandoned farm buildings provide an austere backdrop.

A stone-in-brakes incident involves an innocent bystander and her dog.

and engineering, built to pump water out of the lead mines below. David's involved in its upkeep, and this winter's task is repainting the wheel's buckets – all 400 of them – by hand. I think I'll stick to a spot of gentle off-roading.

We plunge into the heart of the island, on a track that heads straight for Snaefell, the island's highest peak. The terrain becomes more barren the higher you climb, until you eventually leave the tree line behind and succumb to hilly moorland.

Up here there are no houses and few animals, but I do spot a pair of desolate chimneys in the distance. 'Until recently an old woman had lived alone there all her life, though it's empty now,' says Richard. This is a remote spot, there's not a proper road and the old house doesn't have an electricity or water supply. The derelict pit head buildings for the long-defunct lead mines just add to the mystery of this area.

We have to leave the track behind, though, and retrace our tyre tracks. According to Richard and David, the driving will get tougher and, although we've got a farm jack and tow ropes, the risk of getting all three vehicles bogged is just too high. Besides, Richard has something rather special lined up for the afternoon – a beach drive.

This is not an easy task, here or anywhere else. First, you have to find a stretch of beach that you're allowed to drive on (in this case, the long strip of sand from Kirk Michael to Point of Ayre), and then you must get permission from the Department of Transport.

Permission granted, you then have to tell the police and local authorities, and let the DoT see your insurance. It's one-off permission as well, and if you want to return you must re-apply. Not easy, but it does mean that the beach isn't invaded by vehicles, and it also means the authorities can keep an eye on who's doing what.

And if all this sounds a bit too 1984 for you, remember there's no right of way on this beach. They let you drive

there because they're nice people. So we motor up the flat, wide foreshore, keeping in the lead vehicle's tyre tracks.

Driving on wet sand is easy enough, provided you don't stop on a really soft bit. You can almost let the vehicle steer itself, allowing the front tyres to sit in the tracks created by the Land Rover in front. It's a bit like driving a speedboat, really.

Mind you, the boat halfway up the beach we're on didn't have such an easy time. On her maiden voyage in the early 1930s, the trawler *Passage* ran aground and has sat on the beach ever since. There's not much left now, just a collection of rotting iron spars and the shell of the boiler sticking out of the shifting sand, like a partially excavated dinosaur skeleton.

We don't get stuck. Richard has been here before, and knows where to go, so we make it off the beach without having to call the coastguard. The few walkers on the beach don't really seem to care about the three Land Rovers barrelling across the sands towards them.

With the clouds beginning to clear from the sky and some prospect of a sunset in order, we head for a mountain. Once again, I'm struck by how quickly you can go from beach driving to scaling the side of a steep valley, without really noticing how much the surroundings have changed until you're there.

Our last track, another Greenway Road, takes us up the side of Slieau Curn, up a steep climb through enclosing bracken, until we reach the top, where the ground opens out and there's a fantastic view back across the Northern Plains and out to sea.

Cumbria, the Mull of Galloway, and Ireland's west coast are all hazily visible in the distance, and below us the sunlight is sparkling off the little town of Kirk Michael. You can see most of the island from up here.

It's a small place, but sometimes that seems a very good thing.

Wild Rovers

Ireland's varied terrain and wet climate provides off-road challenges galore. The Land Rover Club of Ireland takes Dave Phillips on a guided tour

Words: Dave Phillips
Photographs: Fiona Spencer

THEY CALL IT the Emerald Isle and, every night in dim, smoky bars, locals sing boozily about its 40 shades of green. Ireland's green enough all right – and so it should be, because it's also very wet.

Greenness is no consolation to rain-sodden LRO photographer Fiona, whose drowned camera has just packed up in disgust. Luckily she has a spare to carry on shooting – and just as well, because the lads from the Land Rover Club of Ireland are loving every mud-spattered moment of this deluge. It's great craic, as they say in these parts.

We're driving a maze of forest tracks high up in the Slieve Bloom mountains which, coincidentally, happen to be the coldest place in Ireland in winter, as well as the wettest in summer. Today the seasons must have got muddled, because we've got both at once. Even better, we smile, from within the steamed-up cabins of our Land Rovers.

The mountains here are carpeted in thousands of acres of peat bog, which normally acts as a vast sponge, soaking up the prodigious precipitation. But today even that's overloaded and the excess water is pouring out of the peat and running downhill, turning the tracks into rivers, and creating new wash-outs by the minute.

It all makes the driving more challenging, particularly for me, as I'm driving a Freelander on standard road tyres. Even with traction control on their

side, they're struggling for grip, and the Freelander's lurching around like the Guinness-fuelled regulars who poured out of the bar at closing time last night.

It's a lot easier for Mervyn, Ivor, Trevor, Gary, Patrick and Brendan, whose strictly-utility Solihull hardware copes easily with the deep ruts. Not so for the Freelander, whose inferior ground clearance causes problems every time that tarmac rubber slips and sends me into the ruts. As always, it's the low-slung rear exhaust box that keeps fouling terra firma, and unhooking itself from its mountings. It's easy enough to crawl under and ease the rubbers back into place, but not so pleasant when you have to lie in several inches of very cold water to do it. Ah, how we off-roaders suffer for our craft.

Left top   Our convoy inches its way along the flooded forest tracks.

Left bottom   Only mad dogs and off-roaders would be grinning inanely in weather like this.

A cosy Irish pub looks inviting in the driving rain and howling winds, but we're checking the map for an off-road foray.

This range of mountains, in Co Laois and just an hour's drive from Dublin, boasts no less than 24 forests among its peaks (the highest of them is 514 metres above sea level). We're driving the best of them – Cardtown Forest. It's the best because it's the only one dedicated to off-road driving. And what driving options it offers – over ten miles of designated tracks set in 450 acres, and including virtually every sort of natural obstacle you could expect. There aren't any sand dunes –

Ireland's a tad too wet for desert – but rocks, mud, deep water and peat bog abound, along with wheel-swallowing ruts and steep ascents and descents.

Besides the designated tracks, which are non-damaging to all Land Rovers, including my three-door Freelander, there are also countless miles of rough tracks, bulldozed out by forestry machinery and a much tougher proposition. 'Some of them are hell – there's a mile of track here that would take you two days to winch through,' smiles Mervyn Colton, with the manic eyes of the sort of man who's eager to try. The Milemarker hydraulic winch on the front bumper of his much-abused 200Tdi 90 suggests he probably already has.

Despite the fact that greenlanes as we know them in the UK are virtually non-existent, and off-roading can be carried out only on designated sites, there's a thriving Land Rover scene in Ireland. And that's a bit of a surprise, considering everything conspires against ownership.

For starters, there's the dreaded Irish VRT (vehicle registration tax), otherwise known as DDR (diabolical

Off-road in Eire

OFF-ROADING IN IRELAND is carried out on private property, so you'll need the landowners' permission before you venture into the rough stuff. In practice, this means it's best to drive one of the ever-growing number of off-road sites, springing up all over the country.

We visited Cardtown Forest, where the off-roading activities are run by Wheelbase Ltd. The company was set up two years ago by off-road veteran, Vincent Whelan, himself the driver of a well-preserved early Discovery – a 1991 two-door Tdi.

Vincent drove Land Rovers all over the world during his 40 years' service in the Irish Army, ending up as acting director of the Army Transport Corps, where he was responsible for ordering military vehicles – including hundreds of Land Rovers.

Much of Vincent's time is spent providing off-road training for the emergency services and government agencies, but his site also offers brilliant recreational driving through stunning scenery. Vincent tells us that on a clear day, high up in the mountains above the tree line, you can see five counties. Today, with visibility often down to a few yards, we have to take his word for it.

For further details, contact Wheelbase Ltd at Kildare Road, Mountsterevin, Co Kildare, Eire. Tel 00 353 45 525488 or 00 353 87 273 5985.

The friendly members of the Land Rover Club of Ireland are also more than happy to offer advice to visiting Land Rover enthusiasts. Contact John Redmond on 00 353 87 258 4940.

Raining cats and dogs? The German shepherd cross searching in vain for a lamp-post belongs to Mervyn. Like all Rovers, he shrugs off the wet and gets on with it.

Driver Profiles

MERVYN COLTON TAKES his 1993 200Tdi 90 into the sort of places most folk wouldn't venture, so he makes his vehicle as capable as possible for those times when even the three-inch lift provided from OME springs and Rancho 9000 shock absorbers can't get him unstuck.

That's when the Milemarker hydraulic winch comes in handy. An Alfred Murray auxilliary pump makes it turn faster – and he's very happy to use Plasma synthetic cable rather than traditional steel hawser.

General Grabber mud terrain tyres offer super traction off-road, while seats scavenged from an old Peugeot 205 provide some creature comforts in the cab.

FARMER IVOR CLEGG bought his 90 pick-up brand new in 1984 and it worked hard for its living on the land before he 'retired' it to a less-than-easy life as an off-roader. Out came the original naturally-aspirated 2.5 diesel and in its place he dropped a 3.9 EFi V8 from a 1994 Range Rover, complete with auto transmission. He also replaced the rear axle with one from an early Range Rover, to provide disc brakes all round.

The bull bar, rock sliders and underbody protection are all home-made, while the roll cage came from Safety Devices. Detroit lockers, heavy-duty halfshafts and aggressive Bronco Dirt Devils rubber help make it a go-any-where machine.

TREVOR PEDLOW'S 109-INCH Series III entered military service with the Irish Army in 1974. He bought it five years ago and began transforming it with a new chassis and disc brakes all round – the front from a 90 and the rear set from an early Range Rover. A 3.5-litre carburetted V8 gave it an instant power boost, but he's replaced it since with an even gutsier 3.5 EFi, complete with five-speed manual gearbox and Discovery transfer box.

Heavy-duty springs and halfshafts coupled with steering and diff guards look after the vehicle off-road, while a power-steering conversion and Volvo seats look after the driver. Trevor has fitted three fuel tanks – two in the front and one at the rear – to provide 800 miles range with the thirsty V8.

BELIEVE IT OR not, Gary Parkinson's Series IIA was first registered in 1971 as a tractor by its original farmer owner, and thus attracted minimal road tax levy! When he bought it two years ago, it was in remarkable condition despite being abandoned for five years.

'It needed only new bushes, springs, brake cylinders and pipes,' he says. The original 2.25-litre diesel lump was in running order, but too tardy for modern traffic, so he's replaced it with a gutsier 2.25 petrol. The only other non-original parts are the Rocky Mountain parabolic springs. 'They make a huge difference to the handling,' he says.

PATRICK MULLIGAN FOUNDED the Land Rover Club of Ireland in 1993 after he bought his 110 hard top, then just a year old. Since then, the club has gone from strength to strength – and so has his Defender. It now has 91,000 miles on the clock and the 200Tdi engine is running as sweetly as ever, although he has treated it to a new gearbox and transfer box.

Apart from a cosmetic checker plate – and an extra Alpine roof window – the 110 is very much as Solihull intended, yet Patrick has no hesitation to take it on off-road forays with the more modified machines of fellow club members, proving once again that Land Rovers are competent performers straight out of the box.

daylight robbery). If you buy a new vehicle in Ireland, you'll pay a government levy of 28 per cent on top of the asking price.

Then you face having your pockets emptied by outrageous levels of road tax, based on engine size. A 2.5-litre Discovery will set you back £600 a year, while a V8 Range Rover costs £925. There is one loophole, though – vans and trucks cough up just £160 in Ireland. That explains why there's a disproportionately high number of Discovery Commercials to be found on Ireland's roads.

But it's not all bad news.

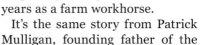

Inferior Japanese 4×4s have been outselling Land Rovers in the Republic for many years now, but luckily there are plenty of older Series vehicles tucked away in barns and farmyards, ripe for restoration. Most have decent chassis and bulkheads, despite that damp climate. According to Ivor Clegg, that's because the Irish authorities seldom use salt on the roads in winter. Certainly, the chassis on Ivor's 1984 90 is solid as a rock, despite spending most of its 18 years as a farm workhorse.

It's the same story from Patrick Mulligan, founding father of the LRCI, and proud owner of a 1992 Defender 110 that's still running on its original chassis, springs, shock absorbers – not to mention an ever-dependable 200Tdi engine.

But most amazing of all is Gary Parkinson's 31-year-old Series IIA, which he picked up for £500 two years ago. The 88-incher had been left to rot behind a shed for five years, but when Gary came to inspect his would-be purchase, he found a pristine original chassis, bodywork and bulkhead. Even the paintwork was in good order once he'd attacked it with T-cut and some elbow grease.

The only vehicle in the convoy that's needed any serious work is Trevor Pedlow's 109-inch ex-Irish Army Series II, which he treated to a new chassis when he bought it five years ago. His passenger today is Brendan Wyse, whose own 110 V8 is currently in pieces on his workshop floor awaiting a rebuild.

Brendan turns out to be a great assistant to me, leaping out of the warm comfort of the cab to stand in the pouring rain and guide me along the narrow, slippery ridges between the deep ruts. One wrong move here and the Freelander won't be going any further. I'd love to crawl along in first gear, low box, but this isn't an option

Water, water everywhere, flowing down the rutted tracks, pouring out of the peat – but nothing's going to stop us enjoying ourselves.

in a vehicle without a transfer box. You are forced to drive far more quickly than you'd like to – and the smell of burning clutch drifts through the fir trees.

It comes through, all right, but there are times when I wonder if I'll ever get it out of that Irish bog again. The Irish lads haven't seen a Freelander venture off-road before and I think they're pleasantly surprised to see it perform so well in terrain where I shouldn't really have taken it.

Our visit is over all too soon, but I'm sure we'll be taking up our Irish friends' invitation to visit again in the warmer months, when the countryside is even more spectacular – and there's even a chance of a suntan. It doesn't always rain in Ireland, but with so much to do and such brilliant off-roading, who cares if it does?

Right top Ballykissangel – we visit Avoca in the Wicklow Mountains, where the popular TV series is set.

Right bottom A warm welcome to a country where time stands still.

Main picture Driving home after a long wet day's exploring.

191

The Last Wilderness

The uplands of County Durham are an unspoilt greenlaners' paradise

Words: Dave Phillips
Photographs: Fiona Richardson

LIFE IS FULL of surprises, especially if you allow preconceptions to cloud your thinking. All of my previous visits to the north-east of England had been to the big urban centres of Newcastle, Sunderland and Middlesbrough – all crumbling shipyards, deserted collieries, back-to-back terraced housing and lively people who live for their football and nightlife.

I knew I wasn't going to encounter much of that once I'd headed inland from the industrial east coast, but I didn't know what to expect. Certainly not the unspoilt oasis of greenlanes and spectacular countryside that I was introduced to by some of LRO's friends from the region.

The original plan had been to take up a long-standing offer from LRO's technical editor, Eddie Evans, to explore the byways of his Cumbrian home patch. That plan had been shelved during the grim months of the recent Foot-and-Mouth epidemic and, even in spring 2002, it was clear that the disease was still a sensitive issue in the area that had been hit as hard as any.

Instead, we decided to team up with LRO contributor Steve Graham and pals and explore the greenlanes the other side of the Pennines, in County Durham, where we were assured we'd get a warmer reception from the locals. But we got a lot more than that.

Our mission was to drive the greenlanes of County Durham, with the North East Rover Owners Club's rights of way officer, Fred Wright, joining us to show us some of the best of them. Oh yes, and we'd sorted a promising off-road centre, too.

We were based outside the lovely market town of Barnard Castle, on the banks of the upper River Tees, just north of the A66 cross-Pennine highway and less than half an hour from Scotch Corner.

We brought along a motley crew of Land Rovers – Steve behind the wheel of a 100-inch Range Rover Series III hybrid, his mate Dave Wells in a 110 and Eddie in his 200Tdi Discovery. I've arrived in a Td4 Freelander, on test from Land Rover, just to see how a so-called soft-roader would cope with the terrain. After all, the object of these forays is to encourage you, the reader, to follow in our tyre tracks. And you wouldn't thank me if you did just that and came unstuck, now would you?

Also on this outing riding shotgun is LRO's photographer, Fiona, who has left her own ex-RAF 90 at home. Instead, she hops from vehicle to vehicle every time we stop to take in the scenery. Her favourite is the back of Steve's hybrid, which offers a good vantage point for photography, while she shelters beneath the canvas tilt.

Heavy metal – most of the old mines are long gone, but this one is now a tourist attraction.

We start by heading north from Teesdale, accompanied by high winds and driving rain, but the latter turns to sleet and eventually snow as we head up beyond the treeline into the high moors of Weardale.

We are surrounded by upland bog, oozing with moisture, yet the tracks are as firm as the rock they're built on. No mud here to dirty our wheels.

Black grouse burst out of the heather at our approach. They're the only sign of life up here, but the magnificent view when the scuttling clouds occasionally clear more than compensates. We even manage to catch a glimpse of the snow-capped peak of Cross Fell – at 893 metres the second-highest mountain in England.

In the dim and distant past, local folk knew it as Fiends' Fell, because they thought it was inhabited by evil spirits that were responsible for the searing, icy winds that blew down from its summit, even in summer. They're known as the Helm winds and are caused by the shape of Cross Fell, which forces warm air from the west upward to meet the cold air at the top, which then rushes down the eastern slopes – often leaving a trail of destruction in

The low ground-clearance Freelander couldn't straddle the deep ruts here due to the narrow gate, so we employed rocks and Steve's plastic waffles to get it through without grounding the exhaust or the transmission.

Driver Profiles

STEVE GRAHAM'S 100-INCH hybrid came about because he happened to have the bits to build it lying around his yard.

He had been dismantling a rather tatty 1981 Range Rover for parts when he arrived at the bare chassis and discovered it was in pristine condition. And he just happened to have a 109-inch ex-military Series III that needed a new chassis, axles and suspension.

The result is a 2.25-litre petrol workhorse that boasts excellent off-road ability thanks to the articulation of the Range Rover coils.

YOU'D BE HARD-PRESSED to find another vehicle as versatile as Dave Wells' One Ten. It's everyday transport and a real workhorse for the plumber, from Stockton-on-Tees, as well as being his weekend off-roader.

It began life with the North East Electricity Board, for working on overhead lines. As that meant traversing some difficult upland terrain, it was fitted with a PTO-powered winch, which Dave puts to good use in sticky off-road situations. He's owned it four years and hasn't bothered to change the original orange electricity board livery, although he has indulged himself in a Webasto heater to pre-heat the engine and cab in winter.

EDDIE EVANS MAY be LRO's much-respected technical editor, but he doesn't spend all his time in his workshop at Cark-in-Cartmel, Cumbria. He loves off-roading, greenlaning, tarmac travelling – in fact any motoring as long as it's in one of his fleet of Land Rovers.

So it's no surprise that Eddie has clocked up 50,000 miles on his 200Tdi Discovery in just two-and-a-half years. It has now covered 150,000 miles on its original engine and gearbox. 'It's the most reliable vehicle I've ever owned,' says Eddie. 'I've fitted a new water pump and lower steering shaft and they're the only significant repairs I've had to do.'

its wake. It would have to be a brave tree to try to get a foothold out here.

You haven't heard of Cross Fell? Not a lot of people have – just as many haven't experienced the splendid desolation of this amazing forgotten wilderness.

It wasn't always like this, though. These lonely moors were once a hive of industry, mined for their rich veins of metals – lead in particular. The worked-out mines and settlements are now largely deserted, but their ruins and heaps of spoil remain, now blending into the landscape.

We're now exploring a UCR (unclassified road) that Fred had reckoned would provide some challenging driving, but Durham County Council's highways department has been along since his last visit and repaired the worst of the wash-outs. Steve grumbles – he'd

Above   Wonderful wide open spaces.

Below top   Wet grass is no problem in the Td4 Freelander fitted with traction control.

Below bottom   Unless you love crawling under the Freelander to hook the exhaust system back onto its mounts, this is the best way to tackle the occasional deep rut.

196

wanted a few holes and ruts to negotiate – but we all admire the council's positive stance.

Trees and green pastures begin to appear again as we descend Galloway Hill, heading for Burnthorpe Reservoir and the valley of the River Wear. We follow the course of the river upstream through stone-built villages and small towns, each with an assortment of Land Rovers parked everywhere. When snow carpets the Pennines through the winter months they will be needed.

There's time to explore two more greenlanes around Alston Moor before we finish the day with some fun at the Weardale Off Road Centre, at nearby Wolsingham.

Yet another surprise here. This isn't your ordinary disused quarry, such as you'd expect in most parts of England. Instead, owner Anthony Todd has turned over 200 acres of his farm to one of the best off-road drives we've ever experienced, with real river crossings, rock climbs, woodland and steep hills. Oh yes, and

Rising to the challenge –steep hills, axle-twisters and deep holes abound at the Weardale Off Road Centre, which also offers scenic drives on private tracks across the fells.

mud holes at last. Steve grins from ear to ear as he points his long-suffering hybrid at the first obstacle.

The Freelander is a bit of a disappointment where the ruts are too deep – it simply doesn't enjoy the same ground clearance as its taller cousins – but it's a great performer on slippery grass slopes, where ETC (electronic traction control) ensures that even on ordinary road tyres it will outclimb the others. You'd really need a whole day to explore this site – there's so much of it. But we take advantage of the long late spring evening and stay until dusk.

The next day we have more exploring to do, taking in some of the sights. The town of Barnard Castle, as its name suggests, boasts the ruins of an impressive 12th

197

Large conifer forests can be explored on the lower slopes of the fells, as here near Forest-in-Teesdale.

Leafing Around – Series Still Rule in County Durham

YOU'LL PROBABLY RUB your eyes in disbelief at your first sighting of a typical Series Land Rover from this neck of the woods. It will most likely be a Series III with a IIA grille, finished in bronze green, with a blue driver's door, a cream passenger door and a red 'un at the back. At the wheel will be a smiling hill farmer.

And if you think of Series vehicles as real rarities – virtual museum pieces that have classic appeal but little practicality in the 21st century, then think again. They are alive and well – thriving in fact – in the north-east. Drive along any lane in County Durham and you'll pass a farm with the obligatory leaf-sprung workhorse in the yard; pay a visit to the nearest market town and you'll see them parked everywhere.

It's a hard life in this tough terrain, and these rugged vehicles work for their living. There are plenty of pretty-much-original Series IIAs and IIIs, plus a lot more mix-and-match combinations. Farmers aren't out to win concours, so cannibalising an old SII or III to keep another running is standard practice.

Fred Wright, rights of way officer for the North East Rover Owners Club, is another fan and reckons a leafer is the ideal vehicle for greenlaning, where go-anywhere ability is its chief asset.

He drives a tax-exempt 1971 109 – one of the last of the Series IIAs. It's on the road seven days a week – five while he works as a maintenance fitter and two as he spends his weekends exploring the maze of lanes

in County Durham, Northumberland and North Yorkshire.

He's been NERO's rights of way officer for the past four years, during which he has built up a good relationship with officers at the local councils. 'The secret is to get them on your side,' he reveals. 'Don't approach them with your hackles up, be diplomatic – but firm when you need to be.'

With Foot-and-Mouth still fresh on the minds of the local farming community, we didn't want to create a bad image by driving a big convoy of Land Rovers across these fields, so we kept vehicle numbers to a minimum. Fred left his SIIA at home – and luckily Steve's mate Karim Jaffer didn't bring his fleet, either. There probably wouldn't be room in County Durham for all of them!

Karim is a leaf-sprung fanatic, currently owning eight Land Rovers – including six Series IIIs and a Series II. The other is a 110.

'I was born in Tanzania in east Africa and the first motor car I ever saw was a Land Rover. I've been hooked on them ever since – especially Series vehicles. I believe they are a lot tougher than the modern coil-sprung Defenders,' says Karim, 40, who now lives in London.

He's a frequent visitor to the north-east, where he loves to explore the countryside and talk Series Land Rovers with Steve Graham. 'I buy all my Land Rovers from Steve because he's an enthusiast. Nobody knows more about how Series Land Rovers work,' he says.

Above Bowes Museum.

Right top The ruins of Barnard Castle.

Right bottom High Force, England's highest waterfall, a must for all visitors to the area.

century fortress, towering over the fast-flowing Tees. It was built by the Baliol family and was home of John Baliol, King of Scotland until he upset England's Edward I, who deposed him in 1296.

Just south of the town, and flanked conveniently by two byways, is the Bowes Museum – a magnificent French-style chateau that looks all the more impressive due to its setting in the north-east of England. It was built by John Bowes, a wealthy mine owner, for his French wife Josephine, who sadly died before it was completed in 1875. The grieving John opened it as a museum, dedicated to her memory, and today it is famous for its art collection.

And finally, before we head for home, we follow the lanes that trace the course of the Tees, upstream to Middleton-on-Tees and High Force, which is England's highest waterfall.

Here, the river suddenly plunges 70 feet over a sheer rock face, accompanied by a thunder roar and clouds of mist, in which mini-rainbows glow every time the sun breaks through the clouds. This is our very own Niagara, England's answer to Victoria Falls, and the biggest tourist attraction in Teesdale. Yet though this is a fine, sunny day we're the only visitors.

And that's the attraction of this neck of the woods. When you visit, you're aware that this unspoilt corner of England will not remain this way for ever. One day the overspill tourist hordes from the Lake District and North Yorkshire's Moors and Dales will surge in to these hills and demand their gift shops.

The local tourist office slogan is 'The North Pennines – England's last wilderness'. And they're right. This is like the best of North Yorkshire, but without the National Park status that's currently threatening the future of greenlanes in the Moors and Dales. This is pure, unspoilt, upland England. Make the most of it – it won't be around for ever.

Telly Addicts

LRO explores the Dales and Moors of Yorkshire, but can't help straying into the world of TV soaps ...

Words: Dave Phillips
Photographs: Fiona Spencer

YORKSHIRE ISN'T JUST Britain's biggest county, it's also the biggest soap opera set imaginable. Emmerdale, Heartbeat and Last of the Summer Wine are some of the favourite TV series filmed here – and they all feature Land Rovers.

This is Land Rover country, all right. So where better to head for some off-roading and sightseeing? At least that's what we thought when we planned this trip, as a chance to test and compare three very different vehicles from the LRO fleet – our 200Tdi Defender 90, 300Tdi Discovery and 1.8 petrol Freelander.

We arrange to meet up in the village of Esholt. Unless you're a soap opera anorak, that might not mean a lot to you, but it is the real name of the fictional TV village where nobody drives anything but Land Rovers. I'm talking, of course, about Emmerdale.

Canny product placement by Solihull's PR department means that everybody in Emmerdale drives them. Even impoverished farmer Jack Sugden, struggling with cash-flow as well as his lines, can somehow afford to drive his brand-new Defender 90 at 7pm on ITV every night of the week.

These days, the Emmerdale film set has been rebuilt in the grounds of Harewood House, north of Leeds, but that doesn't stop tens of thousands of devoted soap fans from descending upon Esholt every year to stroll the streets of the original village. Yet those expecting an isolated settlement in the middle of the Dales are in for a surprise, because Esholt is situated just under a railway viaduct

on the outskirts of Bradford. It's also overshadowed by a huge pay-and-display car park, where coaches constantly disgorge hungry hordes of telly-addicted tourists.

In retrospect, it was probably a mistake for us to park our three Land Rovers outside the Woolpack. The sightseers are now queueing to have their photographs taken alongside the LRO machines, no doubt convinced that our vehicles are part of TV history. This we witness with amusement from within the snug of the Woolpack, where we're enjoying a pint of shandy.

The trouble comes when we leave and the blue-rinsed crowd spots LRO art director, Pete Comely. Suddenly the pink-flushed faces go pale and one old lady looks as though she's about to faint.

'It ... it can't be. Not him. He died last year after the bus crash. Yes, it is ... it's Butch!' It's a big mistake bringing a Butch Dingle lookalike like Pete to Emmerdale. We narrowly escape with our lives and head north.

With Butch – I mean Pete – in the 90 is LRO photographer Fiona Spencer, eager to capture the purple, heather-clad moors and green dales in the moody autumn light. Editor-in-chief, John Pearson, and his partner, Pat, are leading the way in the Project Disco. John knows the greenlanes of Yorkshire like the back of his hand, after years spent exploring them on trials bikes.

I'm sharing the Freelander with off-road driving instructor Amanda Ramsey, who works with LRO Adventure Club leader, Vince Cobley.

Left top   Ready to explore the soap sights of Yorkshire.

Left bottom   The Freelander's underhung exhaust is a headache as soon as you get among the ruts of the byways, but we struggle on anyway.

Above   Ooops ... we didn't notice the sign until eagle-eyed photographer Fiona pointed it out. We reckon the row of Land Rovers gives an otherwise dreary village a touch of ambience.

203

I like industrial West Yorkshire, with its grim, grey-granite mills and terraced houses and, above all, the warmth of the people who live here. It's also where Last of the Summer Wine is filmed (I have it on good authority that Series III-driving Wesley is an avid reader of LRO). But it's still good to escape into the hills, which are always very close wherever you go in Yorkshire. Even in the urban sprawls of Leeds, Bradford and Sheffield, dramatic countryside is never far away.

And that's certainly the case today, as we head along Wharfedale, skirting the Pennines. We make a detour to explore the lanes around the picturesque twin reservoirs of Fewston and Swinsty, constructed in Victorian times by damming the little River Washburn, a tributary of the Wharfe.

Then it's off north again, through Grassington and Kettlewell, as we head for a network of greenlanes just south of Hawes. We're high up in the Pennines now, in

Above left Tech-editor Eddie and editor-editor Dave inspect the damage under the Freelander, but it's only a couple of rubber exhaust hangers that have come unhooked.

Above right The menfolk huddle inside their vehicles …

Below   … while Amanda faces the elements to sort out the kinetic rope.

the heart of the Yorkshire Dales National Park, and the October gales are howling across the treeless hilltops. It's a struggle to stand upright when we reluctantly climb out of the Land Rovers to open and close the gates along the tracks.

The Freelander copes admirably with the terrain – its traction control chattering away reassuringly as we switch from slippery rock to slippery mud to slippery bog. It performs faultlessly until we come to some deeper-than-average ruts … and then we come a cropper due to the inadequate ground clearance. I'm at the wheel, with Amanda out in the elements in front, guiding me along

Top It's getting dark and we can see the road half a mile ahead is badly flooded.

Above A bleak prospect – but we love this open landscape, and the opportunity to explore some more greenlanes.

Below Dave looks suitably determined as he rescues John's stricken Discovery.

the top of the ruts. Amazingly we only get grounded once, by the low-slung rear silencer. It's slung even lower by the time I put my foot down and power it out, but we carry on regardless. With race-trained John surging ahead in the Discovery, it can be a struggle to keep up.

Despite its reputation as an off-road lightweight, the Freelander actually copes very well. The traction control keeps it going through mud and quite deep water that eventually catches out John in the Discovery. He's got cross-axled on some submerged rocks in the middle of a flooded section of track and it takes a hefty heave on the 90, assisted by a kinetic rope, to recover the Disco – which pops out like a cork from a champagne bottle.

Eventually we crest a steep hill and stop to take in the view across the valley beneath us. Unfortunately, it's only too clear that there's heavy flooding on the lower ground and there's no way we're going to get through. So, in the fading light of the evening sun, we about-turn and retrace our route. On one slippery section, uphill this

time, both the 90 and Disco struggle to reach the top and have to make a couple of attempts at the muddy ascent. The traction control on the Freelander, however, allows it to breeze up – despite the fact it's shod with low-profile tarmac tyres. It's not the fluffy hairdressers' car some would have you believe. Mind you, I'd still rather tackle this in a 90.

LRO's technical editor, Eddie Evans, and his wife, Julie, join us this evening in Leyburn, after making the long trek across country from Cumbria. And it's Eddie who crawls under the Freelander with me the next morning to hook the errant exhaust back onto its rubber mounts ready for another off-road foray and, perhaps, some more soap opera sightseeing. Can't wait.

Today we're all heading east into another National Park – this time the North Yorkshire Moors. We'd considered paying a visit to Castle Howard, the setting for early 1980s TV adaptation of Brideshead Revisited, but the estate demands a staggering £500 for us just to

Left top   Surely the intrepid team haven't got lost again? Of course not!

Left bottom   We spotted this brilliant Q-plate Series I recovery vehicle parked by the wayside. It looks like it's still capable of working hard for its living.

Below   Pretty lanes abound in this part of Yorkshire.

Top Negotiations with the farmer's wife give us an alternative route to try.

Middle Watch where you park, or the intrepid Aidensfield police will nick you.

Bottom A forest track in the midst of *Heartbeat* country.

photograph our trio of vehicles in front of their stately pile. Perhaps there has been a little too much TV and movie cash sloshing around these parts. Anyway, we politely decline.

We head instead beyond Thirsk and James Herriott country, taking the A170 towards Sproxton for about five miles, crawling up the precipitous Sutton Bank behind lorries at walking pace, before turning off left onto The Hambleton (aka Cleveland Way) – a spectacular byway that traverses the top of heather-clad Arden Moor and Black Hambleton, before swooping down again to the low plain, far below.

We've been looking forward to this trek, along ten miles of spectacular byway, but early into the journey we grind to a halt by a newly-erected, officious-looking sign, informing us that the section ahead has recently been designated a bridleway by the local council ... meaning that we can legally drive no further. The do-gooders have beaten us to it.

Salvation arrives, however, in the shape of a 110, driven by the local farmer's wife, who stops for a chat. After listening sympathetically to our predicament, she kindly allows us to bypass the prohibited section via her private farm tracks, which include a magical journey through nearby Boltby Forest, before rejoining the byway near Little Moor.

The steep descent down from Black Hambleton to Thimbleby Moor proves to be an excellent test for the

Soap Stops

Esholt
Real name of the original version of fictional TV village Emmerdale. The village used now is in the grounds of Harewood House, north of Leeds. Esholt is situated on the outskirts of Bradford and overshadowed by a large pay-and-and-display car park.

Thirsk
Visit the original surgery of Alf Wight, author of the James Herriot books, and see the World of James Herriot. The popular TV series was filmed in the Yorkshire Dales and North Yorkshire Moors.

Goathland
Visit Heartbeat country, filmed in and around the village of Goathland. The North Yorkshire Railway is used in the series. Also filmed in Whitby and Scarborough.

Holmfirth, Kirklees
Last of the Summer Wine was filmed here In West Yorkshire. See the location of Sid's Café – and Nora Batty fans can stop for a bite to eat at the Wrinkled Stocking Tea Room.

Places to Visit in Yorkshire
Wharram Percy

DESERTED MEDIEVAL VILLAGE near Malton is the extraordinary site of one of the most famous deserted medieval villages. Remains of the medieval church and farm cottages. Evidence of Stone Age occupation and settlement dating back to Bronze Age, with Roman farms and a wealthy Anglo-Saxon estate.

Open any reasonable time. Entry free. Access 6m SE of Malton on minor roads from B1248 half mile S of Wharram le Street. (OS Map 11; ref SE 859645).

For more information phone English Heritage on 0845 3010 003.

Rievaulx Abbey

FOUNDED BY THE holy St Bernard of Clairvaux to bring Christianity to Western Europe in 1132. Dissolved by Henry VIII in 1538. New owner, Thomas Manners, the first Earl of Rutland began systematic destruction of the buildings. Tel 01439 798228. Access In Rievaulx, two and quarter miles W of Helmsley on minor road off B1257 (OS Map 100; ref SE 577849).

Whitby Abbey

CONTAINS SHRINE OF St Hilda, the foundress who died in 680. Overlooks picturesque town and harbour with associations ranging from Victorian jewellery and whaling to Count Dracula. Abbey destroyed by Vikings in 867. Revived by Norman invader Reinfrid in late 1070s. Dissolution in 1538. Tel 01947 603568.

Fountains Abbey and Studley Royal

CISTERCIAN ABBEY FOUNDED in 1132. The largest such remains in Europe. Dramatic focal point for landscape gardens laid-out during the first half of the 18th century. Other features: St Mary's Church and Fountains Hall, and an Elizabethan mansion. Fountains Abbey and Water Garden. Access 4m W of Ripon off B6265. (OS Map 99; ref SE 278703). Tel 01765 608888.

St Mary's Church, Studley Royal

DESIGNED BY WILLIAM Burges in the 1870s. Coloured marble, stained glass, gilded and painted figures and a splendid organ remains. Entry free. Route, see Fountains Abbey.

Freelander's Hill Descent Control (HDC), which clatters along happily as we concentrate on keeping it on the narrow, boulder-strewn track.

With the detours and numerous stops to admire the view, it's taken us nearly three hours to cover ten miles of tricky tracks, so after a village pub lunch we press on – through Malton and across the moors to Goathland, the real village that is the setting for Heartbeat. Da-da-da-da-da ... yes, we're in TV heaven again.

This is the Aidensfield of soapland – the village with an astonishing crime rate higher than a Soweto township, yet where the district nurse drives a ragtop Series I without it ever getting broken into. But then, the hard-pressed Aidensfield police would never catch the MkII Jaguar-driving villains with their 105E Ford Anglia and BSA Bantam motor bike.

We stop at the local hotel – aka the Aidensfield Arms – but there's no sign of Claude Greengrass doing a dodgy deal. Worse still, mini-skirted Scouser barmaid Gina isn't there to pull pints – just a bar full of tourists. We don't stay long.

The next day, we set off for the coast, planning to arrive in Whitby by midday for a fish and chips lunch. We head there via the fabulous tracks of the Dalby Forest, near Scarborough, which led us to the exciting Langdale Quest off-road centre (see next page). John, Eddie and Pete opt to put the 90 and Discos through their paces – and have a

lot of fun in the process – but I decide the Freelander has been punished enough already and take the scenic route to Whitby, via the North Sea coast.

We park to the north of the town, high above the harbour. Our prime objective is to recce the chippies, ready for when the others arrive, but within minutes we stumble across an amazing 1968 Series IIA ice cream van, owned by Neil Trillo. He explains that it has been in the family for over 30 years and its colourful history includes being marooned out on the sands just as the tide was turning. It was completely submerged by the rising water and left overnight, but the next morning the Trillo family recovered the vehicle and restored it. That was 20 years ago – and it's still going strong on its original 2.25 petrol engine. It's teeth-chattering weather and no sane person's buying ice creams, but Amanda and I take pity on Neil and buy a couple of 99s. Delicious they are, too.

Soon the rest of the party arrive, enthusing about the Langdale off-road experience. We've all worked up a hunger for traditional Whitby cod and chips. They're reputed to be the best in the world – and none of us would argue with that as we tuck into them straight out of the wrappers, on the harbour wall.

It's a fitting finale to a great, no-nonsense trip that's been great fun without breaking the bank (or the vehicles). Why don't you give it a go?

Above You're assured a warm welcome from the rangers at Dalby Forest.

Below top The Forest Drive is great fun and it's only a short distance from Scarborough.

Below bottom Clifford's Tower, York, the last remaining part of York Castle and within easy reach.

Langdale Quest

AT 10,000 ACRES, the Langdale Quest is the largest dedicated off-road driving site in the UK. It opened in 1997, supported by both the National Parks and the Forestry Commission. Visitors can either drive their own vehicles or hire one of the Quest's own 4×4s. Unfortunately, there are no Land Rovers on the 12-strong fleet at present.

There are non-damaging routes suitable for novices, as well as the newly-opened Quest Extreme course for experienced off-roaders, comprising twelve different zones within the forest. Each zone provides a new challenge to the driver and vehicle – including winching, comp safari, quarry, massive descents (150 metres), bridge building and obstacle course.

'For groups of over ten vehicles the price drops to 50 per cent,' says Langdale's owner, Andy Young. 'This is done to encourage clubs to organise big groups. Our largest group round the Quest so far has been 57 vehicles in the forest at any one time and we have the capacity for 100 vehicles on the Extreme course.' All prices include a free recovery voucher – just in case you get stuck!

The Quest is open every weekend from the end of March, plus all Bank Holidays and all school holidays (a total of 130 days) until the end of October. For further details, contact Andy Young on 01723 882335 or email langdale-quest@talk21.com

Island Fling

From the Scottish Borders to Lindisfarne in a quartet of Land Rovers – can the intrepid LRO team beat the elements and reach their destination in a day?

Words and Photographs: Dave Phillips

THE LIQUID CALL of a curlew echoes across the lonely sands, exposed at low tide. In the distance a castle perched high on a craggy cliff lies silhouetted between a leaden sky and a stormy sea. Our pilgrimage is almost complete.

Our destination is Holy Island – or Lindisfarne – off the coast of Northumberland. Our starting point this morning, over the border in Roxburghshire, was the equally holy Melrose Abbey. And we've spent the day tracking a saint's footsteps in our four Land Rovers. We're on the trail of St Cuthbert, who lived and died in these parts almost 1,400 years ago.

Our trip was the idea of Colin Bell, who has lived around here just 29 years, but has a wealth of knowledge of the local history and topography. Like the rest of us, he's a Land Rover fanatic, of course.

He's driving a Defender 90 200Tdi. In the passenger seat is his mate, Rob Burbidge. Well, I *think* it's Rob, because also with us is Rob's identical twin, Ian, in a bobtailed Range Rover. I can't tell them apart: let's hope Ian's girlfriend and co-driver, Rachel Hingley, can.

I'm in the Project Discovery, while LRO contributor Steve Graham has also joined the trip, in one of his collection of superb historic Land Rovers. Today he's driving the first Series III diesel ever made – one that's arguably restored to a better standard than it was ever built in the first place. His passenger is Karim Jaffer, who himself owns *six* Series IIIs.

We started our epic journey at Melrose, outside the ruins of what was once Scotland's richest abbey. It's a place dear to the hearts of all Scots, because it's said that the heart of one of their greatest heroes, Robert the Bruce, is buried here. And this is also the place where St Cuthbert started his monastic career, around 650AD.

Some years later, he set out on foot across the hills and moors, eventually arriving at the Northumberland coast, where he founded the first abbey on Lindisfarne and eventually became famous for his healing powers. 'Very nice,' I can hear you say, 'but how does that qualify him for sainthood?' Be patient – all will become clear.

Like all would-be saints, Cuthbert first had to die before achieving beatification. Once he'd passed away, he didn't have long to wait: eleven years later his coffin was opened and his body was found to be perfectly preserved. That miracle was enough for the Pope to give the thumbs-up.

Nobody knows where St Cuthbert's remains are today, because they were removed again – still perfectly preserved – 200 years later when a series of Viking raids threatened the island. The monks carried St Cuthbert away to a secret resting place, but if you're ever digging your garden and your spade hits a stone coffin, don't be surprised if you find yourself face to face with a monk who has stood the test of time.

Today, though, time isn't on our side. It's midwinter, the days are short and we've got a lot of ground to cover and

The team prepare to set off from impressive Melrose Abbey.

Off the beaten track – there are no greenlanes in Scotland, but odd forest tracks like this one near Melrose.

The Tweed is known as the queen of salmon rivers.

sights to see. We duly head east from Melrose, driving a small lane high above the valley of the unspoilt River Tweed, which is the fourth-longest river in Scotland (after the Tay, the Clyde and the Spey), flowing for 97 miles from its source in the Tweedsmuir Hills to the sea at Berwick-upon-Tweed. It's known as the queen of all salmon rivers – a claim disputed only by fans of its more northerly compatriot, the Tay.

Today, the smoke from the peat fires of the cottages in the valley hang in the crisp morning air as we arrive at a beauty spot known as Scott's View. From here there's a stunning view of the Eildon Hills. The viewpoint is named after the novelist Sir Walter Scott, who was born in Edinburgh in 1771 and spent much of his childhood on his grandparents' farm near here. The author of *Ivanhoe* and other historical epics, he's credited with inventing the modern novel.

An abandoned Series II spotted rotting away in a farmyard at Naxton.

Driver Profiles

COLIN BELL'S 1991 Defender 90 has 142,000 miles on the clock, many off-road, but the original 200Tdi engine is as sweet as it's ever been. Since he bought it eighteen months ago, he has added a raised air intake, spotlights and BFG all-terrain tyres.

He lives in Billingham, Teesside, where he grew up with twin brothers, Rob and Ian Burbidge. All three have been Land Rover fanatics since their teens, when all three bought and restored elderly Series vehicles. Ian's driving his distinctive bobtailed 1974 Range Rover, which sits on 235 85–16 mud terrain tyres and suspension lifted by two inches. Six months ago he finished an extensive rebuild, which included fitting an economical 300Tdi diesel engine and a home-made snorkel.

RACHEL HINGLEY (Ian's girlfriend) comes from a Land Rover-mad family. Both her father and mother drive Range Rovers – and she's resigned to the fact that Ian spends long hours toiling in his workshop. Her only gripe is the cash flow: 'He spent half the money we'd saved for a deposit on a house when he rebuilt the Range Rover,' she says.

STEVE GRAHAM has been offered an astonishing £40,000 for his immaculately restored Series III – and turned it down. To him, owning the first SIII diesel off the Lode Lane production line is priceless and no amount of cash will tempt him to part with it. It was built in 1970 and began life as a publicity vehicle for Land Rover, appearing in company adverts at the time, before it was finally registered for the road in 1972 and sold via a dealer in the West Midlands. But although Steve's breathtaking restorations are invariably immaculate, they're never mollycoddled. Rather than mothball them, the specialist enjoys driving them – although he's careful to clean them meticulously after every outing.

KARIM JAFFER lives in London, but regularly makes the long trek north to Steve's workshop to seek advice on his own fleet of Series IIIs. He currently owns four ex-military 109s, as well as a long-wheelbase and 88-incher from civvy street. That would normally be more than enough for anyone, but not a fanatic like Karim. 'I'm about to buy a Discovery for everyday use and I fancy the idea of installing a Td5 engine in a Series III for extra power when I drive long distances,' he says.

He's buried a mile from here at Dryburgh Abbey, also the last resting place of Field Marshal Earl Haig, controversial architect of the British Army's First World War campaign.

It would be really marvellous to go greenlaning in this unspoilt countryside, but sadly it's impossible. Public rights of way for 4×4s are as rare as hens' teeth in Scotland and 'greenlaning' north of the border is done on the tracks of privately owned land. But it's no great loss today, as we've opted for deserted minor roads instead, which twist and turn as they follow the course of the mighty river hundreds of feet below us.

We eventually cross the river at Mertoun Bridge, just north of St Boswells, before venturing off the beaten track again a couple of miles further along the road at Maxton.

Here, in a farmyard behind a low stone wall, we spot two long-dead Land Rovers – a Series II and a IIA. Unlike St Cuthbert, they're very rotten. Even Steve, who's performed some miracle restorations in the past, reckons they're beyond resurrection. No *Wrecks to Riches* here, so we leave them to rust in peace.

Our next port of call is the ruin of Cessford Castle, set on a wild hillside miles from the nearest town. Over the centuries, these border lands have seen countless bloody skirmishes between Romans, Picts, Danes, Vikings, Saxons and Normans – and the remains of keeps and towers are dotted everywhere as reminders of these violent times.

The only aggression today, however, is from a peregrine falcon, which wheels noisily above the battlements, angry that we have disturbed its lonely eyrie with our Land Rovers.

We're still following St Cuthbert's Way, but our Scottish leg is almost complete. We cross the border just beyond Kirk Yetholm and we're now in Northumberland – the magnificent Northumberland National Park, to be exact. It stretches for more than 60 miles from the Cheviot Hills, which we're now driving through, south to the wonder that is Hadrian's Wall.

Over we go – Mertoun Bridge over the River Tweed.

Top Lindisfarne Castle's distinctive profile.
Middle Highland cattle graze the uplands.
Bottom Prop shafted – a rusted hulk on the shoreline.

Northumberland is the least-populated English county. It boasts the UK's largest World Heritage Site (Hadrian's Wall) and the biggest man-made lake in Europe (Kielder Water). Both of those landmarks are too far south for us to explore today, though. We want to get to Lindisfarne before dusk, enjoying this stunning countryside along the way. The speed of our convoy is governed by Steve's SIII. The elderly 2.25-litre diesel is happiest at about 40 mph, bless it.

We cross high moorland *en route* to the market town of Wooler, which is one of those places that begs to be explored. But it will have to put the begging bowl away, because there isn't time. It's not just the fading winter light we're worried about, there's also the North Sea to consider. Holy Island is situated more than a mile offshore and the causeway is negotiable only at low tide. Later this afternoon, it will be cut off by the rising sea.

We head north for Lowick, via a five-mile lane that's so straight it could have been built by the Romans, and on the high ground we catch tantalising glimpses of the coastal sand dunes and white-flecked waves. There's an easterly wind blowing onshore and the sea looks angry.

Northumberland's coastline is noted for its clean, uncrowded beaches. They're clean because there's little pollution and they're certainly going to be uncrowded on a day like this. Stepping out of the vehicle to take some photos of the view, the wind cuts through me like an icy knife.

Lindisfarne now beckons across the mudflats. We take the long route via the causeway, although pilgrims who are literally following in St Cuthbert's footsteps follow the short cut across the sands, which is marked by a mile-long line of wooden posts.

The island itself is about three miles long and barely a mile wide, although much of it consists of barren sand dunes, clothed in marram grass. The rockier eastern end is host to the ruins of St Cuthbert's priory and 16th century Lindisfarne Castle, which is owned by the National Trust.

The island itself, as well as much of the adjacent mainland coastline, is a National Nature Reserve that is renowned for attracting vast numbers of migratory seabirds during the winter months.

We've arrived ... and we duly brave the elements to explore the narrow streets of Lindisfarne village on foot. There are no

St Cuthbert's Way

217

Above   Enjoy it while you can –
some observers reckon that global
warming may put the Holy Island
causeway permanently under water
in years to come.

Bottom left   A statue of St
Cuthbert looking decidedly
miserable.

Bottom right   Set in stone – tourist
information explains the history of
this Holy Island viewpoint.

summer day trippers today and we don't see another soul
as we lean into the wind.

Our only company consists of seabirds – countless
flocks of them – grazing the exposed mud for worms,
shore crabs and shellfish.

Trees are few and far between on the island – the fierce
wind off the sea ensures that the few birches, alders and
willows are stunted. But in the garden of one cottage
there's a sight that makes us stop and smile – a topiary

A Rocky View

The Eildon Hills Scott
admired are what's left of
a chain of volcanic activity
that stretched across the
Borders 300 million years
ago – before the age of the
dinosaurs.

The hills you can see never reached the surface as true volcanoes.
Instead they were forced as great molten blobs into the rock deep
underground, like jam being squirted into a doughnut. There they
cooled slowly, forming rock much harder than the older rocks above.
Since then, the older rocks have been worn away by rivers and glaciers,
leaving the harder rock to form the Eildon Hills.

Many of the walls you see around Borders fields are made of
the hard rock, called whinstone.

Right top Shear magic – a gardener hedges his bets on a 2CV.

Right bottom The Buccleugh Arms Hotel in St Boswells where we stayed – a comfy family-run hotel.

Below Time and tide – the sea starts to flood in over the Holy Island sands.

hedge clipped in the shape of a Citroën 2CV. It's guarded by a line of garden gnomes dressed as Santa Claus. Surreal.

The wind behind us virtually blows us back to the sand-blasted car park, where we celebrate the end of a great day's adventure, hoping that circulation eventually returns to our frozen ears. It's been a wonderful trip (during which our Land Rovers performed faultlessly); one I'd love to repeat in the spring when the days are longer and there's more time to explore. St Cuthbert, we could be coming your Way again.

Resources

The following chapters had no resources in the original articles: RUPPs and Downs, Up and Away, Peak Practice, Exploring the Peaks, Wolds Apart, Notts Landing, Forest Recommissioned, Hidden Heart and Telly Addicts.

General Resources

www.ordnancesurvey.co.uk *All OS maps are available to buy online from the Ordnance Survey website.*

www.glass-uk.org *The Green Lane Association's website is always worth checking out for advice on rights of way and for contact details of area representatives for England and Wales. Better still, you can join up.*

www.laragb.org *The motoring organisations' Land Access and Recreation Association (LARA) is the national forum for country-side motor sport and recreation.*

www.lpga.co.uk *The LP Gas Association has a full list of LPG outlets, constantly updated.*

www.goodguides.co.uk *The Good Pub Guide is available online, with some material from the Good Britain Guide.*

Surf and Turf   pages 10–15

OS Maps and Websites
Explorer OL20 South Devon: Brixham to Newton Ferrers
Explorer 107 St Austell & Liskeard

www.devon.gov.uk *County council site with extensive tourism links, but the rights of way information is not so comprehensive.*

www.cornwalltouristboard.co.uk *If you want to find out more about Cornwall, try this site. Should be just about everything you need to know here.*

Places To Go
The Eden Project *If you've never heard of the Eden Project, welcome back to Earth. Described as the eighth wonder of the modern world, it's the world's biggest greenhouse, housing a fantastic collection of wild and exotic plants. Even if you don't like gardening, go and see it.* Bodelva, St Austell, Cornwall, PL24 2SG (Tel: 01726 811911)

South Devon Railway *Steam trains running on original BR lines that follow the beautiful Dart Valley from Buckfastleigh to Totnes. You can keep going to Kingswear on the Dart Valley Railway. Period stations, Pullman cars and all add to the atmosphere.* The Station, Buckfastleigh, S. Devon, TQ11 0DZ (Tel: 0845 345 1420) www.southdevonrailway.com

Paignton Zoo *One of the country's best and biggest zoos. New exhibits and enclosures a world away from the cramped conditions of 20 years ago. Plenty of interactive stuff for kids and adults – a full day out.* Totnes Road, Paignton, Devon, TQ4 7EU (Tel: 01803 697500)

Off-Road Centres
East Devon 4×4 Off-road Experience, Wessington Farm, Awliscombe, Honiton, East Devon, EX14 3NU (Tel: 01404 42280)

Trax and Trails, South Alston, Stoke Climsland, Callington, Cornwall, PL17 8XL (Tel: 01579 370718)

Get It Fixed
Brookwell's *Independent Land Rover parts and servicing* Pottery Road, Bovery Tracey, Devon (Tel: 01626 832555)

We Stayed At
The Rising Sun Inn *Fairly average pub (interior, rooms) conveniently placed for exploring Dartmoor and the South Hams. Good, extensive menu using local produce.* Woodland, Ashburton, Devon (Tel: 01364 652544)

The Old Ferry Inn *Superb location overlooking the River Fowey – most rooms have river views out to sea. The rest of the pub is decidedly average, and that includes the food we sampled.* Boddinick, Fowey, Cornwall (Tel: 01726 870237)

Land of Contrast   pages 16–23

OS Maps
Explorer OL9 Exmoor
Landranger 181 Glastonbury & the Somerset Levels

Places To Go
Cheddar Caves and Gorge *England's answer to the Grand Canyon, offering activities and attractions including cave tours and a cliff top gorge walk. Rock climbing and abseiling are available, too.* (Tel: 01934 742323) www.cheddarcavers.co.uk

Exmoor Falconry and Animal Farm *Lets visitors get up close and personal with animals ranging from lambs to lizards. Dynamic flying displays are held twice a day – other attractions include nature trails and wildlife ponds.* (Tel: 01643 862816) www.exmoorfalconry.co.uk

Lynton and Lynmouth Cliff Railway *Home to a unique example of a Victorian water-powered lift that still functions, connecting the communities of Lynton and Lynmouth.* (Tel: 01598 753486) www.cliffrailwaylynton.co.uk

We Stayed At
The Yarn Market Hotel *En-suite rooms were well furnished and comfortable. Friendly staff were very helpful and had good local knowledge. Menu was varied and reasonably priced.* 25–31 High Street, Dunster (Tel: 01643 821425) yarnmarket.hotel@virgin.net

Chalk and Trees   pages 24–29

OS Maps and Websites
Explorer 118, 130
Landranger 183, 184

www.visitwiltshire.co.uk *Guide to the whole county.*

www.visitsalisbury.co.uk *Guide to Salisbury and district.*

Places To Go
Stonehenge A303 and A344/360 junction (Tel: 01980 624715)

Tank Museum Bovington, Wool, Dorset (Tel: 01929 405096) www.tankmuseum.co.uk

Stourhead *National Trust 1720 Palladian mansion with beautiful gardens* Stourhead, Stourton, Warminster, Wiltshire (Tel: 01747 841152)

Haynes Motor Museum Sparkford, Yeovil, Somerset (Tel: 01968 550804) www.haynesmotormuseum.co.uk

Fleet Air Museum RNAS Yeovilton, Ilchester, Somerset (Tel: 10935 840565) www.fleetairarm.com

Local Clubs

Salisbury Plain Land Rover Fan Club Keith Brigstock, 9 Vale Road, Pewsey, Wilts, SN9 5HG (Tel: 01672 564562)

Dorset Land Rover and Range Rover Owners Club Mike Mears, 38 Hercules Road, Hamworthy, Poole, Dorset, BH15 4JA (Tel: 01202 681083)

We Stayed At

The Crown *Good, imaginative pub food at reasonable prices and local beers on tap.* Alvediston, nr Shaftesbury (Tel: 01722 780335)

Meet Your Greens pages 30–33

OS Maps

Explorer 144

Contacts

Lasham Gliding Society Lasham Airfield, Alton, GU34 5SS (Tel: 01256 381322)

Watercress Line, The Railway Station, Alresford, Hampshire, SO24 9JG (Tel: 01962 733810)

Alton Information Centre, 7 Cross and Pillory Lane, Alton, GU34 1RQ (Tel: 01420 88448)

Testing Tracks pages 34–43

OS Maps and Websites

Landranger 185 Winchester & Basingstoke, Andover & Romsey
www.eastsussexcc.gov.uk *The local council's highways department* (Tel: 01273 481000)

We Stayed At

Gateway Hotel *Alternatively, there are several pubs and guesthouses in the area, as well as campsites for when the weather gets more friendly.* Eastleigh (Tel: 023 8065 0541)

Contacts

SLRC (Tel: 023 8061 7526)

Defenders of the Realm pages 44–49

OS Maps

Landranger 198 Brighton & Lewes
Landranger 199 Eastbourne and Hastings

Places To Go

Beachy Head *One of Britain's most visited beauty spots – and no wonder. At 530 feet it is the highest chalk sea cliff in Britain, but the main reason for its popularity is the wonderful panoramic view from the top. On a clear day you can see Dungeness, nearly 40 miles away in Kent.*

Beachy Head Countryside Centre *Well worth a visit. Admission is free and it's great for all the family, with interactive displays about the wildlife and history of the area. You can listen to the talking shepherd about farming on the Downland or visit Bronze Age Man in his hut. The wildlife of the Downs can be seen and heard as well as interacted with on the touch-screen computers.*

There's also a gift shop. It's open 10am to 5.30pm. (Tel: 01323 737273)

Beachy Head Pub *Open all day, seven days a week and serves good, honest food. Children are welcome, and there is indoor and outdoor play equipment, as well as baby changing facilities.* (Tel: 01323 728060)

Fishing

The seabed of the English Channel is littered with literally thousands of wrecks, from medieval galleons to warships sunk during the Second World War . Their crumbling hulks are home to huge fish, including giant conger eel, cod, pollack, ling and bass. Charter boat skippers take parties of anglers out to the best wrecks for the rod-bending, fishing trip of a lifetime. In Newhaven, the best known is Frank Shaw, skipper of the Carrick Lee II.

A Winter's Tale pages 50–57

OS Maps and Websites

Explorer 137, 148

www.kent.gov.uk *Kent County Council website that gives brief rights of way information, and links to tourism sites.*

www.kenttourism.co.uk *Attractive site with accommodation lists, places to visit, special offers on accommodation and entry to attractions.*

Places To Go

The Hop Farm Country Park *Big family attraction featuring shire horses, hop farm history, kids' entertainment, adventure playground and military vehicle display. It's also the venue for the War and Peace Show, the world's largest gathering of military vehicles.* Beltring, Paddock Wood, Kent (Tel: 01622 872068) www.thehopfarm.co.uk

Leeds Castle *Norman castle converted to a royal palace by Henry VIII. Open all year round.* Leeds, Maidstone, Kent (Tel: 01622 765400) www.leeds-castle.com

Sissinghurst Castle Garden *Beautiful garden created by the writer Vita Sackville West around an Elizabethan mansion – now a National Trust property. World famous for its use of plants and space – mansion open to visitors.* Sissinghurst, Cranbrook, Kent (Tel: 01580 710700)

Bluewater Greenhithe *Has to be seen to be believed – Europe's largest retail park, jammed with shops. Ten minutes from the Dartford Tunnel. Stop off at the Land Rover store while you're at the centre.* Kent (Tel: 0870 777 0252) www.bluewater.co.uk

Council Contacts

Kent County Council contact for West Kent Byways: Graham Rusling – based at KCC Offices, Kings Hill, West Malling (Tel: 01732 872829)

Big Bucks pages 68–75

OS Maps and Websites

Landranger 165 Aylesbury and Leighton Buzzard
Explorer 181 Chiltern Hills North, Aylesbury

www.informationbritain.co.uk *Tourist website on the UK that is well laid out and full of information. Good for the whole country, not just Buckinghamshire.*

www.aylesburyvale.net *General site on the Aylesbury Vale area (the north of the country), with tourist links and pages.*

Places To Go

Chiltern Open Air Museum *Outdoor museum with historic buildings rescued from destruction and rebuilt on 45-acre site.*

Traditional craft displays, including hands-on sessions. Woodland walks. Newland Park, Gorelands Lane, Chalfont St Giles, Bucks, HP8 4AB (Tel: 01494 871117) www.coam.org.uk

Bletchley Park   Birthplace of modern computing and code breaking: this is where the Enigma machine was cracked, turning the tide of the Second World War. Now a museum dedicated to preserving the brilliance of those who worked there. Also, displays of fire engines, model railways, WWII uniforms and military vehicles. The Mansion, Bletchley, Nr Milton Keynes, Buckinghamshire, MK3 6EB (Tel: 01908 640404) www.bletchleypark.org.uk

Chinnor and Princes Risborough Railway   Preserved steam railway running alongside the Icknield Way and through the base of the Chilterns. Trains run every Sunday, March to October, and there's a licensed buffet on board. 37 Lytham Avenue, Watford, Herts, WD19 6XA (Tel: 01844 354117, talking timetable: 01844 353535)

Off-Road Centres
There seems to be a total lack of "pay and play" off-road sites in Buckinghamshire. There's a Land Rover Experience site at Hounslow Hall, but this facility isn't open to anyone who wants to just turn up and drive around in their own vehicle. A gap in the market for an enterprising landowner, maybe.

Hert of the Matter   pages 76–83

OS Maps and Websites
Explorer OL 1

www.herts.co.uk   Loads of useful information on Hertfordshire – massive list of places to go and things to do, plus accommodation details.

Places To Visit
Knebworth House   Stately home that's become better known for its open air concerts than for it's incredible gothic architecture. Extensive gardens, adventure playground and miniature railway make it good for kids as well. The Estate Office, Knebworth House, Knebworth, Hertfordshire, SG3 6PY (Tel: 01438 812661) www.knebworthhouse.com

Shuttleworth Collection   Aeroplanes from the beginnings of aviation to the 1940s, and vintage and veteran cars set in acres of parkland. Shuttleworth Collection, Old Warden Park, Biggleswade, Bedfordshire, SG18 9EA (Tel: 01767 627288) www.shuttleworth.org enquire@shuttleworth.org

Places To Stay
Camping and Caravanning Club Site   250 pitches. Site open March to October, inclusive. Open to members and non-members of the Camping and Caravanning Club. Mangrove Road, Hertford, SG13 8QF (Tel: 01992 586696) www.campingandcaravanningclub.co.uk

Corner Cottage B&B   Munden Road, Dane End, near Ware, Hertfordshire, SG12 0LH (Tel: 01920 438320)

Council Contacts
Copies of the definitive map are available from the department – the first three A4 copies are free, then they start charging. Rights of Way Unit, Environment Department, County Hall, Pegs Lane, Hertford, SG13 8DN (Tel: 01992 555260)

Lincs with the Past   pages 96–103

OS Maps and Websites
Landranger 113 Grimsby
Landranger 122 Skegness & Horncastle

www.lincswolds.org.uk   For general tourism information on the area, contact the Lincolnshire Wolds Countryside Service. Riverhead Road, Louth (Tel: 01507 609740)

Places To Go
Lincoln Cathedral   Reckoned by many to be the most beautiful in England – and when you consider the quality of the competition, that's quite a compliment. (Tel: 01522 873213)

Lincoln Castle   Open to the public seven days a week. Castle Hill, Lincoln (Tel: 01522 511068)

Museum of Lincolnshire Life   Massive range of exhibits includes the earliest surviving First World War tank, built in Lincoln in 1917. Burton Road, Lincoln (Tel: 01522 528448) lincolnshirelife.museum@lincolnshire.gov.uk

Chequered Flag Karting   Kart racing for all the family   Holton Le Clay, near Grimsby (Tel: 01472 823823) www.chequeredflag-karting.co.uk

Woodside Falconry Centre   Vultures, eagles, owls, hawks and falcons on display. Plus trout fishing ... and pig and ferret racing (yes, really!). Near Langworth, Lincoln (Tel: 01522 754280) www.woodsidefalconry.co.uk

Rushmoor Country Park and Rare Breed Poultry   Includes picnic area and tearoom. Louth Road, North Cockerington (Tel: 01507 327184) www.rushmoorcountrypark.co.uk

We Stayed At
The Kenwick Park Hotel   Old country house set in 300 acres of landscaped grounds, with health and leisure facilities including an indoor heated swimming pool and 18-hole golf course. En-suite rooms were well furnished and comfortable. Friendly staff are very helpful and have good local knowledge. Menu is varied and reasonably priced. Louth, Lincolnshire, LN11 8NR (Tel: 01507 608806) www.kenwick-park.co.uk enquiries@kenwick-park.co.uk

Bordering on Perfection   pages 118–125

OS Maps and Websites
Landranger 137 Church Stretton & Ludlow

www.shropshire-cc.gov.uk   County council site with general tourism and leisure information.

www.shropshiretourism.info   General tourist and accommodation information.

Places To Go
Shropshire Hill Discovery Centre   The ecology, history and culture of the area can be explored in a 25-acre site on the Onny Meadows, which includes a centre with a grass roof. Craven Arms (Tel: 01588 676000)

Ironbridge Gorge Museums   Nine museums in all, in the birthplace of the industrial revolution. Ironbridge (Tel: 01952 884391) www.ironbridge.org.uk

RAF Museum   Free admission. Collection of historic military aircraft as well as a flight simulator. Cosford (Tel: 020 8358 4849) www.rafmuseum.com

Stokesay Castle   The finest and best-preserved 13th century fortified manor house in England. Craven Arms (Tel: 01588 672544)

Weston Park   Ancestral home of the Earls of Bradford. Near Telford (Tel: 01952 852100)

We Stayed At
The Plume of Feathers   Good, honest country pub with en suite accommodation, real ales and hearty meals – all at down-to-earth prices. Harley, near Much Wenlock (Tel: 01952 727360)

Can You Keep a Secret?

OS Maps and Websites

Landranger 191

www.lroac.com *LRO Adventure Club for details of off-road activities at Rockingham Castle and elsewhere in the area.*

www.enlroc.co.uk *East Northants Land Rover Owners Club know the greenlanes around this area like the back of their hands.*

www.northamptonshire.co.uk *General tourist information.*

Places To Go

King's Head *This 16th century pub offers real ales and good food, plus traditional Northamptonshire skittles, played on a table.* Wadenhoe (Tel: 01832 720024)

Fineshade Wood *The Rockingham Forest is famous for its wild-life, including the red kite – a magnificent bird of prey which had been extinct in England for 100 years until re-introduced to the area a decade ago. Today they are commonplace – especially at Fineshade Wood, where there is a viewing centre complete with live video links.* (Tel: 01780 444394)

Santa Pod Raceway *For something more adrenalin induc-ing, come here to watch the drag racers, high-speed cars and bikes.* (Tel: 08700 782828)

The County Set

OS Maps and Websites

Explorer 234 Rutland Water

Landranger 153 Bedford & Huntingdon, St Neots & Biggleswade

www.rutnet.co.uk *Comprehensive Rutland On Line website, with leisure, tourism and accommodation links.*

Places To Go

Rutland Water *There's something for everyone here, with a balance of sport, leisure and wildlife conservation. Fancy wind-surfing or canoeing (01780 720292)? Or maybe hiring a cycle to ride around the 25 miles of perimeter tracks (01780 460705)? There are 22 bird hides from which to view the rare wildfowl and ospreys (01572 770651) and you can even take a cruise on the Rutland Belle steamer (01572 787630). To book a boat for some trout or pike fishing, call 01780 686441.*

Eyebrook Reservoir *To enjoy a spot of trout fishing in quieter surroundings.* (Tel: 01536 770264)

Oakham Castle *The Great Hall is famous for its 12th century stone sculptures.* (Tel: 01572 758440)

Rutland Railway Museum *Steam and diesel locos, plus rolling stock and artefacts.* (Tel: 01572 813203)

Rockingham Castle *Built by William the Conqueror in 1086, it has been home to the Watson family since 1530.* (Tel: 01536 770240) www.rockinghamcastle.com

East of England Land Rover Driving Experience *Run by Vince Cobley, and set in Rockingham Castle's picturesque grounds.* (Tel: 0870 2644463)

Freelanders on Trial

OS Maps

Explorer 124, 125, 134, 144, 149, 150, 151, 152, 153

Freelander Club

The Freelander Club was formed just over two years ago and already has almost 200 members. Anybody can join – for details, phone Julian Read on 02380 269829, or email membership@freelanderclub.co.uk. The club also has a website: www.freelanderclub.co.uk

Topless on the Beach

OS Maps and Websites

Explorer 212 Woodbridge & Saxmundham

Landranger 144 Thetford & Diss

www.suffolkcc.gov.uk *Country council site, with many tourist information links and news on local events.*

www.eastofenglandtouristboard.co.uk *A useful site with a vast range of tourism information.*

Places To Go

East Anglia Transport Museum *Wonderful working museum with tramcars and trolley buses running in a simulated con-temporary environment. Also includes ex-industrial narrow-gauge railway, many vehicles undergoing restoration and static displays.* Chapel Road, Carlton Colville. B1384, about 250 yards from the A146 (Tel: 01502 518959)

Norfolk and Suffolk Aviation Museum *Here you will find over 25 historic aircraft, ranging from pre WWI to the present day. As well as holding various civil and military crafts, the site also holds any other aviation materials.* B1062 Homersfield Road, Flixton (Tel: 01986 896644)

Suffolk Wildlife Park *Get ready to explore more than 100 acres of parkland to find some of Africa's amazing wildlife. See lions, cheetahs, giraffes, zebras, chimpanzees and island colonies of lemur monkeys. With many other animals to see and lots of activities, this wildlife park promises a great day out for all the family.* Kessingland www.suffolkwildlifepark.co.uk

Big Country

OS Maps and Websites

Landranger 89 Cockermouth & Wast Water

www.lakedistrictletsgo.co.uk *It's all here – things to do, places to stay, places to eat, places to drink – and makes a good intro to the Lakes.*

www.cumbria-the-lake-district.co.uk *You'd be forgiven for think-ing all of Cumbria is the Lake District, but this site deals with the whole county, from Hadrian's Wall to Morecambe Bay. Worth a look for another perspective on the area.*

Places To Go

Cars of the Stars *Quirky museum full of famous cars from film and TV, including James Bond's Aston Martin DB5 (complete with ejector seat and smoke dispensers) and Chitty Chitty Bang Bang, eclectic, and very British.* Standish Street, Keswick, Cumbria, CA12 5LS (Tel: 01768 773757) http://members.aol.com/cotsmm/

Lakeland Motor Museum *Thousands of cars, cycles, motorbikes and trucks, including replicas of Donald Campbell's record-break-ing Bluebird cars – part of the Hoker Hall estate.* Holker Hall, Cark-in-Cartmel, Near Grange-over-Sands (Tel: 01539 558509)

Muncaster Castle *Splendid old pile with extensive, unusual gardens and plenty of activities for the family. It's also the HQ of the World Owl Trust, with plenty of these fine birds to admire.* Ravenglass, Cumbria, CA18 1RQ (Tel: 01229 717614) www.muncaster.co.uk

We Stayed At

The Kings Arms *Lively pub in a very popular Lakeland village.* Hawkshead (Tel: 01539 436372)

The George Hotel *Comfortable old coaching inn (now really a pub), popular with outdoors types.* Keswick (Tel: 01768 772076)

Manx for Everything   pages 178–183

OS Maps and Websites
Landranger 95 Isle of Man

www.visitisleofman.com   *Isle of Man Tourist Board's website, with everything you might conceivably need to know about the island. A good starting point for potential visitors.*

Places To Go
Laxey Wheel and Mines   *A monument to Victorian engineering it's the world's biggest water wheel, and it still works. The lead mines it once served are also open to visitors*   (Tel: 01624 675522)

Isle of Man Steam Railway   *The longest (15.5 miles) narrow-gauge steam railway in the British Isles, with services from Douglas to Port Erin in the summer, and an 1874 locomotive. Award-winning railway museum of Port Erin. Isle of Man Transport.*   (Tel: 01624 663366)

The National Museum   *Small but perfectly formed maritime museum in Castletown, featuring on 18th century armed schooner displayed in her original boathouse where she lay undiscovered for 100 years.*   Castletown Harbour (Tel: 01624 648000)

Castle Rushen   *A wonderful medieval castle – one of the best in the British Isles – in Castletown, the ancient capital of the island.*   Castletown Town Hall (Tel: 01624 825005)

We Stayed At
The Sefton Hotel   *Plush, four-star hotel with excellent service and a central location – two minutes from the Seacat terminal, and right on the seafront in Douglas.*   Harris Promenade, Douglas, Isle of Man, IM1 2RW (Tel: 01624 645500) www.seftonhotel.co.im

How To Get There
The Isle of Man Steam Packet company runs ferries from Heysham, Lancashire, and Seacats from Liverpool – both dock in Douglas. Seacats are faster, though ferries are cheaper, but both offer a regular service that can accommodate tall vehicles, such as Land Rovers. Book online at www.steam-packet.com, or call 08705 523523

Wild Rovers   pages 184–191

Websites
www.stenaline.co.uk   *For details of ferry services, check out Stena Line's website.*

www.irelandtravel.co.uk   *Approved accommodation and general tourist information from the Irish Tourist Board.*   info@irishtouristboard.co.uk

www.irlgov.ie/iveagh   *Want to know more about the country you're visiting? The Irish Embassy in London is very helpful.*   (Tel: 020 7225 7700)

We Stayed At
The Killeshin Hotel   *If you want to follow in our tyre tracks and visit the Slieve Bloom mountains in Co Laois, we recommend this hotel.*   Portlaois (Tel: 00353 502 21663) killeshinhotel@eircom.net

Contacts
Wheelbase Ltd   *Set up in 2000 by Vincent Whelan, this company runs off-roading activities in Cardtown Forest.*   Kildare Road, Mountsterevin, Co Kildare, Eire (Tel: 00 353 45 525488)

The friendly members of the Land Rover Club of Ireland are also more than happy to offer advice to visiting Land Rover enthusiasts. Contact John Redmond.   (Tel: 00 353 87 258 4940)

The Last Wilderness   pages 192–199

OS Maps and Websites
Explorer OL 31
Landranger 92

www.thisisthenortheast.co.uk   *Useful guide for visitors to the region.*

Places To Go
Barnard Castle   *Unspoilt market town. Tourist information centre in Flatts Road.*   (Tel: 01833 690909) tourism@teesdale.gov.uk

Bowes Museum   South of Barnard Castle (Tel: 01833 690606) www.durham.gov.uk/bowesmuseum

High Force waterfall   Near Middleton (Tel: 01833 640209) www.rabycastle.com

Island Fling   pages 212–219

OS Maps
Explorer 339, 340
Explorer OL 16
Landranger 73, 74, 95

Places To Go
Melrose Abbey   *Founded in 1136 by King David I of Scotland. The heart of King Robert Bruce is reputed to lie buried within its ruins. It is open daily throughout the year.*   (Tel: 01896 822562)

Dryburgh Abbey   *Also ruined, but contains the graves of Sir Walter Scott and Field Marshal Earl Haig.*   (Tel: 01835 822381)

Abbotsford   *Sir Walter Scott's former home, situated west of Melrose, is open to the public during the summer months. It contains his extensive library and historical artefacts.*   (Tel: 01896 752043)

Mary Queen of Scots Centre   *Tells the story of the tragic queen, who stayed here in 1566. Audio tours available.*   (Tel: 01835 863331)

Heatherslaw Corn Mill   *Driven by a waterwheel and produces stone-ground flour by the traditional methods. It's open to the public daily from April 1 to November 4.*   Wooler (Tel: 01890 820338)

Lindisfarne Priory   *Open all year round.*   (Tel: 01289 389200)

We Stayed At
The Buccleuch Arms Hotel   *A 16th century family-run hotel. Our en-suite rooms were clean and comfy. The menu was extensive and inexpensive, and we got a warm welcome.*   The Green, St Boswells (Tel: 01835 822243) www.buccleucharmshotel.co.uk bucchotel@aol.com